EC Law for
UK Lawyers

Dedication

This book is dedicated to Edwin and Linda
Coppel, to Teresa O'Neill and in loving memory
of the late Jack O'Neill

EC Law for UK Lawyers
The Domestic Impact of EC Law within the UK

Aidan O'Neill   LLB (Edin), LLM (Sydney), LLM (EUI)

Advocate

Jason Coppel   BA (Oxon), LLM (EUI)

of the Inner Temple, Lecturer in European Community Law, Brasenose College, Oxford

Butterworths
London, Dublin, Edinburgh
1994

United Kingdom	Butterworth & Co (Publishers) Ltd, 88 Kingsway, LONDON WC2B 6AB and 4 Hill Street, EDINBURGH EH2 3JZ
Australia	Butterworths, SYDNEY, MELBOURNE, BRISBANE, ADELAIDE, PERTH, CANBERRA and HOBART
Canada	Butterworths Canada Ltd, TORONTO and VANCOUVER
Ireland	Butterworth (Ireland) Ltd, DUBLIN
Malaysia	Malayan Law Journal Sdn Bhd, KUALA LUMPUR
New Zealand	Butterworths of New Zealand Ltd, WELLINGTON and AUCKLAND
Puerto Rico	Butterworth of Puerto Rico, Inc, SAN JUAN
Singapore	Butterworths Asia, SINGAPORE
South Africa	Butterworths Publishers (Pty) Ltd, DURBAN
USA	Butterworth Legal Publishers, CARLSBAD, California and SALEM, New Hampshire

A CIP Catalogue record for this book is available from the British Library.

ISBN 0 406 02459 6

Printed and bound in Great Britain by
Mackays of Chatham PLC, Chatham, Kent

PREFACE

The aim of this book is to introduce legal practitioners to the implications for everyday legal practice of British membership of the European Union. Since 1973, the legal systems of the United Kingdom have been subordinated to a higher supra-national system of law outlined in the Treaty of Rome and developed by the European Court of Justice in Luxembourg. The consequences, for UK law, and for UK lawyers, have been both wide-ranging and profound.

European Community law is a matter which no practitioner can afford to ignore. Contrary to a belief still widespread in the legal profession, EC law does not apply only to those factual situations characterised by a cross-border or international element. Nor is its impact restricted to a limited number of discrete legal areas, such as agriculture and anti-dumping law, which can be easily dismissed as the preserve of 'Euro-specialists'. Rather, EC law is directly applicable to a vast and an ever increasing number of apparently domestic legal fields of practice, ranging from company law to immigration to intellectual property to employment protection to consumer law and the sale of goods. Community law permeates national law. Moreover, it is superior to laws of national provenance and must be considered, and, in appropriate circumstances, applied, by each and every national court and tribunal.

Previous works on EC law, both general guides and more detailed treatments of specialised areas, have tended to treat it as a separate and separable subject of law distinct from the national legal systems of the United Kingdom. In some fields, notably in the area of commercial competition across national boundaries within the European Economic

Area, and to an extent agriculture and fisheries matters, it is indeed arguable that EC law can best be regarded as a separate body of supranational law, distinct from any national legal regimes. However, this book focuses on the domestic impact of Community law within the United Kingdom and examines those aspects of EC law which can only properly be understood as they interact with and apply directly to different areas of national law. The corollary of this approach is that these same areas of national law can themselves only be properly understood and correctly applied by the practitioner if the relevant aspects of EC law are taken into account.

The book therefore approaches the interaction of Community law with national law from the point of view of the latter. We are concerned with the outlook of the UK practitioner who has been presented with a particular legal problem and asked to advise on the relevant law applicable to that problem. Given the broad ambit of Community law, in many cases the relevant law will include aspects of EC law as well as legal provisions of a purely national character.

Accordingly, this book seeks to answer three questions for the practitioner faced with a legal problem: firstly, is there a potential Community aspect to this problem?; secondly, if there would appear to be a potential Community point, what are the basic principles and European cases and provisions to consider?; thirdly, where can further information be found;?

The book is divided into two parts. In the first part, we aim to give a broad outline of how European Community law can, in general, interact and apply to national legal problems. Of particular interest in this regard are the basic EC legal doctrines, such as direct effect and supremacy, and the general principles of EC law, including proportionality and respect for fundamental human rights, which have been developed in the case law of the European Court of Justice. The principal avenues by which actions involving EC law can be pursued are also examined in detail.

In three short chapters we then describe the institutional structure of the European Union, outline the principal methods of European legal research and list the key questions to be addressed by any practitioner faced with a matter with an EC angle.

In the second part, we will look at specific legal areas where the legal practitioner in the United Kingdom may commonly encounter EC legal provisions. Chapters are devoted to the cornerstone policies of the Treaty of Rome, such as free movement of goods, agriculture and competition law, as well as to increasingly important second-generation policies such as public procurement, consumer protection and environmental law. In each section we will discuss the main EC legislative provisions along with the leading case law of the European Court of Justice and give some indication of how national legal provisions should be interpreted and applied in the light of the relevant European Community law.

This book is intended to be a map of the law rather than a detailed guidebook. It is a starting point for what will be, in many cases, a long and complex journey through the mass of EC legal regulation. We hope that it will be of assistance in relation to specific legal problems which arise from day to day and that, more generally, it will help to heighten awareness of an aspect of British legal practice which has not always been given the attention which it deserves in this country.

Our aim was to state the law as at 1 January 1994, but in many cases it has been possible to take account of more recent developments, up until March 1994.

This project was made possible by the generous financial support of the Clark Fund for Legal Education and the European University Institute, Florence. The EUI, and in particular Francis Snyder, also provided invaluable research facilities and logistical assistance. The staff of the Advocates Library in Edinburgh, in particular Kate Flett, have been the model of courtesy, tact and generosity in their responses to many difficult queries and requests. In addition, a number of people brought their individual expertise to bear on various chapters of this book. We would like to thank Roger Alexander, David Anderson, Christine Boch, Louis Charpentier, Laura Dunlop, Lawrence Lumsden, Maureen Lynch, Bill McCann, Bernard Rudden, John Stanton-Ife and David Stevenson. All remaining errors are entirely the responsibility of the authors. Finally, thank you to our handlers at Butterworths for their encouragement and boundless patience.

Aidan O'Neill
Jason Coppel

Edinburgh and London
March 1994

CONTENTS

TABLE OF STATUTES

References in this Table to *Statutes* are to Halsbury's Statutes of England (Fourth Edition) showing the volume and page at which the annotated text of the Act may be found.

TABLE OF
STATUTORY INSTRUMENTS

TABLE OF EC LEGISLATION

PAGE

PAGE

TABLE OF CASES

Decisions of the European Court of Justice are listed both alphabetically and numerically. The numerical Table follows the alphabetical.

PAGE

xxv

B

C

D

PAGE

R

T

W

Decisions of the European Court of Justice are listed below numerically.
These decisions are also included in the preceding alphabetical Table.

PAGE

1 Table of cases

PAGE

PAGE

Part   I

THE GENERAL IMPACT OF COMMUNITY LAW ON THE LEGAL ORDER OF THE UNITED KINGDOM

Chapter 1

THE EUROPEAN LEGAL ORDER

INTRODUCTION

'The EEC Treaty has established its own system of law, integrated in the legal systems of the Member States and which must be applied by their courts.'[1]

When the Royal Assent was given to the European Communities Act 1972, the legal systems of Northern Ireland, Scotland and England and Wales became constituent elements of a supranational legal system governing the activities of both the central institutions and the Member States of the European Communities. The European Community legal system had been in existence for some 20 years before the accession of the United Kingdom. It was already 'a new legal order' capable of creating individual rights directly, without the need for any specific national implementing measures,[2] which proclaimed its supremacy over national laws and which bound national courts to uphold and protect the rights granted under Community law against the provisions of any contrary national laws.[3]

A common misapprehension among lawyers in the United Kingdom is that European Community law is a set of regulations which apply only in certain areas of specialised practice, like competition law and international trade. In fact, its impact is much wider than this. In July 1993 the Department of Trade and Industry stated that:

1   Case 14/68 *Walt Wilhelm v Bundeskartellamt* [1969] ECR 1 at 14, [1969] CMLR 100 at 119.
2   Case 26/62 *Van Gend en Loos v Nederlandse Administratie der Belastingen* [1963] ECR 1 at 12, [1963] CMLR 105.
3   Case 6/64 *Costa v ENEL* [1964] ECR 585 at 593-4.

> 'Over a third of *existing* UK legislation arises from an obligation
> to implement EC law and this proportion is likely to increase.'

and

> '[A]lmost 70 per cent of future business law is likely to be derived
> from the European Community.'[4]

European Community law cannot be regarded (or ignored) as a matter of
particular and peculiar specialist interest. Rather, a consideration of the
relevance of Community law must form an integral part of the whole
range of advice and assistance offered by legal practitioners in the United
Kingdom.

In order to understand how this new legal order works and how it
interrelates with the existing domestic legal systems of the United
Kingdom, some knowledge of the distinctive characteristics of Community
law is required. In this chapter, the information fundamental to a proper
appreciation of the applicability of Community law in everyday practice
is presented.

The following matters will be considered:

- the origins of Community law;
- the objectives of Community law;
- the relationship between Community law and public international
  law;
- the relevance of Community law for the individual;
- the relationship between Community law and the domestic legal
  systems of the Member States;
- the application of Community law to the individual;
- methods of interpretation in Community law;
- the doctrine of precedent in Community law;
- the private international law of the European Community;
- the law of the European Economic Area.

THE ORIGINS OF COMMUNITY LAW

Community law consists in those rights and obligations which can
ultimately be traced to or derived from a set of international treaties
which have been concluded among a number of European countries since
the 1950s.

The principal treaties on which the present European Community is
founded are the 1951 Treaty of Paris which set up the European Coal and

---

4   *Review of the Implementation and Enforcement of EC Law in the UK* (Department of
     Trade and Industry, 1993) at p v, para 1 and p 41, para 4.14 respectively.

Steel Community (ECSC), the 1957 Euratom Treaty which created the European Atomic Energy Community and, most importantly, the 1957 Treaty of Rome which founded the European Economic Community. The Communities created by each of these treaties constitute legal persons distinct from their Member States in both international and domestic law. [5] They have their own rights, powers and duties, independently of the countries which constitute them. Each of the Treaties provided for the creation of four central institutions: a parliamentary Assembly, an inter-governmental Council, an independent Commission and a supervisory Court. The purpose of these institutions was to ensure the better attainment of the objectives of their respective Communities. These institutions do not in general correspond to the classical notion of the division of governmental powers but instead share among themselves judicial, legislative and executive functions.

The foundation treaties were originally concluded among France, West Germany, Italy, Belgium, the Netherlands and Luxembourg. In 1972 a Treaty of Accession was signed whereby Denmark, Ireland and the United Kingdom joined the three Communities with effect from 1 January 1973. Greece joined on 1 January 1981 and Spain and Portugal together became members on 1 January 1986. The 12 countries which currently together make up the European Communities will be referred to throughout this work as 'the Member States'. At the time of writing negotiations were in progress over the possible accession of Austria, Finland, Norway and Sweden to the Communities.

The original foundation treaties have been amended a number of times over the years of the existence of the three Communities. The Single European Act of 1986 made significant and substantial amendments to the original treaties with a particular emphasis on the completion of the single European market, a programme to ensure the abolition of barriers to trade within the Community by 31 December 1992. The Maastricht Treaty, which came into force on 1 November 1993 after some difficulties with its ratification in various Member States, made further changes to the foundation treaties, expanding the competences of the Community and establishing the timetable and conditions for European economic and monetary union. [6]

Although there are in strict law, three distinct European Communities deriving from the three foundation treaties, in practice these three

5 Arts 210 and 211 of the Treaty of Rome.
6 Implemented in the United Kingdom by the European Communities (Amendment) Act 1993. The constitutionality of the UK Government's ratification of the Maastricht Treaty was the subject of an unsuccesful challenge in the English High Court. See *R v Secretary of State for Foreign and Commonwealth Affairs, ex p Lord Rees-Mogg* [1993] 3 CMLR 101. In March 1994 a challenge to the Treaty was mounted in the Scottish Court of Session: see *Hon Christopher Monckton v Lord Advocate* (unreported). The constitutional challenge to Maastricht in Germany is reported as *Brunner v European Union Treaty* [1994] 1 CMLR 57.

Communities are administered as one. The 1965 Merger Treaty provided that all three Communities should share a single Council and Commission. A convention to the Treaty of Rome had already made each Community subject to the same Court and Parliament. While Article 240 of the Treaty of Rome and Article 208 of the Euratom Treaty provided that those treaties were concluded for an unlimited period, Article 97 of the ECSC Treaty provided that it should exist only for a period of 50 years from the date of its entry into force. The ECSC will accordingly come to an end in July 2002. It has been proposed by the Commission that, rather than specifically renewing this treaty, the Member States should simply amend the Treaty of Rome by incorporating in it certain provisions relating to the coal and steel industries.

As well as amending the foundation documents of the European Communities, principally the Treaty of Rome, the treaty concluded at Maastricht also established a European Union superimposed on the existing Communities, and provided for the formal replacement of the term 'European Economic Community' by 'European Community'.

The European Union is an umbrella term which covers three separate areas or pillars: the existing European Communities' structures and law; intergovernmental co-ordination in matters of foreign policy and common external defence; and political intergovernmental co-operation in internal affairs such as criminal justice and policing, immigration and rights of asylum. Article L of the Maastricht Treaty on European Union provides that the second and third pillars should not fall within the Community legal order and that the Court of Justice has jurisdiction only over matters contained within the original foundation treaties of the European Communities, as amended.

Since 'European Union' is a broader political concept, throughout this book the term 'the Community' shall be used to refer to the particular legal order which applies the three original European Communities as a whole. In general, as the basis of the central and most extensive of the three Communities, it is the Treaty of Rome to which reference will generally be made. Specific articles of the other two foundation treaties, or of the Maastricht Treaty on European Union, will be mentioned only where there is a need to draw attention to significant differences in the powers, rights or obligations of the three Communities and/or the European Union. The provisions of the Treaty of Rome will be referred to in their form and numbering following the latest amendments agreed at Maastricht.

Finally, reference to 'the Court' will mean the Court of Justice of the European Communities. There are currently two separate European Community courts, but the lower court, the Court of First Instance, which presides primarily over EC administrative law actions, will be referred to by its full name.

THE OBJECTIVES OF THE EUROPEAN COMMUNITY

The terms of the 1957 Treaty of Rome were integrated with and closely modelled on those of other international trade treaties such as the General Agreement on Tariffs and Trade (GATT) and international monetary arrangements such as the International Monetary Fund (IMF). The provisions of these agreements served as a prototype for the customs union rules of the Community.

Articles 2 and 3 of the Treaty of Rome provided that the purpose of the Treaty was the establishment of a customs union or common market and generally to foster closer relations and increased trade among its Member States. The common market was to be achieved by providing for fair competition and free movement of goods, services, persons and capital throughout the territory of the Community. Common policies were also envisaged in the areas of transport, agriculture and fisheries.

Following the amendments to the Treaty of Rome by both the Single European Act and the Treaty of Maastricht, the objectives of the Community and the corresponding legal competences assigned to it were markedly expanded. The list of Community activities set out in Article 3 of the Treaty doubled from 11 to 20. After the ratification of the Maastricht amendments, the Treaty of Rome provided for the co-ordination of economic and monetary policy by the Member States, leading to eventual economic and monetary union, EMU (Arts 102a to 109m).

The expansion of the objectives and competences of the Community indicate clearly that it must be seen in broader terms than the purely economic. Provision is made in the Treaty of Rome for the Community to be involved in certain areas of social policy, such as the improvement of employment conditions and the health and safety of workers (Art 118a), the achievement of equal pay as between men and women (Art 119), the securing of social security for migrant workers in their host countries (Art 121) and the promotion and funding of vocational training and retraining (Arts 123 and 127). Following the Maastricht amendments a much greater emphasis has been placed on the social sphere.

A protocol and agreement on social policy annexed to the Maastricht Treaty gave the Community competence to adopt measures in the general field of industrial relations. The provisions do not appear in the Treaty proper because the idea of increased Community involvement in the field of employer/employee relations and the status and role of trade unions was politically unacceptable to the United Kingdom Government. Accordingly, the 12 Member States agreed that the machinery and institutions of the Community could be used in proposing and formulating measures under the agreement but that such measures could be adopted by and apply to 11 Member States, excluding the United Kingdom. Given the implications this protocol has for the continued uniformity and coherence of Community law, its legality and that of any provisions made under it, may yet be subject to challenge before the Court of Justice.

Environmental protection became a legitimate area for Community involvement following the Single European Act (Arts 130r to 130t). In addition, after Maastricht, the Community has gained formal competence to make provisions in the fields of town and country planning and land use (Art 130s(2)), public health (Art 129), consumer protection (Art 129a), the development of the European dimension in education (Art 126) and the promotion of Europe's artistic and cultural heritage (Art 128).

The Maastricht Treaty also expanded Community competences in the industrial sphere. The Community is now charged with developing trans-European networks in transport, telecommunications and energy (Art 129b) with encouraging industrial research, development and modernization (Art 130) and with promoting scientific and technological research (Arts 130f to 130p). Provision was also made (Art 130a) for special funding for poorer regions within the Community to improve economic and social cohesion throughout the Community and for the promotion of closer relations with the countries of the developing world (Arts 130u to 130y).

The Community system operates on the basis of the principle of enumerated powers. Those areas of legal regulation which have not been allocated to the Community in the foundation treaties remain the exclusive responsibility of national governments. Subject to this proviso, the competences of the Community and so the scope of Community law are broad indeed. Matters such as health and safety, product liability, sex discrimination, employment protection and company transfers now have a European dimension. Community law is, then, not just for the specialists; it is a matter of importance for each and every legal practitioner in his or her everyday legal practice.

COMMUNITY LAW AND PUBLIC INTERNATIONAL LAW

The European Community was established by means of international agreements between states which were binding in international law. As such, its origins were unremarkable. It took its place in the framework of public international law beside the United Nations, NATO, the Arab League, the Organisation of African Unity, the Council of Europe and countless other international legal structures set up by agreement between states.

At the same time the European Community as an international organisation, is special in many respects. The foundation treaties have given birth to a distinct regional international legal system, with its own legislation and legislative procedures, its own enforcement mechanisms and institutions, and its own court structure. Two aspects in particular take the European Community beyond the constructs of classical public international law.

The effectiveness of Community law

Firstly Community law is normatively very strong. International legal rules, for example those promulgated by the United Nations, are frequently flouted by states with impunity. The judgments of the International Court of Justice at the Hague have been ignored and its jurisdiction repudiated by states unwilling to accept adverse rulings on their conduct. The response to breaches of public international law is frequently limited to public condemnation.

By contrast, Community law seems to be treated by those states subject to it as being normatively strong. There appears to have grown up a general 'habit of obedience' to Community law on the part of Member States. Thus, directives from the Commission or Council are, in general, duly implemented by the Member States. The jurisdiction of the European Court of Justice is respected and its judgments obeyed by the Member States. Since the Maastricht amendments to Article 171, the Court of Justice has the power to impose financial penalties against a Member State for its failure to fulfil an obligation incumbent upon it under the Treaties. Thus, the binding nature of Community law is ensured not simply by political pressure, but also by specific legal sanction.

A central concern of the Court of Justice has been to strengthen the effectiveness of Community law in practice by emphasising the binding nature of Community law on both Member States and private individuals. In consequence the Court itself stresses the distinctiveness of the Community legal order from other systems of public international law. [7]

In general public international law, the default of one party in carrying out his obligations can have the effect of suspending the reciprocal obligations of the other party. [8] However, the Court of Justice has rejected

---

7   See Case 6/64 *Costa v ENEL* [1964] ECR 585 at 593.
8   See Art 60 of the Vienna Convention on the Law of Treaties for the conditions of applicability of this principle in public international law

the contention that obligations under Community law may be contingent on reciprocal performance by some other party. Thus, the Court has held that a Member State's obligations under Community law exist and are enforceable notwithstanding the alleged failure of the Commission to carry out its duties to Member States, [9] or the alleged failure by one Member State to carry out its obligations in relation to another Member State. [10]

Community law is not a matter of contingent or theoretical obligations. It is an overarching legal order binding on and enforced against the Member States.

Membership of the Community may be likened to a form of international citizenship for nations. Just as the citizen cannot select obligations once citizenship has been accepted, so Member States may not reject treaty obligations which prove uncongenial. The Treaty of Rome was created for 'an unlimited period' [11] and contains no provisions for the secession of states from the Community. A state or part thereof may leave the Community but not by unilateral act, but only after negotiation and agreement. Thus, in 1985, Greenland left the Community after formal amendment of the Treaty in accord with the provisions of Article 236 thereof.

Community Law and the individual

Little mention was made in the Community treaties, as originally drafted, of any rights or duties conferred upon private individuals. This is unsurprising since, classically, the law of treaties concerns only the relations between sovereign states. Private individuals are not in general capable of being subjects of international law. Individuals' rights and obligations are, instead, matters for the internal domestic law of States.

However, the Treaty of Rome did provide in Article 189 for secondary legislation to be made by Community institutions. Of the different kinds of secondary provisions, directives were addressed only to Member States but regulations were said to be binding and directly applicable in all Member States and decisions were to be binding upon those to whom they were addressed. In addition, Article 173 specifically provided that any natural or legal person could institute proceedings before the Court

---

9   Joined Cases 90,91/63 *Commission v Luxembourg and Belgium* [1964] ECR 625, [1965] CMLR 58.
10   Case 232/78 *Commission v France* [1979] ECR 2729, [1980] 1 CMLR 418 on France's banning of imports of mutton and lamb.
11   See Art 240 of the Treaty of Rome.

of Justice seeking to review the legality of any Community decisions addressed to him or her or any decisions or regulations of direct and individual concern to him or her.

It was a basic assumption that Community law would not be confined to creating international obligations on the Member States but would also have some relevance for the individual.

In *Van Gend en Loos* [12] the Court of Justice stated that Community law not only could impose obligations on individuals independently of Member States' legislation but could also directly confer rights upon them, both expressly and by implication.

This affirmation by the Court that individuals might be bearers of rights and obligations under the Community legal order was confirmed most recently by the Member States' introduction, in the Maastricht Treaty, of the principle of Community citizenship. Article 8 of the Treaty now provides that every person holding the nationality of a Member State shall be a citizen of the European Union. To be a citizen of the Union means that one enjoys the rights conferred and is subject to the duties imposed on individuals by the treaties.

In creating rights and obligations for individuals, Community law is operating in precisely the same territory as the domestic legal systems of the Member States. The question necessarily arises as to how these different legal orders interrelate with one another.

COMMUNITY LAW AND THE NATIONAL LEGAL ORDER

Conflict between Community law and national law is inevitable. Across the whole range of Community legal regulation individuals find that their rights or duties under national law are less than wholly consistent with the rights and duties laid down by Community law. According to Community law, the solution to such conflict is clear — Community law takes precedence over national law in all situations.

The Court stated in *Costa v ENEL* [13] that membership of the Community entailed a permanent limitation of the sovereign rights of the Member States to the extent that national laws passed after entry into the Community could not be given effect to if and in so far as contrary to Community law. Later, the Court affirmed the supremacy of Community law over the provisions of national constitutions, even those relating to the protection of fundamental rights or to the internal structure of the Member State. [14]

---

12 Case 26/62 *Van Gend en Loos v Nederlandse Administratie der Belastingen* [1963] ECR 1 at 12, [1963] CMLR 105.
13 Case 6/64 *Costa v ENEL* [1964] ECR 585 at 593-4, [1964] CMLR 425.
14 Case 11/70 *Internationale Handelsgesellschaft GmbH v Einfuhr und Vorratstelle fuer Getriede und Futtermittel* [1970] ECR 1125, [1972] CMLR 225.

Member States have a duty to repeal national laws which are contrary to Community law. [15] Where this has not been done, the Court of Justice has repeatedly stressed that it is the duty of national courts to give precedence to Community law in situations of conflict with national law. [16]

Since a national law which has the effect of denying or restricting an individual's Community law rights cannot be enforced before the national courts, it is a good defence to a criminal charge (or a civil action) that the domestic legal instrument which forms the basis of the action is itself in breach of Community law.

In England and Wales this strategy was used by large retailers in a concerted campaign against the enforcement by local authorities of the restrictions on Sunday trading contained in the Shops Act 1950. It was initially argued by the retailers, defending actions brought against them by local authorities seeking to enforce the Sunday trading rules, that national restrictions on Sunday opening constituted a quantitative restriction on imports from other Member States in the Community and so contravened Article 30 of the Treaty of Rome. [17] When this argument was ultimately rejected by the European Court of Justice, [18] a new 'Euro-defence' was found. The retailers then claimed that since the majority of people employed by them on a Sunday in retail outlets were women, restrictions on Sunday opening disproportionately and adversely affected women's employment, contrary to the Community law prohibition on indirect sex discrimination. [19] The restrictions on Sunday trading in England and Wales were liberalised by the UK Parliament before this new defence had run its course.

DIRECT EFFECT: THE APPLICABILITY OF COMMUNITY LAW TO THE INDIVIDUAL

The doctrine of 'direct effect' allows provisions of Community law to be relied upon directly in national courts. Community law is able to confer

---

15 Case 167/73 *Commission v France* [1974] ECR 359.
16 See eg Case C-381/89 *VASKO* [1992] ECR I-2111.
17 See *WH Smith Do-it-All Ltd v Peterborough City Council* [1990] 2 CMLR 577; *B & Q plc v Shrewsbury and Atcham Borough Council* [1990] 3 CMLR 535; *Mendip District Council v B & Q plc* [1991] 1 CMLR 113; *Stoke on Trent City Council v B & Q plc* [1991] Ch 48; *Kirklees Metropolitan Borough Council v Wickes Building Supplies Ltd* [1991] 4 All ER 240, [1992] 2 CMLR 765.
18 Case C-169/91 *Stoke on Trent Borough Council v B & Q plc* [1992] ECR I-6635, [1993] 1 CMLR 426, [1993] 1 All ER 481.
19 *Chisholm v Kirklees Metropolitan Borough Council* [1993] ICR 826.

rights and impose obligations directly upon individuals. National courts have a duty to protect those rights and enforce those obligations. Not all provisions of Community law, however, have this quality of direct effect.

The Treaty of Rome and the secondary legislation issued under it deal primarily with obligations between states. Some provisions of Community law may not be intended to create individual rights. Some provisions may be intended to confer rights but do not adequately specify the parties against whom these rights may be enforced or the precise content of those rights. The Court of Justice has, over the years, developed various criteria to be applied in determining whether or not a particular provision is capable of having direct effect. Three factors have been particularly important:

- the content of the provision must be clear and precise. [20]
- the provision must be self-executing, in the sense that it imposes a specific duty, and neither the Member States nor the Community institutions have any discretion as to whether or not a particular duty is to be carried out. [1]
- the provision must not contain any conditions or qualifications such as to make the existence of an obligation contingent on some further occurrence or external event. [2]

Whether or not a provision of a Community instrument has direct effect depends on the application of the relevant part of the instrument to the particular facts at issue. Direct effect is not something determined in the abstract as regards the whole of a Community instrument. It should also be noted that two recent UK decisions seem to suggest that a Community provision does not have to create specific rights in individuals for it to have direct effect. The direct effect of a Community provision may, in some cases, be relied upon by any person with a recognised interest in the outcome of the action. [3]

Whilst it is possible to elucidate some rules of general application, the attribution of direct effect and the consequences which arise from it

20 Case 6/64 *Costa v ENEL* [1964] ECR 585, [1964] CMLR 425.
1   Case 28/67 *Molkerei-Zentrale Westfalen v Hauptzollamt Paderborn* [1968] ECR 143, [1968] CMLR 187.
2   Case 57/65 *Alfons Luetticke GmbH v Hauptzollamt Saarlouis* [1966] ECR 205, [1971] CMLR 674. See also Case 2/74 *Reyners v Belgium* [1974] ECR 631.
3   Compare *Kincardine and Deeside District Council v Forestry Comrs*, 1992 SLT 1180, [1992] Environmental Law Reports 151 with *Twyford Parish Council v Secretary of State for the Environment* [1992] 1 CMLR 276, [1993] Environmental Law Reports 37. Both cases deal with the question of the direct effect of the Environmental Impact Reports Directive 85/337/EEC, OJ 1985 L175/40. See Ch 13 on Environmental Protection and Planning Law.

varies according to the legislative form of the Community provision at issue. It is necessary, therefore, to consider each of these legislative forms in turn.

Direct effect and articles of the Treaty

Applying the principle that, to be relied upon in national courts, obligations must be clear, precise, unconditional and non-discretionary, the Court has found a substantial number of the provisions of Treaty articles to be directly effective, either separately or read in conjunction with other articles. These include: Article 6 (formerly 7) prohibiting discrimination on grounds of nationality; [4] Article 30 prohibiting quantitative restrictions on imports from Member States; [5] Article 36 prohibiting any arbitrary discrimination or disguised restriction in trade; [6] Article 48 establishing the free movement of workers; [7] Article 52 on the freedom of establishment for the self employed; [8] Article 59 abolishing restrictions on freedom to provide, [9] or to receive, [10] services; Article 85 outlawing anti-competitive agreements; [11] Article 86 prohibiting abuse of a dominant position in the market-place; [12] Article 95 forbidding any indirect protection of home products by Member States' internal tax provision; [13] and Article 119 establishing the principle of equal pay as between men and women. [14]

Applying the same tests to the facts before them the Court has also found a number of Treaty articles not to be directly effective, including: Article 5 on the general duty on Member States to promote the Treaty objectives; [15] Article 59(2) on the freedom to established non-Community

---

4   Case 36/74 *Walrave and Koch v Association Union Cycliste Internationale* [1975] ECR 1405, [1975] 1 CMLR 320.
5   Case 74/76 *Ianelli & Volpi v Paolo Meroni* [1977] ECR 557, [1977] 2 CMLR 688; Case 83/78 *Pig Marketing Board v Redmond* [1978] ECR 2347.
6   Case 120/78 *Rewe-Zentral AG v Bundesmonopolverwaltung fuer Branntwein ('Cassis de Dijon')* [1979] ECR 649. See also Case C-145/88 *Torfaen Borough Council v B & Q* [1989] ECR 3851.
7   Case 118/75 *Watson & Bellman* [1976] ECR 1185.
8   Case 2/74 *Reyners v Belgium* [1974] ECR 631, [1974] 2 CMLR 305.
9   Case 33/74 *Van Binsbergen* [1974] ECR 1299.
10   Joined Cases 286/82, 26/83 *Luisi and Carbone v Italian Ministry of Finance* [1984] ECR 377.
11   Case 127/73 *Belgische Radio en Televisie (BRT) v SABAM* [1974] ECR 51.
12   Case 127/73 *Belgische Radio en Televisie (BRT) v SABAM* [1974] ECR 51. See also Joined Cases T-68,77,78/89 *Societa Italiana Vetro SpA v Commission ('Flat Glass')* [1992] ECR II-1403.
13   Case 27/67 *Fink-Frucht v Hauptzollamt Muenchen* [1968] ECR 223, [1968] CMLR 228.
14   Case 43/75 *Defrenne v SABENA (No 2)* [1976] ECR 455, [1976] 2 CMLR 98.
15   Case 9/73 *Schlueter v Hauptzollamt Loerrach* [1973] ECR 1135.

nationals to provide services;[16] Article 67 on restrictions on the free movement of capital and Article 71 on the liberalization of exchange controls;[17] Article 93 on the supervision and review of State Aids;[18] and Article 117 on improved working conditions and workers' standard of living.[19]

It should be borne in mind that any list of directly effective Treaty articles is not a closed or conclusive one. Articles which in earlier circumstances might have been considered to be insufficiently precise to have direct effect, might in the light of the Court's case law be considered to have become vested with the requisite qualities of definitiveness and unconditionality. The Court's increasing reliance on principles derived from Article 5 of the Treaty may be a case in point. Further, the addition of new and the amendment of existing articles of the foundation treaties may also open up possibilities of arguments as to their direct effect.

Vertical and horizontal direct effect

The issue of direct effect for articles of the Treaty usually arises in actions where an individual seeks to use a provision against the state, or some public authority forming part of the state. This is known as vertical direct effect. However, the Court has held that there is nothing in principle to prevent Treaty articles also having horizontal direct effect, that is, against other private parties. Whether a Treaty article actually does impose obligations upon other individuals is a matter of construction — some, which require the enactment, non-enactment or repeal of legislation, can clearly only bind the state.

As we have seen, the primary provisions of Community competition law, Articles 85 and 86 against cartels and abuse of a dominant position in the market-place, have been held to impose obligations on individuals in relation to other private individuals. Similarly, the Treaty prohibition on discrimination on grounds of nationality and the principle contained in Article 119 of the Treaty that men and women should receive equal pay for equal work have also been held to impose obligations directly on private parties.

In any Community law matter the starting point for a lawyer must be the provision of the Treaty which provides the legal basis for the secondary Community provision in the area. Where a case turns on a

16 Case 52/79 *Procureur du Roi v Debauve* [1980] ECR 833.
17 Case 203/80 *Casati* [1981] ECR 2595, [1982] 1 CMLR 365.
18 Case 6/64 *Costa v ENEL* [1964] ECR 585; [1964] CMLR 425.
19 Case 149/77 *Defrenne v SABENA* [1978] ECR 1365, [1978] 3 CMLR 312.

provision of secondary legislation which is not (horizontally) directly effective, the principle of the Treaty article under which it has been issued may be cited in its place and (horizontal) direct effect attained thereby.

Direct effect and Community regulations

Article 189 of the Treaty provides that 'a regulation shall have general application. It shall be binding in its entirety and directly applicable in all Member States.'

The 'direct applicability' of Community regulations means that no national legislation is required to implement the regulations to give them legal effect in the domestic legal systems of the Member States. Community regulations bind the Member States and have the force of law within the national territories without the intervention of national parliaments.

Whether or not the provisions of a regulation have direct effect, in the sense of creating enforceable rights for individuals which may be relied upon before the national courts, is a matter for the proper construction of the provision in question on the basis of the tests outlined above.[20]   In so far as these regulations can be construed as creating vested rights in individuals they may be said also to be 'directly effective' in the same way as Treaty articles. As with articles of the Treaty, direct effect may, in principle, be either vertical or horizontal.

Direct effect for directives

Article 189 states that 'a directive shall be binding, as to the result to be achieved, upon each Member State to which it is addressed, but shall leave to the national authorities the choice of form and methods.'

Directives are not addressed to individuals. They are instructions to the Member States to ensure the achievement in their national territory of the result envisaged by the directive. The Member States are obliged, within a specified time limit, to enact legislation or to promulgate other legally binding instruments in implementation of the directive. Direct effect serves as a remedy for individuals where their government has failed to implement a directive, or has done so incorrectly. After the

---

20   See the Opinion of Advocate-General Warner in Case 131/79 *R v Secretary of State for Home Affairs, ex p Santillo* [1980] ECR 1585, [1980] 2 CMLR 308.

expiry of the time limit, an individual may rely upon directly effective provisions of directives against national laws which are inconsistent with them.

In order to determine whether or not they have direct effect, provisions of directives must be subjected to the standard tests of suitability. They must be clear, precise and self-executing, and most importantly in this context, they must be unconditional and operate independently of the subsequent discretion of Member States. The obvious problem in relation to directives is that, by definition, they leave to the Member States a margin of discretion in their implementation. Directives lay down ends and leave up to national governments the choice of how they achieve those ends.

The Court of Justice, keen to provide remedies for individuals in the event of non-implementation of directives, has not explicitly modified the established criteria for determining direct effect but, instead, has applied them with a certain flexibility in the case of directives.

Firstly, in considering the direct effectiveness of directives, the Court has emphasised the importance of ends over means. Where the result intended by a directive is clear, the fact that the directive allows a choice of means does not necessarily mean that it is not directly effective.

In *Marshall (No 2)* the provision at issue, Article 6 of the Equal Treatment Directive,[1] required Member States to provide adequate remedies for individuals in the event of discrimination but did not specify what these remedies ought to be. The Court stated that the right of a state to choose among several possible means of achieving the objectives of a directive did not exclude the possibility of individuals enforcing before national courts 'rights whose content can be determined sufficiently precisely on the basis of the provisions of the directive alone.'[2]

Secondly, the Court has held that provisions of directives can be directly effective even where the precise content of the rights to be protected by national legislation, and so the result required by the directive, is subject to a margin of appreciation. Directives may be imprecise as to results in that they frequently lay down only minimum standards which must be achieved by the Member States — national governments are free to accord a greater degree of protection to individuals if they so wish. If a Member State has failed to exercise the discretion given to it by the directive, the Court may apply that requirement which

---

1   Council Directive 76/207/EEC, OJ 1976 L39/40.
2   Case C-271/91 *Marshall v Southampton and SW Hampshire Area Health Authority II*, European Court of Justice, 2 August 1993, at para 37, [1993] IRLR 445. See also Case 286/85 *McDermott & Cotter v Minister for Social Welfare* [1987] ECR 1453 at para 15, [1987] 2 CMLR 607.

imposes the least burdensome obligation upon it so as to confer upon individuals the minimum guaranteed rights.[3]

It now seems that a provision of a directive may have direct effect provided that the intended individual beneficiaries of the directive, the essentials of the substantive rights granted to those individuals, and the identity of the person(s) placed under the correlative obligations can all be identified from its terms.

The most important limitation upon the direct effect of directives is that, in contrast to Treaty articles and Community regulations, their provisions cannot be relied upon by individuals against other private parties. The direct effect of directives is rooted in the obligation of the Member State to pass national legislation in implementation of Community law. Accordingly, the Court has held that it cannot apply as against individuals who have no analogous obligation or competence.[4] This argument applies equally where the state seeks to enforce against a private party the provisions of a directive which it has not implemented.[5]

The provisions of directives can only be vertically directly effective. They may only be directly relied upon as against a Member State. The Court of Justice has mitigated, to a certain extent, the effects of its restriction upon the direct effect of directives by giving a broad interpretation to the concept of the state or an emanation thereof. Bodies regarded by the Court of Justice as unequivocally emanations of the state for the purposes of direct effect are any bodies, whatever their legal form, which are responsible for the provision of some public service and accordingly have greater powers than are normally accorded to private individuals or corporations.[6] These bodies have been held by the Court of Justice to include provide tax authorities,[7] police authorities,[8] health boards,[9] local government bodies,[10] and statutorily established or supported professional bodies.[11]

---

3   Cases C-6,9/90 *Francovich & Bonifaci v Italy* [1991] ECR I-5403 at para 19, [1992] IRLR 84.

4   Case 152/84 *Marshall v Southampton and South West Area Health Authority* [1986] ECR 723.

5   Case 80/86 *Officier van Justitie v Kolpinghuis Nijmegen BV* [1987] ECR 3969, [1989] 2 CMLR 18.

6   Case C-188/89 *Foster v British Gas* [1990] ECR 3313 at 3348, para 20, [1990] CMLR 833. See *Doughty v Rolls-Royce plc* [1992] IRLR 126 for an example of a domestic court, the English Court of Appeal, seeking to apply these principles.

7   Case 8/81 *Becker v Finanzamt Muenster Innenstadt* [1982] ECR 53.

8   Case 222/84 *Johnston v Chief Constable of the Royal Ulster Constabulary* [1986] ECR 1651.

9   Case 152/84 *Marshall v Southampton and South West Area Health Authority* [1986] ECR 723.

10   Case 103/88 *Fratelli Constanzo SpA v Comune di Milano* [1989] ECR 1839, [1990] 3 CMLR 239.

11   Joined Cases 266-7/88 *R v The Royal Pharmaceutical Society of Great Britain* [1989] ECR 1295, [1989] 2 CMLR 751. See also Case 271/82 *Auer v Ministère Public* [1983] ECR 2727 on the nature and authority of the French veterinary association and Case 71/

The denial of horizontal direct effect for directives in this way creates arbitrary distinctions between individuals and has been criticised as threatening the coherence and uniform application of Community law. [12] This limitation in the direct effect of directives results in different standards of protection of Community rights being applied to individuals. [13] Their Community rights derived directly from directives are only protected as against the State or its emanations. In failing properly to implement, for example, the Equal Treatment Directive, [14] the United Kingdom is denying women employed in the private sector rights granted them under Community law. [15]

The Court of Justice has to date resisted calls for it to abandon the distinction between horizontal and vertical direct effect in the context of directives.[15a] Instead, it has developed other remedies for use by individuals who are unable to rely directly upon the terms of a directive. In particular, it has elaborated a duty upon national courts to interpret national law so as to give effect to Community law, and has accepted in principle that individuals can sue Member States in damages for loss caused to them as a result of its failure properly to implement a directive. These alternative remedies are discussed in greater detail in Chapter 2.

Direct effect and decisions of the Council or Commission

Article 189 provides that 'a decision shall be binding in its entirety upon those to whom it is addressed.' Where an individual wishes to challenge the terms of a decision which has been addressed to him, the Treaty provides a remedy in the form of a direct action before the Court of Justice under Article 173 (see Chapter 4). It is possible, however, that individuals may wish to rely upon the terms of a decision addressed to another before their national courts.

76 *Thieffry v Conseil de l'Ordre des Avocats à la Cour de Paris* [1977] ECR 765, [1977] 2 CMLR 373 on the Paris Bar Council.
12 Note the criticisms of Advocate General Van Gerven in his Opinion in Case C-271/91 *Marshall v Southampton and South West Hampshire Area Health Authority (No 2)* [1993] ECR I-4367, [1993] IRLR 445 at 450 ff.
13 Compare for example the result in Case 152/84 *Marshall v Southampton and South West Area Health Authority* [1986] ECR 723, an equal pay claim against a public health authority on the basis of Directive 76/207/EEC, with the decision in *Duke v GEC Reliance Ltd* [1988] 1 All ER 626, a similarly based claim against a private company.
14 Council Directive 76/207/EEC, OJ 1976 L39/40.
15 See the decisions of the House of Lords in *Duke v GEC Reliance* [1988] IRLR 118 and *Finnegan v Clowney Youth Training Programme* [1990] IRLR 299 and the decision of the Northern Ireland Court of Appeal in *Porter v Cannon Hygiene* [1993] IRLR 329.
15a In Case C-91/92 *Dori v Recreb* OJ C107, 1992, p 7 Advocate General Lenz stated (in his Opinion of 9 February 1994) that while considerations of legal certainty required the maintenance of this distinction as regards the past, protection of the legitimate expectation of citizens of the European Union that Community law would apply uniformly and consistently throughout the Single European Market required its abandonment henceforth. The Court of Justice had not yet decided the case at the time of writing.

Where the addressee of a decision is a Member State, and the obligation contained in the decision is clear, precise and unconditional, the European Court has held that the right to invoke the terms of the decision might be exercised by any third parties who can show that they have an identifiable interest in the fulfilment of the obligation.[16] On this basis, the Court found that German long distance road hauliers could rely directly upon the provisions of a Council Decision on the common turnover tax system which applied, among other things, to road freight haulage.

Direct effect and Community recommendations and opinions

Article 189 provides that 'recommendations and opinions shall have no binding force'. These instruments, which are used by the Community to outline general directions of policy, cannot, therefore, give rise to enforceable rights or obligations, directly or otherwise. However, recommendations may, in certain situations, give rise to legitimate expectations on the part of the individual as to the Member State's conduct. The Court of Justice has held that, where this is the case, it is appropriate for national courts to take into account Community recommendations to resolve ambiguities or generally to assist in the interpretation of Community law or national measures which seek to implement Community law. This is particularly the case where recommendations seek to clarify the law or to supplement binding Community measures.[17]

Further, a recent decision of a UK court appears to have taken into account a Community recommendation in interpreting and applying a national statute which did not specifically implement any Community provisions. [18]

Direct effect and international agreements

The Community is, in its own right, a party to a number of international agreements. In respect of certain agreements, notably the General Agreement on Tariffs and Trade (GATT), the Community succeeded to

---

16   Case 9/70 *Grad v Finanzamt Traunstein* [1970] ECR 825, [1971] 1 CMLR 1.
17   Case 322/88 *Grimaldi v Fond des Maladies Professionnelles* [1989] ECR 4407, [1991] 2 CMLR 265.
18   In *Wadman v Carpenter Farrer Partnership* [1993] IRLR 374 the Employment Appeal Tribunal referred to a Commission Recommendation and Code of Practice on the protection of the dignity of employees at work in coming to a view as to whether or not particular conduct constituted sexual harassment, and therefore unlawful and discriminatory conduct for the purposes of the UK Sex Discrimination Act 1975.

the responsibilities and obligations of the Member States.[19]   The Court has also held that the exercise of Community powers internally in particular areas gives rise to Community rights and responsibilities on the international plane.[20]   Further, Article 228 of the Treaty gives the Community capacity to conclude international agreements with third countries on economic and commercial matters. The provisions of these treaties are binding upon the Member States.

The international agreements to which the Community is a party constitute part of the Community legal order and may have direct effect within the Member States to the extent that their provisions are clear, precise, unconditional and non-discretionary. [1]

METHODS OF INTERPRETATION IN COMMUNITY LAW

It will be clear to any lawyer trained in any of the legal systems of the United Kingdom that the European Court of Justice does not approach legal texts in the same way as common law judges. The Court of Justice describes its task of interpreting the law as one of uncovering and furthering the purpose of the particular provision. In performing this task, the Court does not consider itself to be bound by the precise wording of Treaty provisions, or of secondary legislation. The wording of any provision has to be read in context. The context, which includes a consideration of the overall spirit and scheme of the Treaty of Rome, will reveal the purpose of the provision. The wording then has to be re-read in such a way as to ensure the achievement of its purpose. This approach to the legislative text is known as 'teleological' interpretation.[2]

In some ways it is akin to the common law purposive approach to statutory interpretation, or the mischief rule. However, it differs from those techniques in that the Court of Justice sees teleological reasoning as the primary paradigm, rather than, as in the canons of common law statutory interpretation, a method which is resorted to only where there is ambiguity or lack of clarity in the authoritative text.

Although it was the Treaty which originally gave rise to the Community legal order, the articles of the Treaty are themselves interpreted in the

---

19   Joined Cases 21-24/72 *International Fruit Company v Commission* [1972] ECR 1219, [1975] 2 CMLR 1.
20   Case 22/70 *Commission v Council: Re the European Road Transport Agreement (ERTA)* [1971] ECR 263.
1   See Case 104/81 *Hauptzollamt Mainz v CA Kupferberg & Cie KG* [1982] ECR 3641, [1983] 1 CMLR 1. Compare with Case 192/89 *Sevince v Staatssecrataris van Justitie* [1990] ECR I-3461, [1992] 2 CMLR 57.
2   See Millett, 'Rules of Interpretation of EEC Legislation' (1989) 11 *Statute Law Review* 163.

light of what is required of a specifically legal order. Thus, where the Treaty appears to the Court to contain contradictions or gaps the Court, as creator and guardian of this new legal order, feels justified in removing the contradictions and filling in the gaps, even if this results in ignoring or adding to the original wording of the Treaty. As the then Advocate-General (now Judge) Mancini stated in his Opinion in *Les Verts:* [3]

> '[T]he obligation to observe the law takes precedence over the strict terms of the written law. Whenever required in the interests of judicial protection, the Court is prepared to correct or complete rules which limit its powers in the name of the principle which defines its mission.'

In performing its task of 'interpretation', the Court of Justice has, in a variety of contexts, effectively inserted new provisions into the Treaty. The series of cases relating to the involvement of the European Parliament in the Community legislative and judicial processes is a prime example. With no support in the Treaty wording, the Court has found that the European Parliament has a right to intervene in cases before the Court,[4] that it has *locus standi* to raise actions for failure to act under Article 175,[5] that the Court may review the legality of the activities of the Parliament under Article 173,[6] and that the Parliament is competent to bring actions against other Community institutions under Article 173 in order to defend its powers and privileges.[7]

In effect, the Court has re-written the Treaty as regards the position of the European Parliament. The Maastricht Treaty amends Articles 173 and 175 of the Treaty bringing them into line with the case law.

Of more interest for the development of individual rights under Community law has been the manner in which the Court has developed Articles 59 to 66 of the Treaty, which set out the principle that nationals of Member States established in one country should be free to provide services to persons throughout the Community. In *Luisi and Carbone* the Court held that freedom of services throughout the Community was a general principle of Community law. This meant not only that an individual should be free to offer his services to persons outside his own

---

3 Case 294/83 *Parti Ecologiste 'Les Verts' v European Parliament* [1986] ECR 1339 at 1350.
4 Case 139/79 *Maizena v Commission* [1980] ECR 1513.
5 Case 13/83 *Parliament v Council (Transport Policy)* [1985] ECR 1513.
6 Case 294/83 *Les Verts v European Parliament* [1986] ECR 1339. See also Case 34/86 *Council v Parliament (Budget)* [1986] 3 CMLR 94.
7 Case 70/88 *Parliament v Commission (Chernobyl)* [1990] ECR I-2041. See also Case C-295/90 *European Parliament v Council (Students Rights of Residence)* [1992] ECR I-4193.

country, but that individuals should be free to receive services in other Community countries. Any national laws which could have the effect of restricting the freedom of their residents to receive services in other Member States would therefore be subject to review by the Court.[8] Recipients of services, including such broad categories as tourists and cross-border shoppers have, through a process of more or less creative interpretation, been brought under the protective umbrella of the Treaty. [9]

As well as adding to the Treaty, the Court has felt able to contradict the plain wording of Treaty articles in pursuit of its own perception of the goals of the Community. For example, Article 177 of the Treaty plainly contemplates questions as to the validity of acts of the institutions of the Community being raised before and ruled upon by national courts. The national courts, other than those of final instance, have the option of making a reference to the Court of Justice where they consider that a decision by the Court is necessary for them to give judgment. Notwithstanding the terms of Article 177, the Court of Justice held in *Firma Foto-Frost* that while national courts might confirm the validity of Community acts, they had no jurisdiction to declare acts of Community institutions to be invalid.[10] Only the Court of Justice itself could make that decision. To have found otherwise, in accordance with the wording of Article 177, would have prejudiced the uniform application of Community law throughout the Member States since Community acts could become, at least temporarily, valid in some states but invalid in others.

Finally, and perhaps most radically, the Court has suggested that the independence and strength of the Community legal system is such that certain provisions of the Treaty might be unalterable and entrenched against any revision or amendment by the Member States. In its first Opinion on the draft Treaty for a European Economic Area the Court stated: [11]

'Article 238 of the EEC Treaty does not provide any basis for setting up a system of courts which conflicts with Article 164 of the EEC Treaty and, more generally, with the very foundations of Community law.

For the same reasons, an amendment of Article 238 in the way indicated by the Commission could not cure the incompatibility

8   Joined Cases 286/82, 26/83 *Luisi and Carbone v Italian Ministry of Finance* [1984] ECR 377.
9   See Case 186/87 *Cowan v French Treasury* [1989] ECR 195, [1990] 2 CMLR 613.
10 Case 314/85 *Firma Foto-Frost v Hauptzollamt Itzehoe* [1987] ECR 4199, [1988] 3 CMLR 57.
11 *Re a Draft Treaty on the EEA* [1991] ECR I-6079, paras 70-1, [1992] 1 CMLR 245.

with Community law of the system of courts to be set up by the agreement.'

For students of law and legal systems, the performance of the Court of Justice of its function of interpreting the Treaty is an unequivocal example of judicial activism. The result of the Court's jurisprudence is, as one observer of the Court has put it that 'the Member States, although originally the creators of the Communities, are no longer the independent masters of the Treaties but are bound by them.'[12]

For lawyers in practice the primary significance of the Court's approach to interpretation is that the sort of arguments that would appeal to a national court in a particular case are not necessarily the same as those that would appeal to the Court of Justice, and vice versa. In particular, the fact that the Court of Justice is frequently prepared to ignore the literal meaning of a provision in favour of an interpretation which furthers its own view of the guiding objectives of the Treaty, broadens considerably the scope for legal argument about provisions of Community law.

PRECEDENT IN COMMUNITY LAW

Precedent, in the sense of a practice that previous judicial decisions should be regarded as binding on courts at the same level or lower in the judicial hierarchy, is not a general feature of the domestic legal systems of continental Europe. This is a consequence of the codification of those systems and the emphasis on the code as a complete statement of the law which does not require interpretation but only application by the judiciary. Accordingly, judicial decisions are not regarded as being statements of the law in anything except the particular factual situation before the court. Indeed Article 5 of the French Civil Code provides that in deciding the cases before them judges are forbidden to make 'pronouncements of a general and normative kind'.

As we have seen, however, the characteristics of the European legal order have been primarily created in and by the judgments of the European Court, and, as mainly judge-made, Community law resembles in many respects the common law systems of the British Isles. Previous case law is important in such systems because it is in the case law that the guiding principles of the system are found. The need, therefore, arises for some acceptance by the Court of Justice of the binding nature of past

12 See Schwarze *The role of the European Court of Justice in the Interpretation of Uniform Law among the Member States of the European Communities* (1988) at 11.

decisions which have formulated general propositions about the law, if only out of respect for legal certainty.

Some recognition of the binding nature of previous case law is implicit in the Court's acceptance that national courts of final instance are relieved of the obligation to refer a question of Community law to the Court of Justice where they feel that, in view of the Court's previous decisions, the answer is obvious.[13] It is possible to state, in broader terms, that although there is no Community legal doctrine to the effect that its past case law is binding upon it, in practice the Court of Justice seeks to avoid departing from the principles laid down in earlier cases for the sake of consistency in the law. The Court has a tendency to repeat general formulas laid down in its earlier judgments in subsequent cases which raise the same or similar points.

However, in the absence of a doctrine of binding precedent, national courts are not precluded from making a reference to the Court of Justice, notwithstanding that the Court has previously decided on the Community law point at issue. For example, in *Dori v Recreb*,[14] a reference was made by an Italian court to determine whether or not a non-implemented directive concerning the protection of consumers in their dealings with door-to-door and travelling salesmen [15] could be relied upon by an individual against another private party. The reference was made notwithstanding the unequivocal judgment by the Court in *Marshall (No 1)*,[16] and subsequent cases [17] that directives can only have direct effect against public bodies.

Another aspect of the lack of a formal doctrine of precedent is that the distinction between the *ratio* of a decision of the Court and other *obiter* remarks is not recognised in Community law. Instead, everything that is said in the text of the Court's judgment is viewed as an expression of the will of the Court and therefore as an authoritative pronouncement of the law.[18]

The most confusing aspect of the lack of any explicit doctrine of precedent is the apparent unwillingness of the Court to clearly acknowledge in its judgments when its previous decisions are being distinguished, developed, departed from or overruled entirely. The

---

13 Case 283/81 *CILFIT v Ministro della Sanità* [1982] ECR 3415, [1983] 1 CMLR 472.

14 Case C-91/92 *Paola Faccini Dori v Recreb Srl*, notified in OJ 1992 C107/7. Judgment was awaited in this case at the time of writing. Opinion of Advocate General Lenz was delivered on 9 February 1994.

15 Directive 85/577, OJ 1985 L372/31.

16 Case 152/84 *Marshall v Southampton and S.W. Hampshire Area Health Authority* [1986] ECR 723.

17 See, eg Case C-106/89 *Marleasing SA v La Comercial Internacional de Alimentacion SA* [1991] ECR I-4135.

18 Case 9/61 *Netherlands v High Authority of the Coal and Steel Community* [1962] ECR 213, 242, per Advocate-General Roemer.

Court has expressly overruled its previous line of decisions on two occasions. [19] The more typical approach of the Court, however is to ignore inconsistencies with earlier decisions. [20] Thus, in *Francovich*[1] the Court found the proposition that a state was liable in damages to the individual for loss caused through its breach of Community law to be a principle of Community law inherent in the Treaty. However in *Russo v AIMA* [2] the Court had already ruled that the question as to whether or not a Member State was required to pay damages to an individual for loss occasioned to that individual by the state's breach of Community law was a matter for the national law of that state. Although there was an attempt to distinguish *Russo* in the Advocate-General Mischo's Opinion in *Francovich*, the judgment of the Court *Russo* was cited as if it fully supported the new judgment.

Similarly in *Marshall (No 2)* the Court found the provisions of Article 6 of the Equal Treatment Directive to be sufficiently clear and precise so as to be able to deduce a directly effective right to full compensation with interest in the event of an unfair dismissal.[3] This finding conflicts with decision in *Von Colson* [4] where the Court found that although Article 6 required some kind of judicial protection to be provided against sex discrimination it did not prescribe any specific measures to be taken in the event of a breach of the directive but left Member States free to choose among different solutions.[5]

The Court seems sensitive to political, economic and academic reactions to its judgments and it will apparently depart from a previous decision or halt or slow down the development of a line of case law where these have not been well-received in the world outside Luxembourg. [6]

---

19 Case 192/73 *Van Zuylen Freres v HAG AG* [1974] ECR 731, [1974] 2 CMLR 127 on common trademarks and inter-state trade was explicitly departed from in Case C-10/89 *SA CNL-SUCAL v HAG GF AG* [1990] ECR I-3711. In Joined Cases C-267, 268/91 *Keck and Mithouard* 24 November [1993] ECR (not yet reported), the Court stated that it was departing from its line of case law on the proper interpretation of Art 30 of the Treaty of Rome prohibiting 'quantitative restrictions on imports and all measures having equivalent effect'.

20 Compare Case 302/87 *Parliament v Council (Comitology)* [1988] ECR 5615 with Case C-70/88 *Parliament v Council (Chernobyl)* [1990] ECR I-2041.

1 Cases C6,9/90 *Francovich & Bonifaci v Italian State* [1991] ECR I-5403 at para 19, [1992] IRLR 84.

2 Case 60/75 *Russo v AIMA* [1976] ECR 45 at 57.

3 Case C-271/91 *Marshall v Southampton and SW Hampshire Area Health Authority (No 2)*, European Court of Justice 2 August 1993, [1993] ECR I-4367.

4 Case 14/83 *Von Colson v Land Nordrhein-Westfalen* [1984] ECR 1891, [1986] 2 CMLR 430.

5 See also Case 222/84 *Johnston v Chief Constable of the Royal Ulster Constabulary* [1986] ECR 1651.

6 See, for example, the Court's change of position on the relationship between pre-Maastricht Arts 130s and 100a as between Case C-300/89 *Commission v Council*

The case law of the Court is presented and referred to by the Court as a coherent and consistent body of ever developing doctrine. Each judgement of the Court is of equal value and standing as any other. No public dissenting opinions of individual judges disagreeing with the majority are, however, permitted in the Court of Justice. The judgments of the Court are therefore, of necessity, the products of a certain amount of compromise of differing views. Further, the increasing volume of work at the Court of Justice has meant that more and more cases are being dealt with by chambers rather than by the *plenum* of the Court. These chambers may consist of as few as three judges. No matter how many judges are involved, the judgments of the Court are to be regarded by national courts as equally authoritative. It is clear, however, that a difference in the (composition of) chambers dealing with a case might yield a different result. The unity of the Court's approach may therefore be more apparent than real.

PRIVATE INTERNATIONAL LAW IN THE EUROPEAN COMMUNITY

The European legal order encompasses also certain treaties relating to private international law matters which are parallel to the Treaty of Rome and over which the Court of Justice also exercises an interpretative jurisdiction.

To date two principal agreements have been concluded among the Member States of the Community. The first convention, the Brussels Convention of 1968, provides for a common approach among the Member States courts to determining questions of jurisdiction in civil and commercial matters. This convention also deals with the related matter of the recognition and enforcement of judgments of national courts across the Community. The second convention, the Rome Convention of 1980, is concerned with setting up common rules to establishing the national law regime which applies to an international contract. Thus, while application of the rules of the Brussels convention will establish the court in which a case should be held, the rules of the Rome Convention will establish what body of substantive laws should be applied by that court.

('Titanium Dioxide') [1991] ECR I-2867 and Case C-155/91 *Commission v Council: Re the Framework Waste Directives* [1993] ECR I-939. See also the slowing down of the application of the principle of equal treatment to occupation pension heralded in Case 262/88 *Barber v Guardian Royal Exchange* [1990] ECR I-1889 which is evident in the Court's judgment in Case C-152/91 *Neath v Hugh Steeper*, ECJ 22 December, [1993] ECR (not yet reported).

These conventions, as amended, have been incorporated into the domestic law of the United Kingdom by the Civil Jurisdiction and Judgments Act 1982 and the Contracts (Applicable Law) Act 1990. Consideration of the particular rules contained in these conventions and their implementing national legislation is beyond the scope of this work [7] It should be noted that under both conventions, provision is made for national courts to stay their proceedings and to refer questions on the proper interpretation of the conventions to the European Court of Justice. [8] The object of such procedure is, as with Article 177 of the Treaty of Rome, to ensure that national courts adopt a common approach to the interpretation of the conventions. The procedure for such references to the Court of Justice in the case of both conventions is set out in the Brussels Protocol of 1971 which forms Schedule 2 of the 1982 Act. This provides that only the national courts acting in an appellate capacity may make a reference to the Court of Justice.

It may be that further conventions in the sphere of private international law will be concluded within the Community, notably in the spheres of arbitration, bankruptcy and civil wrongs (tort or delict). Any such conventions would be likely to give the Court of Justice similar jurisdiction on interpretation and national courts the same rights of reference.

THE EUROPEAN ECONOMIC AREA

On 1 January 1994 the European Economic Area Agreement came into force between the European Community and Austria, Finland, Sweden, Norway and Iceland, five of the countries which, together with Switzerland and Lichtenstein, formed the European Free Trade Area (EFTA). The aim of this Treaty was to create a European Economic Area (EEA) in which the European Community's free trade rules and competition policy would be enforced. The Treaty provided for a complex system of political and judicial co-operation and information exchange to ensure that these common rules would be interpreted and applied in the same way in both the Community and the relevant EFTA States.[9]

7   Reference may be made to the following works, among others: P Kaye *Private International Law of Tort and Product Liability* (1991) Dartmouth; P Kaye *The New Private International Law of Contract of the European Community* (1993) Dartmouth; D Lasok and P Stone *Conflict of Laws in the European Community* (1987) Professional Books and R Plender *The European Contract Convention* (1991) Sweet & Maxwell.

8   Sections 3(1) and 16(3)(a) of the Civil Jurisdiction and Judgments Act 1982 and s 3 of the Contracts (Applicable Law) Act 1990.

9   See Opinion 1/91 *Re a Draft Treaty on a European Economic Area* [1991] ECR I-6079, [1992] 1 CMLR 245 and Opinion 1/92 *Re a Revised Draft Treaty on a European Economic Area* [1992] ECR I-2821, [1992] 2 CMLR 217.

Chapter 2

THE DUTIES OF NATIONAL COURTS UNDER COMMUNITY LAW

INTRODUCTION

The previous chapter examined the general characteristics of Community law as a new kind of legal order capable of creating rights and obligations not only for states but also for individuals within those states. This chapter considers some of the issues that may arise in practice when an individual seeks to rely upon a Community law right before the national courts of the United Kingdom. In particular, the duties incumbent upon a national judge when faced with a Community law issue are examined.

The United Kingdom became a Member State of the European Communities by virtue of the 1972 Treaty of Accession. From a Community perspective this Treaty resulted in, amongst other things, the bringing of the legal systems of England and Wales, Scotland and Northern Ireland into the existing Community legal order. From a national perspective, the system of Community law was received into the domestic legal systems of the United Kingdom by virtue of an Act of Parliament, the European Communities Act 1972.

Sections 2 and 3 of the 1972 Act required the courts of the United Kingdom to apply Community law as interpreted and applied by the European Court of Justice. National legislation existing prior to the 1972 Act was impliedly repealed in so far as it was inconsistent with Community law.[1] For example, although s 128 of the Employment Protection (Consolidation) Act 1978 apparently limits the jurisdiction of industrial tribunals to those matters specifically conferred upon the tribunals by

---

1 See, eg Case 121/85 *Conegate v Commisioners of Customs & Excise* [1986] ECR 1007, [1987] QB 254 and Case 34/79 *R v Henn & Derby* [1979] ECR 3795, [1981] AC 850 on the implied partial repeal of provisions regarding the powers of Customs officials to order seizure of imports.

statute and (notwithstanding that no national statute has given industrial tribunals such jurisdiction) claims arising directly from Community law, such cases are now regularly heard before these tribunals[2] and Article 177 references have been made by industrial tribunals directly to the European Court of Justice.[3]

From a Community perspective, the duty of national courts to apply Community law in accordance with the decisions and principles of the Court of Justice is found in Article 5 of the Treaty of Rome. In considering how Community law is to be applied, ss 2 and 3 of the 1972 Act should, therefore, be read in the light of the case law of the Court of Justice on the Article 5 duties of national courts.

ARTICLE 5 AND THE EFFECTIVENESS OF COMMUNITY LAW

Article 5 of the Treaty of Rome is set out in the following terms:

> '[i] Member States shall take all appropriate measures, whether general or particular, to ensure fulfilment of the obligations arising out of this Treaty or resulting from action taken by the institutions of the Community.
> [ii] They shall facilitate the achievement of the Community's tasks.
> [iii] They shall abstain from any measure which could jeopardize the attainment of the objectives of this Treaty.'

This article sets out general duties on the Member States to show loyalty and good faith in their dealings with the Community and to co-operate with Community institutions in ensuring the achievement of Community objectives. The Court of Justice has held that the duties set out in Article 5 to promote the objectives of the Community apply to all public institutions and authorities within the Member State. In *Fratelli Costanzo*,[4] for example, the Court held that the municipal and regional authorities of a Member State were bound by the provisions of a directly effective directive notwithstanding the fact that the directive had not been properly implemented into national law by the central government.[5]

2   *Wright and Hannah* [1991] IRLR 187.
3   See, eg *Smith v Avdel Systems Ltd* [1993] 1 CMLR 554 and Case C-152/91 *Neath v Hugh Steeper Ltd*, 22 December, [1993] ECR (not yet reported), [1994] IRLR 91.
4   Case 103/88 *Fratelli Costanzo v Comune di Milano* [1989] ECR 1839, [1990] 3 CMLR 239.
5   See also Case 8/88 *Germany v Commission: Re Suckler Cows* [1990] ECR I-2321, [1992] 1 CMLR 409 and Case C-33/90 *Commission v Italy: Toxic Waste in Campania* [1991] ECR I-5987, [1992] 2 CMLR 353.

Most importantly from the point of view of the practising lawyer, the duty to promote the effectiveness of Community law applies directly and equally to all the national courts of the Member States. National courts must ensure the full and proper effect of Community provisions.

The performance of this duty involves essentially a two-stage process. Firstly, the national court must establish the aims or objectives of the Community provision at issue and so understand the result which would be sought by Community law. To this end, the national judge must become a Community judge and apply Community legal principles and methods of interpretation.

Having established the result to be achieved by the application of the relevant Community law to the facts before it, the national court must, secondly, consider the mechanism whereby this result might be achieved whether by direct or indirect effect.

In view of the supremacy of Community law over national law,[6] the paramount duty of fidelity or loyalty is owed by each national court to the Court of Justice, rather than to other courts in the national hierarchy.[7] If a lower court doubts the correctness of the decision of a higher court on a point of Community law, then it should either distinguish the higher court ruling or make a reference to the Court of Justice under Article 177. The Court of Justice has stated that any rule of national law whereby a court is bound on points of law by the rulings of a superior court cannot deprive lower courts of their power to refer to the Court of Justice questions of interpretation of Community law.[8]

INDIRECT EFFECT: THE DUTY TO INTERPRET NATIONAL LAW IN ACCORDANCE WITH COMMUNITY LAW

The Von Colson principle

The obligation of national courts under Article 5 to interpret national law in accordance with Community law was first elaborated by the Court of Justice in *Von Colson v Land Nordrhein-Westfalen.*[9] The Court held that in respect of national legislation which implements Community law, domestic courts should interpret these in the light of the wording and purpose of the relevant directive, so as to achieve the result intended by the Community provision. Thus, national courts in the United Kingdom

6   Case 6/64 *Costa v ENEL* [1964] ECR 585, [1964] CMLR 425. See Ch 1.
7   Case 106/77*Amministrazione delle Finanze dello Stato v Simmenthal* [1978] ECR 629, 643.
8   Case 166/73 *Rheinmuehlen-Duesseldorf* [1974] ECR 33 at 38.
9   Case 14/83 *Von Colson v Land Nordrhein-Westfalen* [1984] ECR 1891, [1986] 2 CMLR 430.

have power under Community law to add to, delete from or hold ineffective provisions of implementing national legislation in order to ensure that they give full and accurate effect to Community law.[10] As Lord Oliver of Aylmerton stated in a seminal judgment in the House of Lords in a case which turned on the correct interpretation of the Transfer of Undertakings (Protection of Employment) Regulations 1981 (TUPE)[11] in the light of the Community directive[12] which the national regulations purported to implement:

> '[T]he greater flexibility available to the court in applying a purposive construction to legislation designed to give effect to the United Kingdom's Treaty obligations to the Community enables the court, where necessary, to supply by implication words appropriate to comply with those obligations ... Having regard to the manifest purpose of the regulations I do not for my part feel inhibited from making such an implication in the instant case.'[13]

It should be noted that in *Litster* there was no ambiguity in the UK regulations.[14] The judges were not confronted with two or more possible constructions and invited to choose the one which reflected the requirements of Community law. Rather, the national regulations were simply inadequately drafted in so far as they were intended to implement the Community directive. The Lords accordingly did not interpret the text of the national regulation, they re-drafted it.

Not only does the national court or tribunal have the power to interpret national legislation in this radical, purposive way, but it has a duty to do so under Community law. A purposive reading of national regulations may require the national court, even where there is no ambiguity in the plain wording of the regulations, to add or delete provisions with a view to achieving the objective of the directive. In the United Kingdom

10 See *Pickstone v Freemans plc* [1989] AC 66. The question as to how national courts should deal with non-implementing national legislation which conflicts with Community law is dealt with below.

11 SI 1981/1794.

12 Council Directive 77/187/EEC, OJ 1977 L61/27.

13 *Litster v Forth Dry Dock Co Ltd* [1990] 1 AC 546 at 577.

14 Lord Slynn, formerly UK judge on the Court of Justice has noted in 'Looking at European Community Texts' (1993) *Statute Law Review* 12 at 26 that:
    '[I]t is necessary for the national court to take account of the terms of the directive where implemented by specific legislation at all times. It would not be consistent with the obligation for a national court to be subject to a precondition such as a requirement that it may not look behind the text of a national implementing measure unless it is found to be ambiguous. For a court to tie its hands in this way might lead to a 'wrecking' interpretation of national provisions which might needlessly bring them into conflict with Community law rules.'

context, this does not involve *contra legem* interpretation or a usurpation of parliamentary authority since Parliament's avowed purpose in passing the national legislation was to implement fully the Community directive.

The issue of the direct effect of the provisions of the directive never arose in *Litster*. The respondent company was a private party, and the doctrine of vertical direct effect meant that the provisions of the directive could not be directly applied against it. Instead, the national court's obligation to read the national implementing legislation in the light of the wording and purpose of the relevant Community provision gave rise to the 'indirect effect' of Community law. The provisions of implemented directives could thereby be made effective against all parties, public and private.

In *Kolpinghuis Nijmegen* [15] the Advocate-General suggested, further, that where a Member State stated that its existing legislation was sufficient to implement the provisions of a directive, then such legislation should be treated in the same way as specific implementing legislation. It should also be noted that, in this case, the Court of Justice held that the duty of a national court to interpret national law in the light of a Community directive did not extend to an interpretation which had the effect of, retrospectively, creating a criminal offence.

National legislation which does not implement Community law

The decision in *Von Colson* seemed to leave open the question of whether the duty to interpret national law in accordance with Community law applied also to national legislation which was not specifically intended to implement Community provisions.

The broader view of the interpretative obligation presents particular problems for national judges who are constrained by the common law rules of statutory construction and by the traditional doctrine of the role of the courts in relation to Parliament.

While the creative interpretation of implementing legislation might be justified on the grounds that it was Parliament's intention to implement fully Community law, it is less easy to take a liberal view in respect of other legislation where the specific intention to implement is not present. This notwithstanding, broader claims about the proper interpretation of national law in the context of Community law have been made by national judges. For example, in *Garland v British Rail Engineering* Lord Diplock stated that unless an Act of Parliament passed after the

15 Case 80/86 *Officier van Justitie v Kolpinghuis Nijmegen* [1987] ECR 3969, [1989] 2 CMLR 18.

United Kingdom's accession to the European Community expressly stated that it was passed with the intention of breaching Community obligations, then UK legislation should be construed in a manner consistent with Community law 'however wide the departure from the *prima facie* meaning of the language of the provision might be needed to achieve consistency.'[16]

The argument that Parliament intends to comply with Community law in all circumstances unless it expressly says otherwise would provide the courts with a general background intention upon which to fasten and so permit a purposive interpretation of all national legislation. It is not, however, an argument which has been consistently adopted by the House of Lords.[17]

Any restriction of the national court's interpretative obligation only to such national legislation as was passed with a view to implementing a particular Community provision would not appear to be correct under Community law in the light of the decision of the Court of Justice in *Marleasing v La Comercial*[18] in which the Court held that:

> '[I]n applying national law, *whether the provisions in question were adopted before or after the directive,* the national court called upon to interpret it is required to do so, so far as possible, in the light of the wording and the purpose of the directive in order to achieve the result pursued by the latter.'

The obligation to interpret national law in accordance with Community law expressed in *Von Colson* is thereby explicitly extended to cover national provisions which pre-dated, and accordingly did not implement, Community law.

---

16 *Garland v British Rail Engineering* [1983] 2 AC 751 at 770-1. See also Lord Oliver in *Litster*, [1990] 1 AC 546 at 563:
'If your Lordships are in fact compelled to the conclusion [that the regulations are gravely defective and the Government of the United Kingdom has failed to comply with its mandatory obligations under the Directive], so be it; but it is not, I venture to think, a conclusion which any of your Lordships would willingly embrace in the absence of the most compulsive context rendering any other conclusion impossible.'

17 In both *Duke v GEC Reliance* [1988] AC 618, [1988] 1 CMLR 719 and *Finnegan v Clowney Youth Training Programme* [1990] 2 AC 407, [1990] 2 CMLR 859 the House of Lords refused to 'distort the plain meaning of the [national] legislation' so as to find that an employer's policy of compulsory retirement of men and women employees at different ages might constitute unlawful sex discrimination.

18 Case C-106/89 *Marleasing SA v La Comercial Internacional de Alimentacion SA* [1990] ECR I-4153 at 4159, [1992] 1 CMLR 305 at 322-3.

The need for ambiguity in the national legislation ?

The other main issue which arises out of the *Von Colson* principle is to what extent the interpretative obligation is conditional upon ambiguity in the provision of national law which is subject to interpretation. Does the obligation only operate where a statute is reasonably capable of construction in conformity with Community law, or must the national judge distort the plain words of a statute where this is necessary to achieve the result prescribed by Community law?

In *Von Colson* itself, national judges were instructed to interpret national law in accordance with Community law in so far as they had discretion to do so under national law. In *Marleasing*, sympathetic interpretation was required 'as far as possible'.

In the United Kingdom there is a long-established presumption in the common law that Parliament intends to legislate in conformity with its international commitments and that where a statutory provision is susceptible of more than one interpretation the court should give it the construction which complies most closely with those commitments. However, a judicial power to read statutes *contra legem*, which arguably would go beyond even the widest view of interpretation, is difficult to reconcile with common law doctrine.[19]

In *Webb v EMO Cargo*[20] the Lords accepted that it was their duty, as national judges within the Community, to construe domestic legislation in any field covered by a Community directive so as to accord with the meaning of the directive as interpreted by the Court of Justice. This duty applied to domestic legislation regardless of whether it preceded or was subsequent to the directive. This duty was stressed to be one of interpretation rather than interstitial legislation. Where the national law was not intended to implement Community provision the duty of the national court did not extend to distorting the otherwise plain meaning of the legislation. Rather, such a statute should only be read in conformity with Community law where it is open to divergent interpretations.

The extent of the interpretative obligation of national courts with respect to non-implementing legislation appears, then, to be as follows: where there are two possible interpretations of the domestic provision, one of which accords with the wording and purpose of the relevant directive and the other which does not, the national court should prefer and apply that interpretation which best accords with the Community law.[1]

19 *Salomon v Customs and Excise Comrs* [1967] 2 QB 116.
20 *Webb v EMO Cargo* [1993] 1 CMLR 259. The case was referred by the House of Lords to the Court of Justice: Case C32/93, OJ 1993 C75/13.
1   See also *Porter v Cannon Hygiene* [1993] IRLR 329.

At the time of writing *Webb v EMO* represented the state of UK law on the obligation of national courts to interpret domestic law in accordance with Community law. It remains possible to argue, however, that the House of Lords in *Webb* took an unduly narrow view of its Article 5 duties; that is, that Community law does not in fact recognise its distinction between implementing and non-implementing legislation, but rather rejects any requirement for ambiguity in the national legislation statute. Clearly, the UK position may be subject to modification in the light of future judgments of the Court of Justice. However, it may currently be summarised as follows:

- Where the UK legislation specifically implements a Community provision, a purposive reading should be given to the national law regardless of whether or not the wording of its provisions can be said to be ambiguous.[2]
- Where existing national measures were re-enacted or consolidated subsequent to the adoption of a directive, but no amendments or further implementing legislation were made on the grounds that the national authorities considered that the existing legislation duly complied with the directive, then a broad purposive reading in line with the relevant Community provision should be given to this national law, regardless of the question of any ambiguity in its text.[3]
- Where no specific implementing measures have been taken by the UK Government and no existing legislation is presented by it as already complying with the relevant Community provision, then the United Kingdom is in default of its obligations under Community law. In such a situation, it remains the duty of the domestic courts under Article 5 of the Treaty, to minimise the executive's default by interpreting the existing UK law, wherever possible, in conformity with the relevant Community law.[4] In fulfilment of this duty the national court requires to determine the result sought by the relevant Community law. The relevant national law has to be read in the light of the objectives of this Community law insofar as it is in the power of the national court so to do.

---

2   *Litster v Forth Dry Dock & Engineering Co Ltd* [1990] 1 AC 546, [1989] 1 All ER 1134, [1989] 1 All ER 1134.

3   See *Bell Concord Educational Trust Ltd v Customs and Excise Comrs* [1989] 1 CMLR 845, CA; *Bethway & Moss v Customs and Excise Comrs* [1988] 3 CMLR 44.

4   See *R v Secretary of State for the Home Department, ex p Brind* [1991] 1 AC 696 on the duty of national courts to interpret domestic law in conformity with non-Community treaties, specifically the European Convention on Human Rights and Fundamental Freedoms.

Comparison with direct effect

The next section considers the implication for national courts of the principle of the direct effect of Community law. Certain distinctions between the characteristics of direct effect and approach of indirect effect through sympathetic interpretation should, however, be noted at this stage:

- Sympathetic interpretation or indirect effect is a remedy in national law, which seeks to assert rights under national legislation. Direct effect, on the other hand, involves the assertion of rights which have been conferred by Community law but which, by definition, national law does not adequately reflect. It requires the national court to displace, rather than to uphold, the terms of national law.
- An argument for direct effect is an argument that the Member State is in breach of its obligations under Article 5 and/or Article 189 of the Treaty, faithfully to implement Community law. Since a state cannot be allowed to profit from its own failure to implement Community law, the relevant Community provision should be invoked to override any inconsistent national provisions. The argument for sympathetic interpretation asserts precisely the opposite, that national legislation does indeed fully reflect the demands of Community law, if only the national court would interpret it in the manner requested. It is the court which may be in breach of its obligations under Article 5 if such an interpretation is not given.
- Direct effect cannot, in the context of directives, be invoked against an individual. This is a potentially serious limitation on its usefulness. As we have seen, however, the *Von Colson* approach may allow the terms of directives to be enforced indirectly against both public bodies and private individuals.[5]
- Direct effect cannot operate until the expiry of the time limit for implementation of the Community provisions at issue. Until this point, the Member State is not in breach of its Community law obligations. In *Kolpinghuis Nijmegen*, however, the Court of Justice held that the obligation to interpret national law in conformity with Community law operates independently of any time limits.[6] The provisions of Community directives can, therefore,

---

5   See, eg Case C-106/89 *Marleasing SA v La Comercial Internacional de Alimentacion SA* [1990] ECR I-4153, [1992] 1 CMLR 305.
6   Case 80/86 *Officier van Justitie v Kolpinghuis Nijmegen* [1987] ECR 3969, [1989] 2 CMLR 18.

be brought to bear upon national law from the date of the directive's adoption.

DIRECT EFFECT: THE DUTY TO DISAPPLY CONTRARY RULES OF NATIONAL LAW

Even if a national court or tribunal finds itself unable to give effect to Community law through a process of interpretation of national law, the relevant Community provisions may have direct effect. A finding of direct effect allows litigants before national courts to by-pass national legislation and rely directly on the terms of Community instruments. All domestic courts and tribunals, from industrial tribunals up to the House of Lords have a duty to 'disapply' any rules of national law which are inconsistent with the full and proper enjoyment of rights directly conferred under Community law.[7] This duty is distinct from the interpretative obligation outlined above, which applies regardless of any finding of direct effect of the relevant Community provisions.

Judicial review of primary legislation is a requirement of Community law itself, notwithstanding that it is in direct conflict with the common law principle of the national courts' respect for the sovereignty of Parliament. The principle that courts in the United Kingdom can and must explicitly review national legislation for its conformity with Community law, has only gradually been accepted.[8]

CASE STUDY: *SPANISH FISHERMEN V PARLIAMENT*

In 1988 Parliament passed the Merchant Shipping Act in order, it was claimed, to implement and to enforce the national quota system established by the Community's Common Fisheries Policy. The Merchant Shipping (Registration of Fishing Vessels) Regulations 1988 issued under the Act required all vessels previously registered under the Merchant Shipping Act 1894 to re-register under new conditions which were designed to exclude foreign owned and operated fishing boats from eligibility for registration as British vessels. Registration was the prerequisite to obtaining a licence to fish under the quota permitted the United Kingdom under the Community's Common Fisheries Policy. The Act came into

---

7   Case 106/77 *Amministrazione delle Finanze dello Stato v Simmenthal* [1978] ECR 629 at 644.

8   *R v Secretary of State for Transport, ex p Factortame* [1990] 3 WLR 818, in particular, Lord Bridge at 857-8.

force on 1 December 1988 and it was provided that the validity of registrations under the previous Act would expire on 31 March 1989.

In *R v Secretary of State for Transport, ex p Factortame*, [9] the applicants requested judicial review of the refusal of the Secretary of State, in accordance with the Act, to re-register certain Spanish controlled boats. The basis for judicial review was that the Act itself (and the regulations and administrative acts issued under it) contravened Article 7 (now 6) of the Treaty of Rome preventing discrimination on grounds of nationality and Article 52 on the freedom of the nationals of one Member State to pursue their trade in another Member State.

The Divisional Court requested the guidance of the Court of Justice on the proper interpretation of, among other things, Article 52 of the Treaty. Pending that decision, the Divisional Court also made an interim order purporting to 'disapply' the operation of both the principal Act and the disputed regulations made under it and forbidding the Secretary of State to enforce those regulations as against the parties to the case, thereby allowing their previous registrations under the 1894 Act to continue until the final determination of the case.

The interim order was appealed to the House of Lords which held that no such order could be granted against the Crown because of two rules of English law: that Acts of Parliament were to be presumed to be valid and compatible with Community law unless and until the matter was otherwise decided by the European Court of Justice; and that, in any event, the courts in England had no power or jurisdiction to grant any injunction against the Crown. [10]

However, their Lordships considered that a second reference was needed to the European Court to ascertain whether Community law required that these procedural rules of English law would themselves have to be set aside as a matter of Community law so that interim protection could be granted to putative Community rights.

On 19 June 1990 the Court of Justice replied to the House of Lords as follows: [11]

> 'Community law must be interpreted as meaning that a national court which, in a case before it concerning Community law, considers that the sole obstacle which prevents it from granting interim relief is a rule of national law must set aside that rule.'

---

9   *R v Secretary of State for Transport, ex p Factortame* [1989] 2 CMLR 353, QBD.
10   *R v Secretary of State for Transport, ex p Factortame (No 1)* [1990] 2 AC 85.
11   Case C-213/89 *R v Secretary of State for Transport, ex p Factortame (No 2)* [1990] ECR I-2433, [1990] 3 CMLR 1.

On receiving this reference back from the Court of Justice, the Lords then granted an order restraining the Secretary of State 'from withholding or withdrawing registration in the Register of British Fishing Vessels maintained by him pursuant to the Merchant Shipping (Registration of Fishing Vessels) Regulations 1988.'[12]

In granting this order, the House of Lords, as required by Community law, set aside the rule of English law that injunctions could not be pronounced against the Crown.[13] No clearer illustration can be given of the obligations of courts in the United Kingdom to protect Community law rights as against conflicting common law and statutory provisions.

THE DUTY TO AWARD DAMAGES AGAINST THE STATE FOR BREACH OF COMMUNITY LAW

The *Francovich* case

The remedies of direct effect and sympathetic interpretation of national law will be sufficient to protect rights under Community law in the great majority of cases. As has been noted, however, the *Von Colson* principle of indirect effect does not operate in all circumstances. Reliance on direct effect, too, is precluded where the relevant provision is not sufficiently clear, precise and unconditional, or, in the case of provisions of directives, where the other party to the case is a private individual or corporation. Where neither direct effect nor indirect effect could be pleaded in aid, the individual was left with a bare Community law right but no remedy by which to enforce it.

In *Francovich* the Court of Justice sought to close this disjunction between individuals' rights and individuals' remedies by ruling that, under Community law, an individual may claim damages against a Member State for loss caused by its failure properly to implement Community law.[14] In a case where an individual cannot rely directly upon a directive against a private party, and the national court refuses to give the directive indirect effect, the correct recourse is an action in damages

---

12 See *R v Secretary of State for Transport, ex p Factortame (No 2)* [1991] 1 AC 603.

13 Significantly, in the face of the consequent disparity of treatment between those cases involving an element of Community law and those which did not, the House of Lords have now overruled their finding in *Factortame 1* that as a matter of English law no injunction could be pronounced against the Crown. See *M v Home Office* [1993] 3 All ER 537.

14 Joined Cases C-6,9/90 *Francovich and Bonifaci v Italy* [1991] ECR I-5357, [1992] IRLR 69, [1993] 2 CMLR 66.

against the Member State for failure to implement the terms of the directive.

The relevant directive in *Francovich* was intended to protect employees in the event of their employer becoming insolvent by providing for a guarantee fund to ensure that the employees received backpay which was due to them under their contracts of employment.[15] The Italian Government failed to implement this directive, even after a ruling against it by the Court of Justice in Article 169 proceedings.[16] Two Italian companies went into liquidation leaving substantial sums by way of unpaid wages due to their employees. Had the directive been implemented in Italy, this money would have been recoverable by the employees from a guarantee fund set up for precisely this situation. No such guarantee fund existed in Italy however, and there was little chance of recovering any backpay from the companies' liquidators. The ill-served employees accordingly brought actions against the Italian Government claiming either the monies which would have been due to them had the directive been duly implemented or damages to compensate them for their losses resulting from the state's failure to implement the directive. These actions were referred by the Italian Courts to the Court of Justice.

The Court of Justice held, firstly, that the Directive in question was not sufficiently clear and precise to have direct effect, since it did not identify the national institution which was to be responsible for administering the guarantee fund. This was a matter which had been left to the discretion of the Member States. The Court went on to hold, however, (at paragraph 36 of their judgement) that Community law itself contained a general principle to the effect that a Member State is obliged to make good the damage to individuals caused by a breach of Community law for which that Member State was responsible.

This obligation was said to arise out of Article 5 of the Treaty of Rome which places a general duty on Member States to take all appropriate measures to ensure fulfilment of their obligations under Community law. Having made its general statement of principle, the Court laid down more specific criteria for liability in damages in respect of the individual case of non-implementation of a directive. Liability would arise where:

- the directive conferred rights on individuals;
- the content of those rights was identifiable from the provisions of the directive; and
- there was a causal link between the failure of the Member State to fulfil its obligations and the damage suffered by the individual.

15 Council Directive 80/987/EEC, OJ 1980 L283/23.
16 Case 22/87 *Commission v Italy* [1989] ECR 143.

The implications of the *Francovich* judgment are enormous. The Court did not limit its judgment to a prospective ruling, applying only to breaches of Community law subsequent to the decision in *Francovich*, as was suggested by the Advocate-General in the case. The right in damages is not restricted to the nationals of the particular Member States in breach. For example, the Spanish trawlermen who were prevented from fishing from their British registered vessels during the currency of the legislation which was ultimately declared contrary to Community law in the *Factortame* litigation have raised an action in damages against the United Kingdom Government for their loss of profits resulting from the enforced laying-up of their boats in the period before the Act was disapplied.[17]

The principle of liability in damages was stated in general terms and the Court clearly envisaged that other types of breach, beside non-implementation of directives, would be covered. The Court stated that the availability of damages in a particular case would depend on the nature of the breach of Community law, but it only elaborated conditions of liability for the specific case of non-implementation. It is arguable that damages may now be sought in all instances of breach of Community law by a Member State, not only non-implementation of directives but also faulty implementation, breach of directly effective Treaty articles, failure to respect general principles of Community law, and so on. Following this line, anybody who could establish that they had suffered loss as a result of the actions of a Member State which adversely affected their individual rights under Community law will have grounds for a *Francovich* action. The Court of Justice has already ruled that, where national law cannot be interpreted in such a way as to achieve the result envisaged by a particular directive, then the Member State will be liable under the Francovich principle for damages resulting from its incorrect or incomplete implementation of the directive.[18] The most pressing issue to be resolved is, therefore, the establishment of detailed criteria for liability for other types of breach of Community law.

There is some concern among the Member States that *Francovich* damages should not be available where a Member State has simply made a misjudgment as to the demands of Community law. The criteria set out in *Francovich* are notable for excluding any consideration of fault on the part of the Member State, but a regime of strict liability for all types of breach could be financially disastrous for public authorities.

---

17 Case C-48/93 *R v Secretary of State for Transport, ex p Factortame (No 3)*, notified in OJ 1993 C94/13: an Article 177 reference to the Court of Justice from the English High Court on questions as to the types of loss recoverable and the criteria for liability to be applied in *Francovich* damages actions.

18 Case C-334/92 *Teodoro Wagner Miret v Fondo de garanatia salarial* ECJ, 16 December [1993] ECR (not yet reported).

Some have argued, for example, that the Court of Justice ought to apply the same criteria to damages actions against national authorities as it does to those against the Community institutions under Article 215.[19] These criteria are notoriously narrow. On the other hand, it is arguable that the imperative of ensuring the full protection of Community law rights, which, after all, gave rise to *Francovich*, would seem to require that damages be more easily available.

Further, it may be argued that the *Francovich* action, as a general action for damages for breach of Community law, could also lie against individuals.[20] Clearly, there are certain forms of breach, including the non-implementation of directives, which can only be perpetrated by, and could only be actionable against, the State. Others, such as a breach of the Treaty articles on competition law or equal pay relate specifically to the activities of private parties, and raise important questions as to the future development of the damages action. Until further notice from the Court of Justice, it would seem that a *Francovich* action only lies against the state, although this does not mean that damages will never be available against an individual for breach of Community law.

CASE STUDY: *FRANCOVICH* DAMAGES AND PRIVATISATION

The Transfer of Undertakings (Protection of Employment) Regulations 1981[21] were intended to provide the same rights to employees in national law as were guaranteed under the EC Acquired Rights Directive 77/187. A significant feature of the national regulations, however, was that the protection which they afforded was restricted to persons employed in commercial undertakings (reg 2(1)).

Over the years following the adoption of the directive, the Court of Justice dealt with a significant number of Article 177 references as regards the proper interpretation of the directive. It became increasingly clear that the directive had to be interpreted broadly, with a view to achieving its stated aim of protecting employees' rights.

In October 1992 the European Commission took the United Kingdom before the Court of Justice under Article 169 for its alleged failure to fulfil its obligations under the Treaty in respect of its full and proper implementation of the Acquired Rights Directive.[1] One of the matters

19 See, for example, the Opinion of Advocate-General Mischo in *Francovich*. Compare on this point Parker, LJ in *Bourgoin v Ministry of Agriculture* [1986] QB 716, [1985] 3 All ER 585, [1986] 1 CMLR 267.
20 This has been explicitly argued for by Advocate-General Van Gerven in his Opinion in *H J Banks & Co Ltd v British Coal Corpn* Case C-128/92, dated 27 October 1993. The judgment of the Court was awaited at the time of writing.
21 SI 1981/1794.
1   Case C-382/92 *Commission v United Kingdom*, notified OJ 1992 C306/11. Advocate-General's Opinion delivered 2 March 1994; judgment of the Court awaited at the time of writing.

complained of was the exclusion of employees of non-commercial undertakings from the protection of the directive.

The UK Government responded by passing the Trade Union Reform and Employment Rights Act 1993 intended, among other things, to 'bring detailed provisions of UK legislation on employees' rights on transfer of undertakings ... fully into line with the EC Acquired Rights Directive.' Section 33 of this Act amended the Transfer of Undertakings Regulations so that non-commercial ventures were no longer excluded from the protection of the Regulations. There was, however, no provision in the Act that this amendment should be retrospective.

In the 14 years from the expiry of the time limit for implementation of the directive and the date of the Royal Assent to the 1993 Act, the commercial undertakings rule was applied and interpreted by courts in the United Kingdom in such a way as to exclude large numbers of employees from the protection of the Regulations, particularly those persons who were employed in enterprises which were subject to privatisation.[2] Following *Teodoro Wagner Miret*[3], which concerned the implementation in Spain of the Employers' Insolvency Directive 80/987, it is arguable that those people who have suffered loss as a result of the UK's non-commercial undertakings exclusion can now claim *Francovich* damages against the UK Government for its failure properly to implement the directive.

The position in UK law

Before *Francovich* the creation of a remedy in damages for breach of Community law was a matter for national legal systems.[4] The nature and extent of any such right in the domestic law of the United Kingdom was a matter of some controversy since the question was viewed in the light of the complex doctrines surrounding liability for breach of statutory duty. This was primarily because Community law is given force of law in the United Kingdom by statute, the European Communities Act 1972.

Thus, in *Garden Cottage Foods v Milk Marketing Board*[5] the House of Lords found that breach of a directly effective article of the Treaty of

---

2   See for example *Expro Services v Smith* [1991] IRLR 156, [1991] ICR 577; *Stirling v Dietsmann Management Systems* [1991] IRLR 368. Compare with *Kenny v South Manchester College* [1993] IRLR 265.

3   Case C-334/92 *Teodoro Wagner Miret v Fondo de garanatia salarial* ECJ, 16 December [1993] ECR (not yet reported).

4   Case 60/75 *Russo v AIMA* [1976] ECR 45, 57.

5   *Garden Cottage Foods v Milk Marketing Board* [1984] AC 130, [1983] 2 All ER 770.

Rome, namely Article 86 on abuse of a dominant position in the market place, could be categorised in English law as a breach of a statutory duty. The same remedies which were available in the case of a breach of a statutory duty, including damages, could in principle be available in respect of a contravention of Community law.

In *Bourgoin SA v Ministry of Agriculture*,[6] a French company sought compensation from the UK Government, claiming that a ban on the import of turkeys from other Community countries, which had been found by the Court of Justice to contravene Article 30 of the Treaty, had resulted in damage to the plaintiff's business. The majority of the Court of Appeal held that, as a matter of English law, the plaintiff did not have a private law claim to damages in respect of action by the Minister which was merely *ultra vires*. There was no tort giving rise to strict liability in damages for loss occasioned by an *ultra vires* act. The proper remedy against a public body was judicial review and damages could be available only under the tort of misfeasance in public office, which requires the plaintiff to show that the decision complained of was taken either maliciously or in the full knowledge that it was *ultra vires*.[7] This is notoriously difficult to prove, reflecting the traditional concern of courts in this country to limit the financial liabilities of public authorities. In Scots law, too, considerations of public policy have been held to limit the liability of public authorities to cases of malicious breach of a statutory duty.

Following *Francovich*, courts in the United Kingdom are required, as a matter of Community law, to provide a remedy in damages and the problem, in practical terms, is how to deal with the precedent of *Bourgoin*. In *Kirklees Borough Council v Wickes Building Supplies*, Lord Goff accepted that since the decision of the Court of Justice in *Francovich* it was doubtful that *Bourgoin* had been correctly decided, but the matter was not considered at length.[8] At present, *Bourgoin* can only be reconciled with the demands of Community law if the non-implementation of directives is equated with misfeasance in public office. This is at least arguable. However, in respect of other types of breach it is difficult to see how any criteria for liability laid down in the future by the Court of Justice, even on analogy with Article 215, could approximate to those of misfeasance in public office and, on this view, the principle of *Bourgoin* cannot stand. In the absence of *Bourgoin*, it would seem that the *Francovich* action could be integrated into the

---

6 *Bourgoin v Ministry of Agriculture, Fisheries and Food* [1986] QB 716, [1986] 1 CMLR 267.
7 See also *Jones v Department of Employment* [1989] QB 1 at 25.
8 *Kirklees Borough Council v Wickes Building Supplies Ltd* [1992] 2 CMLR 765 at 785, HL.

national systems of remedies most easily under the head of breach of statutory duty, by analogy with the *Garden Cottage Foods* case.[8a]

SPECIFIC PROCEDURAL DUTIES UNDER ARTICLE 5

The Court of Justice has derived an increasing number of procedural duties from the principle that Community law rights must be effectively protected. National courts must have regard to these duties in all matters which have a Community law element, regardless of any prior inquiry as to whether or not the substantive Community rights which they seek to vindicate and protect themselves have direct effect.

The duty to provide interim protection to Community rights

Community rights do not exist in a vacuum but are claimed and protected within the context of the existing rules and procedures of national courts. The Court has held, however, that any rules, including procedural rules, which might impair, even temporarily, the full force and effect of Community law must be set aside.[9] Hence, in *Factortame*,[10] the Court ruled that the effective protection of Community law rights meant that national courts should have the power to grant interim orders protecting such rights. Any national procedural rules which prevented the interim protection of Community rights must be disapplied.

The following propositions relating to interim protection may be derived from the decisions in *Factortame*:

- in any case in which an individual claims to have a right protected under Community law, the national courts have an immediate duty to consider the merits of the claim under Community law and to reach a view thereon;
- if it appears to the court that the claim is a good one, then all national rules which impede the enjoyment of that directly effective right should be set aside;
- if it appears to the national court that there may be some merit in the claim, but that a final decision on the matter requires an authoritative interpretation of the Community law from the

---

8a See, most recently, Case C-5/94 *R v Ministry of Agriculture, Fisheries and Food, ex p Hedley Lomas (Ireland) Ltd* notified in 1994 OJ C59/14 in which the Divisional Court has sought guidance from the Court of Justice as to the conditions of liability and measure of damages under Community law where national authorities refused a trader an export licence contrary to Article 34 of the Treaty. Judgment awaited at the time of writing.

9   Case 106/77 *Amministrazione delle Finanze dello Stato v Simmenthal* [1978] ECR 629, [1978] 3 CMLR 263.

10   Case C-213/89 *R v Secretary of State for Transport, ex p Factortame* [1990] ECR I-2433, [1991] 1 AC 603, [1990] 3 CMLR 1.

European Court, then a reference should be made to that Court under Article 177;
- pending the outcome of this reference, the putative right under Community law should be protected by the national court granting all and any such orders as are necessary to ensure proper protection of the claimed Community right;
- any national rules, be they procedural or substantive, which would otherwise impede the interim protection of the putative Community law right should be set aside by the national court while awaiting the final judgment of the Court of Justice.

In the United Kingdom issue of interim protection in Community law cases is assessed on the standard principles laid down in *American Cyanamid.* [11] The plaintiff or pursuer must show that there is a *prima facie* case indicating a serious issue to be tried on the merits. The court should then consider whether damages would be an adequate remedy, and, if not, whether the balance of convenience favours the grant of an injunction or, in Scotland, an interdict.

In *R v Secretary of State for the National Heritage, ex p Continental Television BV* [12] the UK Government's order under s 177 of the Broadcasting Act 1990 proscribing hard core pornographic programmes broadcast from Denmark to the UK by way of satellite was subject to challenge on a number of grounds, among them that Community law permitted a Member State to suspend only those broadcasts from another Member State which had been re-transmitted within its own territory. The Divisional Court held that the case raised questions as to the correct interpretation of the Community Broadcasting Directive 89/552 and referred the matter to the Court of Justice. After seeing some of the proscribed broadcasts, however, the Divisional Court refused an application for an interim injunction of the Minister's order on the bases that some of the acts shown were contrary to English law and that the protection of the moral welfare of minors outweighed the potential damage to the broadcasters' profits.

It had been assumed throughout the *Factortame* litigation that the fishermen would not be able to recover financial compensation from the UK Government in the event of their claim being vindicated. Following *Francovich*, however, damages are available in principle and, as we have noted, the fishermen filed a claim for damages which was, at the time of writing, being considered by the Court of Justice. If Continental Television BV are successful in their arguments before the Court of Justice, then a

11 *American Cyanamid Co v Ethicon Ltd* [1975] 1 All ER 504, HL.
12 *R v Secretary of State for the National Heritage, ex p Continental Television BV* [1993] 2 CMLR 333.

damages claim against the UK Government in respect of their lost profits would seem to be open to them.

The duty to provide effective procedures

It is a basic principle of Community law that national courts should ensure the existence of an effective judicial remedy to enforce and protect individuals' rights under Community law.[13] The conditions governing the availability of this judicial remedy are matters for national law. There is no common code of procedure detailing how national courts should deal with Community law claims. The possibility of the development of Community procedural rules is hinted at by the Court of Justice in *Francovich* in its discussion of the individual's right, founded directly on Community law, to obtain compensation in respect of the State's breaches of his Community law rights. The Court states:[14]

> '[I]t is in accordance with the rules of national law on liability that the State must make reparation for the consequences of the harm caused. *In the absence of any Community legislation*, it is a matter for the internal order of each Member State to determine the competent courts and lay down the detailed procedural rules for legal proceedings intended fully to safeguard the rights which individual derive from Community law.'

In the absence of such procedural harmonisation the domestic legal systems of the Member States may designate which of their courts have jurisdiction in, and what procedural conditions apply to, actions seeking to invoke Community law directly. [15] This procedural autonomy is, however, limited in certain respects by Community rules:

– National procedural rules should not be applied in such a manner as to make the enforcement of Community rights more difficult than the enforcement of analogous national rights. That is, there should be no procedural discrimination between national law and Community law rights.[16]

13 Case 222/84 *Johnston v Chief Constable of the Royal Ulster Constabulary* [1986] ECR 1651; Case 222/86 *Union National des Entraineurs et Cadres Techniques Professionnels du Football (UNECTEF) v Heylens* [1987] ECR 4097.
14 Joined Cases C-6,9/90 *Francovich & Bonifaci v Italy* [1991] ECR I-5357 at para 42.
15 Case 13/68 *Salgoil v Italian Ministry for Foreign Trade* [1968] ECR 453.
16 Case 33/76 *Rewe v Landwirtschaftskammer für Saarland* [1976] ECR 1989, [1977] 1 CMLR 533.

- Even where they apply equally both to national and to Community law rights, national procedural rules should not have the effect of making it impossible in practice,[17] or even excessively difficult,[18] to exercise rights guaranteed under Community law.
- The Court has stated that the Treaty of Rome was not intended to create new remedies in the national courts to ensure the observance of Community law.[19] The 'no new remedies' principle is not, however, a serious obstacle to procedural effectiveness since, as in *Factortame*, the creation of a new remedy can be treated as simply the extension of an existing one.

The effective protection of Community law rights may require national courts to modify or suspend aspects of their existing national procedural rules. This power to modify or suspend rules of national procedure is not based on national law, but results instead from the national court's application of the Community law principle of the effective protection of Community law rights.[20]

The general principle of effective protection of Community rights has been applied directly in procedural matters by UK courts. It has been held, for example, that the principle of effective protection was sufficient to confer jurisdiction on industrial tribunals in relation to claims brought solely and directly under Community law,[1] notwithstanding the fact that no specific jurisdiction in purely Community matters had been granted to them under the domestic statutes by which the tribunals were constituted.[2] In accordance with the rule against procedural discrimination as between national and Community law claims, it has been held that when industrial tribunals are faced with claims of sex discrimination contrary to Community law, the same procedures and time limits should be applied to the Community law claim as would be applied in a claim for breach of the analogous domestic legislation, the Sex Discrimination Act 1975.[3] Similarly, claims alleging unfair dismissal or a change in conditions of employment contrary to the provisions of the Acquired Rights Directive 77/187 might be brought under the same conditions and

---

17 Case 45/76 *Comet v Produktschaap voor Siergewasen* [1976] ECR 2043, [1977] 1 CMLR 533.

18 Case 199/82 *Amministrazione delle Finanze dello Stato v San Giorgio* [1983] ECR 3595.

19 Case 158/80 *Rewe Handelsgesellschaft Nord v Hauptzollamt Kiel ('Butterboats')* [1981] ECR 1805, [1982] 1 CMLR 449.

20 Case C-213/89 *R v Secretary of State for Transport, ex p Factortame* [1990] ECR I-2433.

1 *Secretary of State for Scotland v Wright and Hannah* [1991] IRLR 187.

2 See the Employment Protection (Consolidation) Act 1978, s 128(1).

3 *Livingstone v Hepworth Refractories* [1992] IRLR 63. See also *McKechnie v UBM Building Supplies* [1991] IRLR 283.

procedures as apply to similar claims brought under purely national employment protection legislation. [4]

Although it now appears generally accepted that industrial tribunals may be used in claims based directly on Community law, it does not follow that claims based on the direct effect of provisions of Community in the field of employment protection or sex discrimination must, therefore, be brought these tribunals. No specific code or procedure for the protection before national court of rights based on Community law has, as yet, been provided by the national authorities in the United Kingdom. It is arguable that such failure to provide a code of procedure is itself contrary to Community law, in particular the principles of effective protection and of legal certainty.

Industrial tribunals are available in Community law claims only because of the direct application by those tribunals of the Community law principle of effective protection. It would be paradoxical for a national court to rely on this particular application of a Community law principle, to itself deny the effective protection of Community law rights. Such a situation would arise if a claim based on the direct effect of Community law were dismissed by an ordinary court on the grounds that it should have been brought in an industrial tribunal. Such a decision would, in effect, be to permit the national authorities to profit from their own failure properly to implement Community law by explicitly providing for appropriate procedures. As is clear from *Kolpinghuis Nijmegen*,[5] however, national authorities of the state may not rely on their own state's failure to give proper respect to (principles of) Community law. Accordingly, in the absence of specific procedural rules regarding the protection of Community law rights, the possibility of the effective protection of Community law rights by other specialist tribunals should not, in itself, be regarded as sufficient grounds for an ordinary court of general jurisdiction to decline jurisdiction in a case involving Community law rights.

The duty to provide effective sanctions

National legal systems are also permitted a measure of discretion as to the sanctions which they provide for breach of Community law rights. The Court of Justice stated in *Amsterdam Bulb* that in the absence of

---

4   *National Union of Public Employees v the Secretary of State for Employment*, 5 May 1993, [1993] *The Times Law Reports* 250.

5   Case 80/86 *Officier van Justitie v Kolpinghuis Nijmegen* [1987] ECR 3969, [1989] 2 CMLR 18.

provisions in Community rules providing for specific sanctions to be imposed on individuals for failure to observe those rules, Member States were free to adopt such sanctions as appeared to them appropriate.[6]

Again, the discretion of the Member States is not absolute but is limited by the principles of non-discrimination as between national and Community rights in relation to the sanctions for breach and the principle that the sanction should provide for effective protection of those rights. The effective protection of Community rights has been held to mean that the sanctions available in national law for breach of a Community law right must have a 'real deterrent effect ... such as to guarantee real and effective judicial protection.'[7] Therefore, any award of damages for breach of Community law should provide proper compensation for loss suffered, rather than simply a nominal award.[8]

In *Anklagemyndigheden v Hansen*, a case concerning the Danish implementation of the Community tachograph regulations, the Community law in relation to sanctions was summarised as requiring Member States to take all measures necessary to guarantee the application and effectiveness of Community law. For that purpose, while the choice of penalties remains within their discretion, the Member States were to ensure that infringements of Community law were penalized under conditions, both procedural and substantive, which are analogous to those applicable to infringements of a national law of a similar nature and importance and which, in any event, made the penalty 'effective, proportionate and dissuasive:'[9]

- an 'effective' sanction is one which is in fact aimed at achieving the objective of the Community provision in question.
- a 'proportionate' sanction is one which is not, in all the circumstances of the case, excessive.
- a 'dissuasive' sanction is one which is not so minimal as to fail to deter a breach of Community law.

In summary, any sanction or penalty which is not aimed at achieving the same objective as the Community provision or which is, in all the circumstances, either excessive or derisory, will, therefore, be incompatible with Community law.

---

6   Case 50/76 *Amsterdam Bulb v Produktschap voor Siergewassen* [1977] ECR 137 at para 32.
7   Case 79/83 *Harz v Deutsche Tradax* [1984] ECR 1921.
8   Case 14/83 *Von Colson v Land Nordrhein-Westfalen* [1984] ECR 1891, [1986] 2 CMLR 430.
9   Case 326/88 *Anklagemyndigheden v Hansen & Sons I/S* [1990] ECR I-2911.

Member States' discretion in stipulating sanctions has been narrowed further by the judgment of the Court of Justice in *Marshall (No 2)*.[10] The House of Lords referred questions as to the validity under Community law of provisions of the Sex Discrimination Act which placed a ceiling on the amount of damages available in the event of discriminatory treatment and did not provide for an award of interest.

The Court of Justice held that, with respect to the Community right to equal treatment embodied in the Equal Treatment Directive, effective protection entailed that Member States should provide for measures designed to restore such equality when it had not been observed. In the case of an act of discrimination which expressed itself in dismissal from employment, the appropriate measures would either be an order for reinstatement to employment or an award of compensation for the full loss and damage actually sustained as a result of the discriminatory dismissal. In addition, an award of interest on the capital sum awarded by way of compensation was held to be required in order to make the remedy a truly effective one.

This right to full compensation with interest was found to flow from or be implicit within the terms of Article 6 of the Directive[11] which provided that:

> 'Member States shall introduce into their legal systems such measures as are necessary to enable all persons who consider themselves wronged by a failure to apply to them the principle of equal treatment ... to pursue their claims by judicial process after possible recourse to other competent authorities.'

This Article appears to be no more than an expression of the general principle of effective protection in the particular context of equal treatment. However Article 6 of the Directive was found by the Court to be sufficiently precise and unconditional to have direct effect when read in the context of the whole Directive. Accordingly, the House of Lords was required, as a matter of Community law, to over-ride those provisions of the Sex Discrimination Act which imposed a maximum limit on compensation and which did not provide for an award of interest to run thereon.

For the moment it would appear that the precise elements and amount of restitution claimed under Community law remains a matter for the national courts applying their national rules. However, it is possible to

---

10 Case C271/91 *Marshall v Southampton and South West Hampshire Area Health Authority (No 2)*, 2 August 1993, [1993] ECR I-4367, [1993] IRLR 445.
11 Directive 76/207/EEC, OJ 1976 L39/40.

foresee pressure for general Community harmonization in this area. Article 177 references might be submitted to the Court of Justice as to whether or not Community law requires that proper restitution should include an award for moral damage for hurt feelings or *solatium*, or the degree (if any) to which Community law requires or permits unforeseen losses to be taken into account.[12]

The duty to allow recovery of illegal charges

If any charges have been levied upon an individual by reason of national provisions which are found subsequently to be contravene to Community law, the Court of Justice has held that, as a matter of Community law, the individual has a right to repayment of the sums already paid by him.[13] For example, national charges found by the Court to have equivalent effect to customs duties on imports from,[14] or exports to,[15] other Member States are recoverable in the national courts.

The right to restitution of monies paid under a mistake in law, must be protected by national courts as a matter of Community law, regardless of the domestic rules on the recoverability of such payments. Following the decision of the House of Lords in *Woolwich Building Society v Inland Revenue Commissioners*,[16] English law appears to be falling into line with Community law by allowing recovery of money paid under a mistake in law even where there is no Community element.

The duty in relation to time bar and prescription of claims

Judgments of the Court of Justice are declaratory of existing Community rights; they do not create new rights. Accordingly, the Court's decisions,

---

12   See the reference to the Court of Justice in the case of the *Factortame* fishermen's action for damages against the Crown, Case C-48/93 at OJ 1993 C94/13. The matters referred to the Court of Justice include questions as to whether or not *Francovich* damages includes exemplary damages, expenses incurred in an attempt to mitigate loss, losses consequent upon the need to provide bonds, fines and legal expenses for alleged offences connected with the exclusion of the Spanish controlled vessels from the British Register.

13   Case 61/79 *Amministrazione delle Finanze dello Stato v Denkavit Italiana* [1980] ECR 1205, [1981] 3 CMLR 694; *Amministrazione delle Finanze dello Stato v Ariete SpA* [1980] ECR 2545, [1981] 1 CMLR 316; Case 68/79 *Hans Just I/S v Ministry for Fiscal Affairs* [1980] ECR 501, [1981] 2 CMLR 714.

14   Case 77/72 *Capolongo v Azienda Agricola Maya* [1973] ECR 611.

15   Case 18/71 *Eunomia v Ministro dell'Istruzione* [1971] ECR 811.

16   *Woolwich Building Society v Inland Revenue Commissioners* [1993] AC 70, [1992] 3 All ER 737.

for example as to the direct effect or the invalidity of a particular Community provision, generally have retrospective effect and apply even to legal relationships arising and established before the judgment.[17] In exceptional circumstances the Court has limited its rulings so that they have general effect only from the date of judgment.[18] Such a limitation in the temporal effect a judgment is, however, within the exclusive jurisdiction of the Court of Justice. It is not open to national courts to limit the effects of a ruling of the Court of Justice in this way.[19]

The question of the application of national rules of prescription and limitation to rights created and guaranteed under Community law is a vexed one. The Court of Justice has consistently stressed that individual rights must be fully and uniformly protected in the Member States from the date of the creation of those rights, and not from the date of any explicit ruling as to the direct effectiveness or applicability of those rights within the Member States.[20] Yet individuals are only assured of the protection of Community law once the Court has ruled, and at this point they may be out of time.

Thus in *Emmott v Minister of Social Welfare*,[1] the Court held that national limitation periods cannot be used to prevent actions being raised by litigants seeking to enforce their rights under a directive which has not been properly transposed into national law. The Court reasoned that until a directive has been fully implemented by national measures, individuals will be uncertain as to the extent of their rights and it would be unfair if time was to begin to run before then.

In line with this approach, the Court of Appeal in *R v Minister of Agriculture, Fisheries and Food, ex p Bostock* [2] set aside the three month limitation period for judicial review in a case relating to a claim to compensation following the surrender of a milk quota. The right to compensation on the surrender of a milk quota had only been established by the decision of the Court of Justice in *Wachauf v Germany*,[3] more than four years after the original English tenant had surrendered his quota.[4]

---

17 *Amministrazione delle Finanze dello Stato v Denkavit* [1980] ECR 1205 at 1223.
18 See, eg Case 43/75 *Defrenne v Sabena (No. 2)* [1976] ECR 455; Case 262/88 *Barber v Guardian Royal Exchange Assurance Group* [1990] ECR I-1889, [1991] 1 QB 344.
19 Cases 66,127,128/79 *Amministrazione delle Finanze dello Stato v Meridionale Industria Salumi* [1980] ECR 1237.
20 Case 106/77 *Amministrazione delle Finanze dello Stato v Simmenthal* [1978] ECR 629.
1 Case C-208/90, *Emmott v Minister of Social Welfare* [1991] ECR I-4269, [1991] IRLR 387, [1991] 3 CMLR 894.
2 *R v Minister of Agriculture, Fisheries and Food, ex p Bostock* [1991] CMLR 687.
3 Case 5/88 *Wachauf v Germany* [1989] ECR 2609, [1991] 1 CMLR 328.
4 The substantive points in *Bostock* are now before the Court of Justice: Case C2/92, OJ 1992 C33/9.

Emmott was also considered by the Employment Appeal Tribunal in *Cannon v Barnsley Metropolitan Council.* [5] Ms Cannon was made redundant from her employment as a headmistress in August 1985. Under the then applicable domestic legislation[6] her redundancy payment was reduced because she was only two months from her normal retirement age of sixty. A man's redundancy payment would have been similarly reduced immediately prior to his normal retirement age of sixty-five. In January 1990, amending legislation abolished this different treatment and equalized the age at which such reduction should occur. Within two months of this provision coming into force Ms Cannon raised an action seeking a redundancy payment equal to that which a man of her age would have received. The industrial tribunal ruled her application out of time as having been made more than three months from the date of the payment, according to the time limit set out in the Sex Discrimination Act 1975. The Employment Appeal Tribunal applied *Emmott* and held that, since Ms Cannon's claim to equal payment was made under Community law,[7] the limitation period would begin to run only from the date in January 1990 on which the national provision correctly implementing Community law came into force. Her claim was therefore made in due time.

Although the judgment in *Emmott* makes relatively clear the time from which prescription periods or time limits are to begin to run, the question of how long the relevant period should be is left open. It remains a matter for national law, with the proviso that no time limit which renders the exercise of the Community right excessively difficult may be applied. It remains unclear, however, which of the various time limits set out in UK statutes for claims under national law should be applied, by analogy, to claims based on Community law.

The duty not to rule on the validity of Community acts

One of the most basic concerns of the Court of Justice has been that Community law should be applied uniformly throughout the Member States. It is felt that divergences in the interpretation and application of Community law by national courts would call into question the very integrity of Community law as a coherent legal system. Accordingly, the Court of Justice has laid great emphasis on the duty of national courts,

---

5   *Cannon v Barnsley Metropolitan Council* [1992] IRLR 474.
6   Employment Protection (Consolidation) Act 1978, Sch 4, para 4.
7   Specifically the Treaty of Rome, Art 119, the Equal Pay Directive 75/117/EEC (OJ 1975, L45/19) and the Equal Treatment Directive 76/207/EEC (OJ 1976, L39/40).

under Article 5, faithfully to apply Community law in its entirety. Article 177 of the Treaty of Rome clearly envisages national courts considering and ruling on the validity of the acts of Community institutions. The Court of Justice has held, however, that whilst national courts may confirm the validity of Community acts called into question before them, they have an obligation, flowing from Article 5, to refer any doubts about the validity of Community legislation to Luxembourg.[8]

The prohibition on national courts calling into doubt the validity of Community acts was relaxed slightly in a subsequent case. In *Zuckerfabrik Suderdithmarschen v Hauptzollamt Itzehoe*,[9] the question arose as to whether or not national courts might still have the power under Community law to grant interim suspension of national administrative measures which were based upon a Community regulation, pending a decision on the validity of that regulation by the Court of Justice. The decision illustrates the development of a common Community procedural law to be applied by national courts when dealing with Community issues. The Court held that national courts do indeed have the power, in effect, to suspend the operation of Community law *ad interim*, provided that the following conditions are met:

- the national court has serious doubts as to the validity of the Community act. The basis for these doubts must be specified to the European Court;
- the suspension of the national regulations should be provisional and for the shortest possible period. The national court is obliged immediately to make a reference to the European Court seeking a final ruling on the validity of the disputed measure, unless the same issue is already before the Court;
- the interim suspension is absolutely necessary to avoid serious and irreparable damage to the applicant. It should be noted that pecuniary damage is not generally to be considered irreparable;
- the interests of the Community should be taken into account in ruling upon the application. Where suspension of the measures would result in serious financial damage to the Community, guarantees or other security may be required of the applicant pending a final determination of the validity of the Community act.

---

8 *Firma Foto-Frost v Hauptzollamt Lübeck Ost* [1987] ECR 4199, [1988] 3 CMLR 57.
9 Cases C-143/88 and C92/89 *Zuckerfabrik Suderdithmarschen v Hauptzollamt Itzehoe* [1991] ECR I-415.

DUTIES OF RESPECT FOR THE GENERAL PRINCIPLES OF COMMUNITY LAW

In interpreting and applying the treaties, the Court of Justice has developed a whole body of unwritten law, consisting mainly in principles of administrative justice and the protection of fundamental human rights. These doctrines, which had no explicit basis in the Treaty of Rome, have been termed the general principles of Community law.

General principles are applied by the Court in order to determine the boundaries of proper or lawful administrative action by both Community institutions and by national governments acting in the sphere of Community law.[10] Where a Community law issue arises in respect of national administrative action, the general principles of Community law must be applied by national courts in the same manner as they would be applied by the Court of Justice.[11] Domestic courts and national lawyers have, accordingly, to be aware of these principles and the manner in which they have been applied by the Court to date.

Protection of fundamental rights

The Court of Justice has held that respect for human rights forms an integral part of Community law and that it is required to ensure that fundamental human rights, as enumerated in particular in the European Convention on Human Rights, are duly protected in all areas covered by Community law.[12] On this basis, it would appear that rules of national law in areas which are also subject to Community regulation should incorporate respect for human rights.[13]

National legislation which seeks to implement Community law,[14] or to derogate from Community law,[15] or indeed to have general effects in

---

10 Case C-260/89 *Elleniki Radiophonia Tileorassi (ERT) v Dimotiki Eatairia Pliroforissis (DEP)* [1991] ECR I-2925.
11 See the Opinion of Advocate General Mancini in Case 237/82 *Jongeneel Kaas v Netherlands* [1984] ECR 483 at 520, 522.
12 See, eg Case 44/79 *Hauer v Land Rheinland-Pfalz* [1979] ECR 3727.
13 Article F2 of the Treaty on European Union, which does not fall within the jurisdiction of the Court of Justice, provides:
 'The Union shall respect fundamental rights as guaranteed by the European Convention on Human Rights and Fundamental Freedoms . . . and as they result from the constitutional traditions common to the Member States, as general principles of Community law.'
14 Case 5/88 *Wachauf v Germany* [1989] ECR 2609.
15 Case C260/89 *Elleniki Radiophonia Tileorassi (ERT) v Dimotiki Etairia Pliroforissis (DEP)* [1991] ECR I-2925.

areas also covered by Community law,[16] must be subject to review on human rights grounds. National courts, therefore, have a duty to ensure that national legislation falling within the field of operation of Community law accords with respect for human rights, as this is understood and applied by the Court of Justice.[17] The European Convention on Human Rights, which has not been formally incorporated into domestic law in the United Kingdom, is therefore fully effective in UK courts in those areas covered by Community law.

As a result of the effective incorporation into Community law of the provisions of the European Convention on Human Rights (ECHR) by the Court of Justice it would appear that Community law protects, among others, the right to a fair and public hearing (ECHR, Art 6), the right to respect for private and family life (ECHR, Art 8), the right to freedom of thought, conscience and religion (ECHR, Art 9), the right to freedom of expression (ECHR, Art 10), the right to peaceful assembly (ECHR, Art 11), a procedural right to an effective remedy before national courts for violation of substantive rights (ECHR, Art 13); and a right to freedom from discrimination on grounds of sex, race, colour, language, religion, political or other opinion, national or social origin, association with a national minority, property, birth or other status (ECHR, Art 14). Member State action in the field of Community law is subject then to assessment for its compatibility with human rights protection. [18] The opportunity to invoke the ECHR, which is otherwise strictly circumscribed in the domestic law of the United Kingdom,[19] provides a whole new range of arguments for lawyers in cases with a Community law element. [20]

---

16   Case 159/90 *SPUC v Grogan* [1991] ECR I-4685, [1991] 3 CMLR 849, in particular the Opinion of Advocate-General Van Gerven.

17   See, however, the Opinion of 20 April 1993 of Advocate-General Gulmann in Case C-2/92 *R v Minister of Agriculture, Fisheries and Food, ex p Bostock*, OJ 1992 C33/9 in which he counsels caution on the part of the European Court in developing this line of human rights jurisprudence. In the Advocate-General's view, given that all the Member States are governed by the rule of law and are signatories to the European Convention on Human Rights, their national courts can be trusted to ensure the protection of fundamental rights without the help or interference of the Court of Justice.

18   See Case C-260/89 *Elleniki Radiophonia Tileorassi (ERT) v Dimotiki Eatairia Pliroforissis (DEP)* [1991] ECR I-2925 at paras 43-45 in which a national derogation from Community law was assessed for its compatibility with freedom of expression guaranteed by Article 10 of the European Convention.

19   *R v Home Secretary, ex p Brind* [1991] 1 All ER 720.

20   For example in *W Emmett & Son Ltd v The Commissioners of Customs and Excise* London VAT Tribunal, LON/90/1316Z, unreported, 7 October 1991 it was argued, albeit unsuccessfully, that the strict liability and fixed penalties laid down in s 14 of the Finance Act 1985 for failure to submit correct VAT returns contravened Community law in offending against the basic right of the individual for respect for his or her private property.

Proportionality

Proportionality, a principle originating in German administrative law, requires that there should be a proper relationship between means and ends in administrative and legislative measures.[1] The principle has been applied by the Court of Justice to assess the compatibility with Community law of Member State's legislation intended to limit and provide penalties in relation to the free movement throughout the Community of goods, services, workers and capital as guaranteed under the Treaty of Rome.[2]

Proportionality is a complex doctrine and involves the application of three distinct tests:

- the measure should be shown to be appropriately and effectively aimed at a legitimate end, in the sense that the relationship between means and ends is neither impossible or unlawful;
- the measure should be demonstrated to be a necessary one, in the sense that there are no less restrictive means which might achieve the same purpose;
- the measure should be seen to be proportionate or balanced, in the sense that any injury or restriction on the individual caused by the act should be offset by the gain to the general public or the community as a whole.

A lawful measure under Community law must, therefore, be shown not only to be aimed at a legitimate objective permitted by Community law, but also to be the least burdensome measure appropriate to that task and should not, in any event, disproportionately affect any of the general objectives of the Community.[3] The application of the test of proportionality requires the judge to engage in a complex assessment of competing legislative policies, and the consequent need for judicial activism has prompted a degree of resistance to the test in the United Kingdom courts.[4]

---

1 Case 181/84 *R v Intervention Board for Agricultural Produce, ex p Man (Sugar)* [1985] ECR 2889, [1985] 3 CMLR 759.
2 See Case 118/75 *Watson & Bellman* [1976] ECR 1185 on free movement of persons and Case 41/76 *Donckerwolke v Procureur de la République* [1976] ECR 1921, [1977] 2 CMLR 535 on free movement of goods.
3 See, eg Case C-331/88 *R v Minister of Agriculture, Fisheries and Food, ex p Fédération Européene de la Santé Animale (FEDESA)* [1990] ECR I-4023, [1991] 1 CMLR 507.
4 See, for example, Hoffman J in *Stoke on Trent Borough Council v B & Q* [1991] 2 WLR 42, 57.

The test has, however, been held applied by UK judges in assessing the validity of both national executive decisions [5] and the lawfulness of Acts of Parliament.[6]

The House of Lords has, however, rejected the application of the proportionality test in the review of legislative or administrative acts where there is no matter of Community law at issue. [7] Proportionality is regarded, rightly, as qualitatively different from the tests set out in *Associated Provincial Picture Houses v Wednesbury* [8] in that it involves the judges, substituting their judgment of what is reasonable for that of the lawful decision-maker or, indeed, the legislature.

The protection of legitimate expectations

A legitimate expectation to be treated in a certain way by the administration is something less than an enforceable right. It may arise where, for example, a particular course of action has regularly been followed by the administration; the courts may protect the expectation that such conduct will continue. The Court of Justice may also uphold legitimate expectations against otherwise binding obligations. The past conduct of the executive or the administration is held to fetter their discretion in the future. [9] The Community principle of the protection of legitimate expectation is, in this way, similar to the doctrine of personal bar or estoppel.

This principle been adopted by the courts in the United Kingdom,[10] although in the United Kingdom the judiciary is markedly more reluctant to enforce expectations as to the substantive conduct of the administration. Generally, it is legitimate expectations as to the procedure to be followed by the administration in making its decisions which will be upheld.

The preservation of legal certainty

The principle of legal certainty entails that Community law should be clear and predictable and able to be relied upon by those subject to it,

---

5   *R v Minister of Agriculture, Fisheries and Food, ex p Bell Lines* [1984] 2 CMLR 502.
6   See, eg *B & Q v Shrewsbury and Atcham Borough Council* [1990] 3 CMLR 535 in relation to the Sunday trading restrictions in the Shops Act 1950 and *R v Secretary of State for Employment, ex p the Equal Opportunities Commission* [1992] 1 All ER 545, QBD on the matter of the lawfulness of the difference of treatment between part-time and full-time workers contained in UK employment protection legislation.
7   *R v Home Secretary, ex p Brind* [1991] 1 AC 696.
8   *Associated Provincial Picture Houses Ltd v Wednesbury Corpn* [1948] 1 KB 223.
9   Case 81/72 *Commission v Council: Re Staff Salaries* [1973] ECR 575.
10 *Council for Civil Service Unions v Minister for the Civil Service* [1985] AC 374.

whether individuals or Member States. It is a general principle of wide application. Legal certainty requires, for example, that Community measures should only apply to individuals after the legislative texts have been duly published and affected individuals given the opportunity to acquaint themselves with the contents.[11] It has also been held to follow from the principle of legal certainty that ambiguous provisions of tax legislation should be read *contra proferentem* and given the interpretation which favours the rights of the individual against those of the public authority.[12]

In general, the Court of Justice will strike down provisions which seek retrospectively to impose or validate criminal or penal sanctions on past conduct.[13] Exceptionally, however, retroactive legislation which is necessary to achieve a particular lawful purpose and which respects the legitimate expectations of those affected by it may be permitted by the Court.[14]

By contrast, judgments of the Court of Justice are generally retroactive in effect. They are said to be declaratory of what the law always was rather than creative of new law. For example, when the Court finds that a Community provision has direct effect it is generally said to have direct effect as from the date of the adoption of the measure, rather than from the date of judgment. The Court has, however, claimed the power to limit the effect of certain of its judgments such that they apply retrospectively only to the case at hand and to any actions actually commenced before the delivery of judgment. This power has been used sparingly, in cases where the Court's new decision which would otherwise have a substantial economic impact.[15]

---

11 Case 98/78 *Racke v Hauptzollamt Mainz* [1979] ECR 69.
12 Case 169/80 *Gondrand Frères* [1981] ECR 1931.
13 Case 63/83 *R v Kirk* [1984] ECR 2689, [1984] 3 CMLR 522.
14 Case 99/78 *Weingut Gustav Decker AG v Hauptzollamt Landau* [1979] ECR 101.
15 The Court has limited the effect of its judgements in this way as regards the direct effect of Art 119 (Case 43/75 *Defrenne v SABENA (No 2)* [1976] ECR 455); in finding that a University registration fee payable by non-nationals in Belgium was contrary to Community law (Case 24/86 *Blaizot v University of Liege* [1988] ECR 379) and in holding that Art 119 applied to the payment of employment pensions (Case 262/88 *Barber v Guardian Royal Exchange Assurance Group plc* [1990] ECR I-1889).

The standard of formal equality

The principle of equality is a general principle of Community law and is not confined to matters of discrimination on grounds of sex [16] or nationality.[17] Rather it is the principle that like cases should be treated alike, and that differences in treatment which rest on distinctions which cannot be objectively justified are unlawful.[18]

Procedural due process and rights of natural justice

This is a developing area of Community law. The Court of Justice has specified a number of rights in the area of administrative justice and judicial review. These include the following.

THE RIGHT TO LEGAL REPRESENTATION

In a staff case,[19] the Court stated that the Commission's refusal to allow either the staff member or his lawyer access to his disciplinary file in order to prepare a defence in disciplinary proceedings constituted a breach of the right to defend oneself through legal assistance.

THE PROTECTION FROM SELF-INCRIMINATION

It is for the Community authorities to establish a breach of Community law. An individual cannot be compelled to answer questions, the replies to which would constitute admissions of unlawful activity.[20] In a recent decision of the European Court of Human Rights, it was held that under Article 6(1) of the European Convention which guarantees a right to fair trial, a person was entitled to remain silent and not incriminate himself and that any attempt to use pecuniary sanction to force an individual to

16   The principle of equal treatment without regard to sex is specifically provided for in Art 119 of the Treaty and subsequent Directives. See Case 43/75 *Defrenne v SABENA (No 2)* [1976] ECR 455 and Ch 17 on Sex Discrimination.

17   See Art 6 of the post-Maastricht Treaty of Rome (formerly Art 7), applied in, eg in Case 186/87 *Cowan v Trésor Public* [1989] ECR 195, [1990] 2 CMLR 613.

18   See Cases 117/76, 16/77 *Ruckdeschel* [1977] ECR 1753 at 1769; Case 41/84 *Pinna v Caisse d'Allocations Familiales de la Savoie (No 1)* [1986] ECR 1.

19   Case 115/80 *Demont v Commission* [1981] ECR 3147.

20   Case 374/87 *Orkem v Commission* [1989] ECR 3283, [1991] ECR 3283. Cf Case C-60/92 *Otto BV v Postbank NV* ECJ, 10 November [1993] ECR (not yet reported) in which the Court held that this right to silence applied only in the context of administrative proceedings before Community authorities and did not extend to civil litigation in national courts between private parties.

produce potentially incriminating documents was in breach of this article.[1]

THE CONFIDENTIALITY OF COMMUNICATIONS BETWEEN LAWYER AND CLIENT

Following a comparative survey of the laws of the Member States, the Court concluded that the Commission's extensive powers of investigation, search and seizure in the context of suspected breaches of Community fair competition law were subject to the principle that communications between lawyer and client were to be respected as confidential. The Commission could not therefore require the production of business records concerning such communications. The Court held, however, that the principle of confidentiality applied only in relation to communications with independent counsel rather than with in-house lawyers or legal departments.[2]

THE RIGHT TO A HEARING

An individual is entitled to be informed of the case against him and to be heard in his own defence when a decision is proposed which the administrative authority knows will cause substantial detriment or will otherwise seriously affect the interests of that person by, for example, the imposition of substantial penalties or fines.[3]

THE RIGHT TO JUDICIAL REVIEW OF ADMINISTRATIVE DECISIONS

The Court has stated that the conferral of a right under Community law necessarily implies that there also exists a right to a remedy of a judicial nature against any decision of a national authority withholding the benefit of that right. Thus, in *Johnston v Chief Constable of the Royal Ulster Constabulary*[4] the Court of Justice held that a provision of UK law which treated a certificate issued by the Secretary of State as 'conclusive evidence' that an act was done for the purpose of safeguarding national security was contrary to Community law since it had the effect of preventing individuals from pursuing their claims to Community rights by judicial process.

---

1 *Funke v France* [1993] 1 CMLR 897.
2 Case 155/79 *AM & S Europe Ltd v Commission* [1982] ECR 1575 at 1610-3.
3 Case 17/74 *Transocean Marine Paint* [1974] ECR 1063. See also Case 85/76 *Hoffman La Roche & Co AG v Commission* [1979] ECR 461, [1979] 3 CMLR 211.
4 Case 222/84 *Johnston v Chief Constable of the Royal Ulster Constabulary* [1986] ECR 1651.

THE RIGHT TO REASONS FOR A DECISION

Following from its decision that there exists a right to judicial review of national administrative decisions which affect an individual's rights under Community law, the Court has held that effective judicial review must be able to review the legality of the reasons for the contested decision. Accordingly, in *Heylens* the Court found that a national administrative authority owes a duty to the individual under Community law to inform him of the reasons upon which their final decision affecting his Community rights was based. Failure to give such reasons is a contravention of Community law.[5]

It should be noted that all the above rights apply without distinction between natural and legal persons, individuals and corporations.

THE JUDICIAL REVIEW OF NATIONAL LEGISLATION

Although a successful claim to a right under Community law may require the suspension of an Act of Parliament, courts in the United Kingdom have until recently been unwilling to contemplate the development of a specific procedure for the judicial review of national legislation. Rather than concede in general that legislation could be reviewed as a matter of general public law, the courts in both England,[6] and Scotland[7] preferred such review to be carried out only in the particular context of individual claims: either in relation to a claim to the direct enforcement of a Community right such as equal treatment,[8] or in using Community considerations to challenge individual administrative decisions.[9] This reluctance to embrace the judicial review of legislation was, perhaps, understandable in the light of the classical common law doctrine of parliamentary sovereignty.[10]

5   Case 222/86 *Union National des Entraineurs et Cadres Techniques Professionnels du Football (UNECTEF) v Heylens* [1987] ECR 4097.
6   *R v Secretary of State for Employment, ex p the Equal Opportunities Commission* [1993] 1 CMLR 915, [1993] IRLR 10, CA.
7   *National Union of Public Employees v Secretary of State for Employment*, 5 May 1993, [1993] *The Times Law Reports* 250.
8   Case C-271/91 *Marshall v Southampton and South West Hampshire Area Health Authority (No 2)*, European Court of Justice 2 August 1993, [1993] ECR I-4367, [1993] IRLR 445.
9   See *R v Secretary of State for Social Security, ex p Bowmore Medical Supplies* [1986] 1 CMLR 228, CA; *R v Minister of Agriculture, ex p Bell Lines* [1984] 2 CMLR 502; *R v Secretary of State for Social Services, ex p Clarke* [1988] 1 CMLR 279.
10   In *Stoke on Trent City Council v B & Q plc* [1991] 2 WLR 42, 57 Hoffman J. stated:
     'The function of this court is to review the acts of the legislature but not to substitute its

With the increasing realisation among domestic lawyers of the fact that arguments based on Community law could be used actually to challenge the validity (or at least applicability) of Acts of Parliament, there was growing pressure for the development by the courts of a general procedure for the judicial review of national legislation. In *R v Secretary of State for Employment, ex p the Equal Opportunities Commission* [11] it was claimed on behalf of the Equal Opportunities Commission that the continued differentiation between full-time and part-time employees in the qualifying thresholds (two years and five years respectively) for employment protection in national law constituted indirect sex discrimination, contrary to principles of Community law developed in the case law of the Court of Justice.

The Equal Opportunities Commission sought to use the mechanism of judicial review of administrative acts, in this case the relevant government department's expression of opinion in a letter to the Equal Opportunities Commission that existing UK legislation did not breach Community law, to develop a procedure for the judicial review of legislation. They sought, then, to have the national court:

- compare existing UK legislation with developments in Community law;
- to find this national legislation to be contrary to Community law;
- to pronounce an order declaring the UK Government to be in breach of its obligations under Community law in failing to introduce appropriate amending national legislation.

In the Divisional Court, the Equal Opportunities Commission was successful in persuading the court to take the first of these steps. The court, however, found the national legislation to be objectively justified under Community law. When the matter was taken to the Court of Appeal, this court refused to take even the first of these steps on a variety of grounds. The Court of Appeal suggested that, constitutionally, it was not open to individuals or interest groups to use the machinery of judicial review to seek to challenge the general validity, under Community law, of UK legislation abstracted from particular factual circumstances of individual cases. The matter was taken to the House of Lords. A hearing took place in the summer of 1993 and judgment was issued in early March 1994. Their Lordships, relying on the precedent set by the Court

own policies or values. This is not an abdication of judicial responsibility. The primacy of the democratic process is far more important than the question of whether our . . . laws could or could not be improved.'

11 *R v Secretary of State for Employment, ex p the Equal Opportunities Commission* 3 March 1994, House of Lords, not yet reported.

of Justice in *Factortame 2*, reversed the judgment of the Court of Appeal on the procedural point and held that judicial review should be available for the purpose of obtaining a declaration from a national court that UK primary legislation was incompatible with Community law. They also overturned the decision of the divisional court on the substantive issue and found the part-time/full-time distinction in UK employment protection law to be contrary to the Comunity law principle of equal treatment of the sexes. This judgment marks the unequivocal acceptance by the courts of the United Kingdom of the supremacy of Community law. From now on, all laws applying within the United Kingdom will be open to be challenged by way of judicial review before national courts charged by the European Court of Justice with ensuring the 'Euro-constitutionality' of Member States' legislation.

CONCLUSION

In this chapter it has been made clear that Community law has had the effect of creating a whole new series of duties to be applied by national courts. It requires national courts when dealing with Community law to become Community courts applying the principles and techniques of Community law.

As was seen in Chapter 1, the fundamental characteristics of Community law — direct effect, supremacy, uniformity and efficacy — are in large part the result of activist interpretation by the Court of Justice. The Court of Justice is the lynch-pin of the Community legal system. On this basis, it might be said that the primary duty of national courts under Community law is to co-operate with the Court of Justice and faithfully to use the reference procedure provided by Article 177 of the Treaty so as to allow Community law to be developed consistently and coherently. It is, therefore, Article 177 procedure that is now examined.

Chapter 3

PRELIMINARY REFERENCES TO THE EUROPEAN COURT OF JUSTICE

INTRODUCTION

The majority of cases in European Community law reach the Court of Justice as preliminary references from national courts under Article 177 of the Treaty and it is through Article 177 that the practitioner is most likely to have contact with and access to the Court. All references from national courts are ruled upon by the Court of Justice. The Court of First Instance has no jurisdiction in this respect even in competition law matters, with which it is primarily concerned.

Under Article 177, when national courts are faced with a question of Community law, the resolution of which is necessary for them to give judgment, they may, and in some cases they must, suspend the proceedings before them and refer the matter to the Court of Justice for a ruling. Once the Court has ruled on the issue, the proceedings return to the national court which will apply the ruling to the particular facts of the case and decide accordingly. The intention of the procedure is to foster the uniform interpretation and application of Community law throughout the Member States, although it should be noted that an Article 177 reference is a request for assistance, not an appeal from the national court to the Court of Justice.

The Article 177 procedure draws a distinction between lower courts and courts of last resort. When a lower court feels that a decision is necessary on a point of Community law, it has the option of referring the matter to the Court of Justice. Courts of last resort, on the other hand, *must* refer points of Community law where a decision upon them is necessary.

The first matter to clarify is which bodies are to be considered to be lower courts and tribunals and which are to be courts of last resort.

LOWER COURTS AND TRIBUNALS

All those bodies exercising a judicial function are entitled to make references to the Court of Justice. In Britain, this would clearly cover all levels of the court structure, from the magistrates' courts in England, and the Sheriff and District Courts in Scotland to the House of Lords, to specialist bodies such as the Patents Court. It also takes in a wide range of administrative tribunals, including industrial, VAT and social security tribunals.[1] Arbitrators appointed by statute may have the power to refer on the basis of the official authority with which they are endowed but private arbitrators, operating under a clause in a private contract, cannot make references to the Court.[2]

The Court of Justice has also answered questions referred to it by professional disciplinary bodies,[3] primarily because no right of appeal lay from the professional body to the ordinary courts. On this basis, bodies such as the Law Society and the Bar Council, whose decisions are subject to judicial review are unlikely to qualify.

COURTS OF FINAL RESORT

National courts against whose decisions there is no judicial remedy under national law have not merely a discretion but an obligation to refer questions of Community law to the Court of Justice. Clearly this refers to the House of Lords in the British system but it arguably also includes any court or tribunal against whose decision there is no appeal in the instant case.[4] An example would be the Scottish Court of Criminal Appeal, given that in Scotland appeal only lies to the House of Lords in civil matters. There is some debate as to whether or not the Court of Appeal could also be regarded as a court of last resort given that leave to appeal to the House of Lords may be refused.[5]

---

1   For the principles see Case 61/65 *Vaassen v Beambtenfonds Mijnbedrijf* [1966] ECR 261.
2   Case 102/81 *Nordsee Deutsche Hochseefischerei v Reederei Mond* [1982] ECR 1095. It may be possible, however, for an appeal on a point of law to be made to an ordinary court which can then make a reference.
3   Case 246/80 *Broekmeulen v Huisarts Registratie Commissie* [1981] ECR 2311.
4   Case 6/64 *Costa v ENEL* [1964] ECR 585.
5   For the contrary view, see *Generics (UK) v Smith, Kline and French Laboratories* [1990] 1 CMLR 416. See also *Magnavision v General Optical Council* [1987] 1 CMLR 887 on the unreviewable power of the Divisional Court to certify in criminal proceedings that there exists a point for consideration by the House of Lords.

THE EXERCISE BY LOWER COURTS OF THE POWER TO REFER

When is a reference necessary?

One of the most important factors in the decision to make a reference is whether the matter at issue is such as to require the assistance of the Court of Justice. The Court of Appeal, in the *Stock Exchange* case,[6] stated that where a court has found the facts of a case and considers that the Community law issue is critical to its final decision, it should ordinarily make a reference, unless it can with complete confidence resolve the issue itself. Such confidence can only be justified after a full consideration of the differences between national and Community legislation, of the pitfalls of venturing into a potentially unfamiliar field, of the need for uniform interpretation of the law throughout the Community and of the expertise and logistical advantages enjoyed by the Court of Justice.

The Court of Appeal's approach approximates to that of the Court of Justice, which has also stressed the need for uniformity of Community law and the difficulties which national judges face in deciding questions of Community law for themselves.[7]

Following the *Stock Exchange* case and in contrast to previous formulations of principle on this point,[8] there now seems to be a presumption in favour of the referral to Luxembourg of points of Community law. Lower courts do, nevertheless, retain a discretion not to refer. Factors which may be significant in this regard include the expense and delay involved in the reference procedure, the wishes of the parties (although this is not required under Community law),[9] and the general importance of the point of law which is at issue.

The discretion to refer is not fettered by national rules of precedent: lower courts remain free to consult the Court of Justice even if a higher national court has ruled on the matter previously.[10] Nor is it fettered by previous rulings of the Court of Justice itself. The Court not being bound

---

6   *R v International Stock Exchange of the United Kingdom and the Republic of Ireland, ex p Else* [1993] 1 All ER 420.
7   Case 283/81 *CILFIT v Ministero della Sanità* [1982] ECR 3415, concerning the *obligation* to refer of courts of final resort. See *infra*.
8   *Bulmer v Bollinger* [1974] 2 All ER 1226.
9   *Bulmer v Bollinger*, [1974] 2 All ER 1226. But for a contrary view, see *Portsmouth City Council v Richards* [1989] 1 CMLR 673.
10 Case 166/73 *Rheinmühlen-Düsseldorf v Einfuhr- und Vorratsstelle für Getreide und Futtermittel* [1974] ECR 33, 139.

by precedent, and having in the past reversed its earlier rulings, national courts remain free to ask questions on which the Court has already made its views known.

Challenging Community measures

Notwithstanding the terms of Article 177, the Court has ruled that a lower court must make a reference in one particular situation — where it has doubts about the validity of a Community measure called into question before it. Community measures are frequently immune from direct challenge before the Court of Justice because of the restrictive standing requirements of the Article 173 action for annulment (see Chapter 4). For many private parties, the best way to challenge the validity of a Community measure is to bring an action for judicial review of a national decision based on the Community measure. The legal basis of the national decision is then called into question and the national court is then faced with a question of Community law. Approximately one in seven preliminary references have been directed towards this end.

National courts are quite entitled to confirm the validity of the Community measure, but only the Court of Justice can declare Community measures to be invalid, so a reference must be made where the national court is in any doubt.[11] It is possible, however, for a national court to order the interim suspension of a national measure which is based on a Community regulation, despite the implications which this may have for the uniform of application of European Community law throughout the Member States.[12]

Appealing against the decision to refer

According to the Rules of the Supreme Court (RSC), an order of a lower court making a reference to the Court of Justice is a final order, so parties may appeal against it to the Court of Appeal without leave.[13] References made by the Court of Appeal can only be appealed to the House of Lords under the normal leave requirements. The reference will not usually go to the Court of Justice until the time for appealing has expired or any appeal has been resolved but the referring court may order the reference

---

11 Case 314/85 *Foto-Frost v Hauptzollamt Lübeck-Ost* [1987] ECR 4199.
12 Cases C143/88 and C92/89 *Zuckerfabrik Süderdithmarschen v Haumptzollampt Itzehoe* [1991] ECR I-415.
13 RSC Ord 114, r 1.

to be sent anyway.[14] The situation is less complicated in Scotland given that there is, in general, no requirement to seek leave to appeal against a final judgment of a Scottish court. Decisions not to refer are only interlocutory and leave to appeal is required.

Following the *Stock Exchange* case,[15] a decision to refer will be overturned where the higher court comes to the conclusion that the referring court could indeed have decided the question of Community law with complete confidence.[16] The reverse presumably applies in the case of decision not to refer. It has been successfully argued in Ireland, however, that rules providing for appeal from a decision to make a reference could not be applied because they fettered the unqualified jurisdiction to refer of the lower court.[17]

THE EXERCISE BY FINAL COURTS OF THE OBLIGATION TO REFER

In *CILFIT*,[18] the Court held that a national court of last resort need not refer a question in three situations. Firstly, where the question of Community law is irrelevant to the proceedings before it. Secondly, where the question has already been decided by the Court of Justice, and thirdly, where the correct application of Community law in a particular case is so obvious as to leave no room for reasonable doubt. The latter is known as the doctrine of *acte claire*. Before citing *acte claire*, however, the national court should consider whether the answer would be as obvious to courts in other Member States, noting linguistic difficulties, the special character and terminology of Community law and contextual and policy considerations.

The ruling of the Court of Justice in *CILFIT* to the effect that even final courts need not refer a question where the answer is clear, has the effect of conferring a discretion upon these courts similar to that possessed by lower courts and tribunals. The House of Lords has in the past availed itself of this discretion. In *Litster*, for example, a question of Community law arose relating to the interpretation of the Acquired Rights Directive, which guarantees the rights of employees when their company changes hands. The Lords did not refer the question to Luxembourg because an almost identical point had already been dealt with by the Court.[19]

14 RSC Ord 114, r 5.
15 *R v International Stock Exchange of the United Kingdom and the Republic of Ireland, ex p Else* [1993] 1 All ER 420.
16 See, however, *Procurator Fiscal, Elgin v Cowie* [1990] 3 CMLR 445 (High Court of Justiciary): orders to refer should only be overruled where they are plainly wrong.
17 *Campus Oil v Minister for Industry and Energy* [1984] 1 CMLR 479.
18 Case 283/81 *CILFIT v Ministero della Sanità* [1982] ECR 3415.
19 *Litster v Forth Dry Dock* [1989] 1 All ER 1134; [1989] 2 CMLR 194.

REFERENCES IN INTERLOCUTORY PROCEEDINGS

Article 177 references can be made in the course of interlocutory proceedings.[20] Nevertheless, certain practical considerations, such as the need for prompt resolution of the matter and that no factual findings will have been made at this stage, dictate that they will rarely be appropriate. The fact that a grant or refusal of interim relief is not a final judgment on the substantive point, and indeed that the interlocutory issue can be reopened during the substantive proceedings, may help to persuade a lower court that a decision on the point of Community law is not necessary, within the terms of Article 177. It also has the effect of removing any obligation to refer on the part of courts of last resort.[1] An issue of Community law relating to the very availability of interim relief would, however, require a reference.[2]

INTERIM RELIEF

The sheer length of the Article 177 process means that obtaining interim relief is frequently of the utmost importance if the rights claimed under Community law are to have any real substance. British courts are required to take all necessary steps to protect putative Community law rights for the duration of the reference process, even to the extent of ordering the interim suspension of the operation of a statute.[3] As has already been noted, they may also suspend the operation of national provisions which implement Community legislation within the United Kingdom.

WHICH QUESTIONS CAN BE REFERRED?

The review of a decision to refer a matter to the Court of Justice has already been examined in context of the English and Scottish systems. The national court's exercise of its discretion to refer may also be reviewed by the Court of Justice, which has refused to answer a variety of questions sent to it by national judges. The list of questions to be referred to the Court of Justice is fixed by the national judge in consultation with the parties to the case. No fixed procedure is followed; sometimes

---

20   Case 107/76 *Hoffman-La Roche v Centrafarm* [1977] ECR 957.
1   Ibid.
2   *R v Secretary of State for Transport, ex p Factortame* [1990] 2 AC 85, [1989] 2 All ER 692, HL; Case C213/89, [1990] ECR I-2433.
3   Ibid.

the parties will agree upon a set of questions which are then presented to the court, sometimes they will make opposing suggestions which form the basis for the judge's own list. The Court of Justice need not, however, answer all questions which are referred to it and the chances of obtaining useful answers will be greatly enhanced by consideration of the following rules.

- According to Article 177 itself, the Court of Justice will rule upon issues relating to the interpretation of the Treaty, the validity and interpretation of acts of the institutions and the interpretation of the statutes of bodies established by an act of the Council where those statutes so provide. The Court will interpret a wide range of Community legal provisions including Treaty articles, acts of subsidiary conventions such as the Brussels Convention on Jurisdiction and the Enforcement of Judgments in Civil and Commercial Matters which makes specific provision for preliminary references to the Court of Justice, Community secondary legislation and Agreements with non-Member States such as Association Agreements and the General Agreement on Tariffs and Trade (GATT).
- The Court will only rule upon questions of interpretation. It will not apply its interpretation to the facts of the particular case. Nevertheless, the line between interpretation and application is frequently more apparent than real. The Court naturally interprets the law in the light of the facts of the case and its rulings can leave little or no discretion to the national court.
- The Court will not interpret national law or rule upon its compatibility with Community law. The latter function is, in theory at least, reserved for direct enforcement actions whereby the Commission brings Member States which it believes to be in breach of Community law before the Court under Article 169 (see Chapter 4). In the course of an Article 177 reference the Court will only interpret provisions of Community, which the national court then applies to the national law at issue. The rule has been modified slightly in that the Court will expressly interpret a provision of national law which incorporates by reference terms of Community law and so applies them even in purely internal situations.[4]

This rule is also something of a fiction which reflects more the Court's practice of giving judgments in the abstract, than any reluctance to validate the compatibility of national law with

---

4   Cases C297/88 and C197/89 *Dzodzi v Belgium* [1990] ECR I-3763; see also Case C231/89 *Gmurzynska-Bscher v Oberfinanzdirektion Köln* [1990] ECR I-4003.

Community law. Indeed, the majority of the cases dealt with by the Court under the Article 177 procedure are concerned with exactly this. In the Sunday trading references, for example, the basic issue was the compatibility with Community law of the Shops Act 1950, which restricted Sunday opening in England and Wales. Questions from the British courts and answers from the Court of Justice did not, however, mention the Shops Act, but were phrased in terms of an unnamed national law.[5]

- The Court will not rule upon questions which it regards as unnecessary or irrelevant,[6] although it will normally accept the national court's own opinion as to the relevance of a particular issue, the national court being best placed to assess what is necessary to enable it to give judgment.[7] It is important, therefore, to ensure that the national court explains in its reference why it considers a reply to its questions necessary for the resolution of the dispute before it. On the other hand, the Court will consider provisions of Community law which have not been raised by the referring court but which seem necessary to enable it to give a useful decision.[8]

- The Court is reluctant to give judgment on issues which have not been raised by the national court and which are not directly relevant to the case at hand but which it would nevertheless be sensible to resolve.[9] It has, however, on occasion answered questions bearing little resemblance to those originally referred to it and no firm rules can be suggested for predicting when it will exercise this discretion.[10]

- The Court will not rule on questions about which it feels it has been provided with insufficient information about the factual and legal circumstances to enable it to give useful answers.[11] This implies in particular that the facts of a case, and the questions of national law which it raises should be settled before a reference is made.[12]

---

5   See, eg Case 145/88 *Torfaen BC v B&Q* [1989] ECR 3851.

6   Case C343/90 *Lourenço Dias v Director da Alfândega do Porto*[1992] ECR I-4673.

7   Case C83/78 *Pigs Marketing Board v Redmond* [1978] ECR 2347.

8   See, eg Case 280/91 *Finanzamt Kassel-Goethestraße v Viessmann* [1993] ECR I-971; [1993] 3 CMLR 153.

9   Case C163/90 *Administration des Douanes et Droits Indirects v Legros* [1992] ECR I-4625.

10 See, eg C106/89 *Marleasing v La Comercial Internacional de Alimentación* [1991] ECR I-4135.

11 Cases C320-322/90 *Telemarzi Cabruzzo v Circostel* [1993] ECR I-393, ECJ.

12 See Cases 36 and 71/80 *Irish Creamery Milk Suppliers Association v Ireland* [1981] ECR 735.

- The Court will only rule on those issues which arise out of a genuine dispute between the parties. In *Foglia v Novello*,[13] the Court asserted its right to look into the circumstances surrounding references from national courts and to refuse to give judgment where it felt that it was being asked to deliver a consultative opinion on a general or hypothetical question rather than to assist in the administration of justice in the Member States. The Court refused to rule on what it seems to have regarded as a friendly action, set up by the two parties to the case who were in fact in agreement as to the desired result.[14]

These rules are tempered by the fact that the Court will extract an admissible question from one which is imperfectly formulated, although most of the cases in which this was done were in the early days of the Community when the Court was keen to maximise the number of references which it received from the national courts.[15] The Court currently receives more references than it can comfortably deal with, and has proved noticeably less accommodating in recent years.

PROCEDURE

The procedure for references to the Court of Justice from a British court can be found in the ordinary rules of procedure for that court.[16] An order for reference should give a clear and succinct statement of the case giving rise to the request for the ruling of the European Court of Justice, including the following information: the particulars of the parties; the history of the dispute between the parties; the history of the proceedings; the relevant facts as agreed by the parties or found by the court or, failing such agreement or finding, the contentions of the parties on such facts; the nature of the issues of law and fact between the parties; the domestic law, so far as is relevant; and the Treaty provisions or other acts, instruments or rules of Community law concerned.

The rules of the procedure of the Court of Justice are set out in the Protocol on the Statute of the Court of Justice annexed to each of the

---

13 Case 104/79 *Foglia v Novello (No 1)* [1980] ECR 745; Case 244/80 *Foglia v Novello (No 2)* [1981] ECR 3045.
14 Case C83/91 *Meilicke v ADV/ORGA* [1992] ECR I-4871; (1992) Times, 20 October.
15 See, eg *Costa v ENEL* [1964] ECR 585.
16 In England, references from the High Court are governed by RSC Ord 114, r 1; the form of the reference is governed by Ord 114, r 2 which is Form 109 in the Supreme Court Practice. The rules for other courts and tribunals do not differ greatly from this basic model. In Scotalnd, see RC 296 A-E.

Community treaties and in the Court's own Rules of Procedure.[17] Queries can be addressed to the British Registry at the Court of Justice.

Once a question has reached the Court of Justice, the terms of the reference are translated into the other eight official Community languages, notified to the Member States and the Community institutions and published in the 'C' series of the Official Journal. Following the service of the papers upon the participating parties they have two months to submit written observations to the Court under Article 20 of the Statute of the Court. The written pleadings before the Court of Justice are considerably more important than the written stage of proceedings before an English court, and accordingly should be set out in some detail. The Member States, the European Parliament, the Commission, which participates in virtually all cases, and the Council, where the case concerns the validity or interpretation of one of its acts, are also allowed to give their views. No other interested parties are permitted to submit their views.

At the end of the written phase, one of the judges of the Court, designated the 'judge rapporteur' prepares a preliminary report on the case, which is private to the Court. This report contains an assessment of the issues raised by the case as well as, occasionally, the judge's suggestions for any preliminary enquiries, with respect to witnesses or experts' reports, to be carried out.

The oral procedure comprises, firstly, a report for the hearing prepared by the judge rapporteur setting out the facts of the case and the respective contentions of the parties. Following this a hearing before the Court takes place where oral observations, usually limited to 30 minutes for each party are submitted. Thirdly, the Court's Advocate General gives his opinion on the case, which is often but not always followed by the Court in its own ruling. An interesting point to note is that the Court of Justice recognises the rights of audience of all British lawyers, solicitors included.

A major feature of the reference procedure is the length of time which is required between the making of the reference and the eventual decision of the case by the national court or tribunal. The process usually takes between eighteen months to two years, but is sometimes longer. As a consequence, the pleading of Community law issues which then have to be sent to Luxembourg for resolution is an increasingly important tactical ploy. Defence lawyers in the Sunday trading saga used this strategy to good effect, justifying their clients' breach of the Shops Act on the basis that the Act was in breach of Community rules on the free movement of goods. The defendant companies continued to trade on

17 The procedure of the Court is set out fully in 'Selected Instruments Relating to the Organisation, Jurisdiction and Procedure of the Court' published by the Community's Official Publications Office.

Sundays whilst several references, over a number of years, went to and from Luxembourg and not long after the Court finally upheld the validity of the Shops Act 1950, the Government announced that the Act itself was to be replaced by more liberal shopping legislation.

The costs of the reference procedure are incidental to the national proceedings and the court will reserve the matter to the national court to decide. Where legal aid has been granted in a criminal case, it will extend automatically to cover the costs of the reference; in civil cases, special authorisation is needed. The Court of Justice may itself grant legal aid in special circumstances to a party who is wholly or in part unable to meet the costs of the proceedings.[18]

BIBLIOGRAPHY

K Lasok *The European Court of Justice — Practice and Procedure* (2nd edn, 1993) Butterworths.

18 Article 104 of the Court's Rules of Procedure.

Chapter 4

DIRECT ACTIONS

INTRODUCTION

Under the EC Treaty, the jurisdiction of the Court of Justice is defined in terms of enumerated forms of action. The action which accounts for the majority of cases, the Article 177 reference from national courts, has already been dealt with. This chapter outlines the various forms of so-called direct action, which do not involve proceedings in national courts, but only before the Luxembourg courts. From 1 August 1993, jurisdiction over all direct actions, except for enforcement actions by the Commission and the Member States, has been transferred to the Court of First Instance.[1]

COMMISSION ENFORCEMENT ACTIONS

One of the primary functions of the Commission is to monitor and enforce the compliance of Member States with the obligations imposed upon them by Community law. Much of this task is performed unobtrusively, in behind-the-scenes negotiations with national administrations but where this proves insufficient, the Treaty provides the Commission with a legal remedy. Article 169 of the Treaty requires that the Commission deliver a reasoned opinion to a Member State which it believes has failed to fulfil a Treaty obligation, having given the state concerned the opportunity to submit its objections. The vast majority of disputes are settled at or before this stage but if the state concerned does

---

1 Council Decision 93/350/EEC, OJ 1993 L144/21. The transfer of direct actions relating to dumping and subsidies has been agreed in principle but deferred.

not comply with the terms of the opinion, the Commission may bring the matter before the Court of Justice.[2]

The United Kingdom has a better record than most states in fulfilling its Community law obligations, but has nevertheless been before the Court of Justice a number of times in recent years. The Court has ruled, for example, that certain British beaches failed to meet the standards of hygiene laid down in a Community directive,[3] and that Britain must amend the Patents Act 1977 in respect of the issue of compulsory licences where a patent has been not been sufficiently exploited. The Act appeared to discriminate against imports from other Member States and so infringed Community law on the free movement of goods.[4]

Once a dispute has reached the judicial stage it is extremely difficult for a Member State to justify its failure to comply with the demands of Community law. Various imaginative excuses have been pleaded and summarily rejected by the Court. A state may, nevertheless, persuade the Court that the Commission's view of what it has done, or of the demands of Community law, is mistaken.

The Article 169 action is, however, a weak remedy against violations of Community law by the Member States. It entails a long and cumbersome process which is frequently held up or abandoned altogether for political reasons and ultimately, the Court of Justice can make only a declaration that the state is in breach of Community law. These declarations have frequently been ignored. In an effort to alleviate the latter problem, the Maastricht Treaty confers new powers upon the Court to impose monetary penalties on Member States who do not comply with its judgments in Article 169 proceedings (Art 171(2)). The practical effect of strengthening the Article 169 remedy will not, however, become apparent for a number of years.

Although the Article 169 action involves only the Commission and the Member States it may have an importance for individuals. Making a complaint to the Commission is the cheapest and easiest, although certainly not the most reliable, means of attacking the actions of a Member State government on the basis of Community law. The Commission, which in fact relies to a considerable extent on assistance from the public in detecting breaches of Community law, may then exercise its discretion to investigate the matter, negotiate with the government concerned and ultimately bring an Article 169 action. In the

2   Once an action has been brought before the Court the Commission may request interim measures, usually in the form of an injunction to suspend the operation of the national law at issue. See, eg Case 246/89R *Commission v United Kingdom* [1989] ECR 3125. The Treaty also provides for an enforcement action to be brought by one Member State against another. Art 170, however, has rarely been used.

3   Case C56/90 *Commission v United Kingdom*, Judgment of 14 July 1993; [1993] ECR I-4109.

4   Cases C235/89 and C30/90 *Commission v United Kingdom and Italy: Re Compulsory Patent Licences* [1992] ECR I-829; [1992] 2 CMLR 709.

event of an action being brought, individual complainants may also prompt the Commission to request temporary suspension of the national measures. Nevertheless, the Commission cannot be forced to investigate a matter and whilst it may often be profitable, in challenging national measures, to obtain the support of the Commission, other avenues of challenge should always be pursued.

ACTION FOR ANNULMENT OF COMMUNITY MEASURES

Where the grievance of the individual is with a measure adopted by one of the Community institutions, the most direct recourse is to bring an action before the Court of First Instance for its annulment, under Article 173. On annulment the measure will be deprived of all legal effect, although the Court's powers are flexible in this respect.[5] Aside from intra-institutional staff disputes, the action is probably used most frequently to challenge Commission decisions in competition law matters.

An action for annulment must be brought within two months of either the publication of the disputed act, its notification to the applicant or the date on which it came to his attention. Assuming that this requirement is met, a successful action under Article 173 consists of three elements. Firstly, an act of a Community institution which is susceptible to review; secondly, standing to challenge that act; thirdly, a substantive ground on which to base the annulment of the act.

Measures which can be challenged

With respect to reviewable acts, Article 173, provides that the Court shall review the legality of acts of the Council, the Commission and the European Central Bank, other than recommendations and opinions, which do not have binding force. Regulations, directives and decisions are the remaining categories of act laid out in the Treaty but the Court has interpreted its jurisdiction more broadly, to include 'all measures adopted by the institutions, whatever their nature or form, which are intended to have legal effects.'[6] Acts of the European Parliament which are intended to have legal effects vis-à-vis third parties are also reviewable.[7]

---

5 See, eg Case C295/90 *Parliament v Council: Re Students' Right of Residence* [1992] ECR I-4193, where a directive was declared void only from the point at which another measure could be enacted to replace it.

6 Case 22/70 *Commission v Council: Re European Road Transport Agreement* [1971] ECR 263.

7 This codifies the result of Case 294/83 *Partie Ecologiste ('Les Verts') v European Parliament* [1986] ECR 1339.

The need to cite an act which is reviewable may be the greatest obstacle to challenging the Commission in competition law matters. In a large number of matters the Commission will not take a formal decision, but will proceed informally, by way of administrative letters which are said not to produce legal effects and are probably not, therefore, susceptible to review. Where a complaint is made to the Commission and the Commission does not wish to proceed to a formal investigation, the complainant may not challenge the Commission's first, preliminary opinion on the complaint.[8] The complainant may, however, insist upon a final, definitive opinion, which will be susceptible to challenge under Article 173.[9]

Standing to challenge

The Member States, the Council and the Commission are known as privileged applicants and automatically have standing to challenge reviewable acts regardless of whether they can demonstrate an interest in so doing. The European Parliament and the Central Bank are semi-privileged applicants, entitled to bring actions for the purpose of protecting their prerogatives. Private individuals, however, are non-privileged and must fulfil stringent criteria of *locus standi* in order to get into court. The result is that whilst a wide range of acts are reviewable, most can be challenged only by states and institutions. In practice, only decisions and regulations which are successfully argued to be decisions in disguise, are open to challenge by private parties.

DECISIONS, REGULATIONS, DIRECTIVES

An individual has standing to challenge a decision of a Community institution which is addressed to him. This is frequently the scenario in competition law proceedings — the Commission has issued a decision fining a company and the company then challenges that decision before the Court of First Instance. Problems arise when an individual seeks to challenge a decision which is addressed to someone else, or a regulation, which is a general instrument without specific addressees. In these instances the individual must establish that he is directly and individually concerned by the measure which he wishes to challenge.

---

8   Case T64/89 *Automec v Commission (No 1)* [1990] ECR II-367.
9   Case T24/90 *Automec v Commission (No 2)* [1992] ECR II-2223; [1992] 5 CMLR 431.

The result is that regulations, which are not normally challengeable under Article 173 by individuals because they are general measures which do not, by definition, directly and individually concern any individual or group of individuals, may be open to attack where their object or content is sufficiently individuated as to be analogous to that of a decision. The Court of Justice will, in short, look behind the form in which a measure has been adopted. In *Roquette Frères v Council*, for example, the regulation affected a group of isoglucose producers who had previously been awarded quotas, and included an annex listing the affected producers by name and detailing how their quotas would be affected.[10] The regulation appeared to be a bundle of individual decisions and was therefore open to challenge. A regulation may also be hybrid in nature, a measure of general application which is nevertheless specific so far as certain people are concerned.[11] The same rules appear to apply also to the challenge of directives.[12]

It is crucial, therefore, to establish that the individual is seeking to challenge what is, so far as he is concerned, a decision. Where this decision is not formally addressed to him, the tests of direct and individual concern must be satisfied.

DIRECT CONCERN

Direct concern is essentially a matter of causation and will be satisfied where it is certain that a measure will affect the applicant in a particular way. The test is generally concerned with examining whether a Member State has a measure of discretion in the implementation of a measure, in which case the causative link is lost. In *Alcan*, the applicants challenged a decision of the Commission which rejected a request of the Belgian Government for an aluminium import quota. Had the quota been granted, however, the Belgians would have had discretion as to whether or not they used it and the applicants were therefore not directly concerned.[13] It seems that discretion must not only exist but the manner of its exercise must be unpredictable.[14] Direct concern can also be established where the Community measure merely authorises or confirms action which has already been taken by the Member State.[15]

---

10 Case 138/79, [1980] ECR 3333.
11 See, eg Cases 239 and 275/82 *Allied Corpn v Commission* [1984] ECR 1005.
12 Case C298/89 *Government of Gibraltar v Council* [1993] ECR I-3605, ECJ.
13 Case 69/69 *Alcan v Commission* [1970] ECR 385.
14 Case 11/82 *Piraiki-Patraiki v Commission* [1985] ECR 207.
15 See Case 62/70 *Bock v Commission* [1971] ECR 897; Cases 106 and 107/63 *Toepfer v Commission* [1965] ECR 405.

INDIVIDUAL CONCERN

The requirement of individual concern has been interpreted strictly by the Court. It is satisfied where the measure in question affects the legal interests of the applicant because of a factual situation which differentiates him from all other persons and distinguishes him individually in the same way as a person to whom a measure is explicitly addressed.[16] This has meant in practice that the applicant must belong to a closed category of people, which is generally only the case where the measure has retroactive effects. In *International Fruit Company*, for example, the measure related to applications for import licences which had been made during the previous week. It applied, then, to a category of importers which was closed and each importer in the category was found to be individually concerned by it.[17] This case concerned a regulation which was found by the Court to be, in reality, a bundle of individual decisions.

Closed categories of applicants are, however, few and far between, and the requirement of individual concern will prove insurmountable for the vast majority of potential applicants. It is not sufficient to show that an applicant's business interests have been affected by a measure, nor that they were affected in a different way or more seriously than those of other traders, nor that the applicant's identity and his interest in the matter was known to or was ascertainable by the Commission at the time that the measure was passed, nor that the measure was in fact passed partly in order to deal with the applicant's situation.[18] It is not even enough to prove that the applicant is the only person affected by the measure.[19]

Moreover, there have been other cases where membership of a category which is definitively closed has not been enough to demonstrate individual concern. These cases have involved regulations which the applicant seeks to argue are in fact disguised decisions. The Court has, on occasion, applied a preliminary test to determine whether a measure is in fact a true regulation, based upon whether it is worded in abstract terms. The result is that regulations with even the most specific effects can appear unchallengeable because they are worded in general terms.[20]

There are, in addition, a number of special cases of individual concern. Private parties whose complaints to the Commission initiate investigations leading to possible enforcement action in the areas of restrictive practices and anti-dumping will be allowed to challenge any measures issued as a

16 Case 25/62 *Plaumann v Commission* [1963] ECR 95.
17 Cases 41-44/70 *International Fruit Company v Commission* [1971] ECR 411.
18 See, eg *Plaumann v Commission* [1963] ECR 95; Case 231/82 *Spijker v Commission* [1983] ECR 2559.
19 Case 1/64 *Glucoseries Réunis v Commission* [1964] ECR 413.
20 Case 789/79 *Calpak Commission* [1980] ECR 1949.

result of their complaint. Undertakings which complain about the activities of their competitors will frequently want to challenge Commission decisions not to take action. An undertaking must have a legitimate interest in the matter in order to lodge a complaint in the first place and no further standing requirements are imposed.[1]

The rules on individual concern are complex and cannot really be explained by one overarching theory. Nevertheless, a useful rule of thumb is that an applicant will only be individually concerned by a measure if it has been framed to take account of his particular situation or of it should have been so framed. In *International Fruit Company*, for example, the Commission's regulation was framed with regard to a known list of importers.[2] On the other hand, in *Sofrimport,* Commission regulations intervening in the import of apples from Chile did not, as they were required to do under empowering measures, take into account the special position of those importers who had apples in transit. The interests of the applicants should have been taken into account and they were allowed to bring an Article 173 challenge.[3]

Substantive grounds for challenge

Article 173 sets out four substantive grounds of review. They have tended to become subsumed under the broadest heading, infringement of the Treaty or of any rule of law relating to its application, and it is not always clear on which ground the Court has acted. All potentially applicable grounds for challenge should, nonetheless, be pleaded.

The first ground, lack of competence, refers to the situation where an institution has acted ultra vires, beyond the limits of the competences attributed to it. The institutions are, however, presumed to possess all the powers which are necessary to enable them to carry out the tasks allocated to them by the Treaty and it is unusual for this claim to succeed. In passing a measure, the institution concerned must state the legal basis for its competence, in the form of a Treaty article and/or previous enabling legislation, and challenges to legal basis are frequently brought by the institutions and the Member States.

---

1 See, eg Case 26/76 *Metro v Commission* [1977] ECR 1875 (restrictive practices); Case 264/82 *Timex v Commission* [1985] ECR 849 (anti-dumping). Importers, who have to pay anti-dumping duties must prove individual concern on the normal rules: Case C358/89 *Extramet v Commission* [1991] ECR I-2501. See also Case 169/84 *COFAZ v Commission* [1986] ECR 391 on the regime for state aids to industry, under which complainants do not have a formal status.
2 Cases 41-44/70 *International Fruit Company v Commission* [1971] ECR 411.
3 Case C152/88 *Sofrimport v Commission* [190] ECR I-2477.

Infringement of an essential procedural requirement is equivalent to procedural ultra vires in English and Scottish administrative law. Successful invocations of this ground in the past have cited, for example, inadequacies in the statement of reasons which must accompany all secondary legislation, and a failure to consult affected parties where this is required.

It is often difficult to differentiate between this ground of review and the main ground, infringement of the Treaty of any rule of law relating to its application, since the latter may include the breach of requirements which are essentially procedural. Most of the bases for review under the latter heading stem from the general principles of Community law, which include equality, proportionality, legal certainty, the right to a fair hearing and respect for fundamental human rights. These have been discussed in greater detail in Chapter 2. Virtually any rule of Community law, whether originating in the Treaty of Rome, in secondary legislation, in international treaties which are binding upon the Community, or in the general principles can be cited under this heading.

The final ground for challenge, misuse of powers, is analogous to the English doctrine of improper purpose. It is difficult to prove since it requires evidence of the actual subjective intention of the authority when it acted and it has given rise to little case law.[4]

Interim suspension of the Community measure

In the course of proceedings under Article 173 an application for interim relief may be made to the Court of First Instance which has the discretion to suspend the operation of the contested act (Article 185) and to order such other measures as may be necessary (Article 186). The Court must be satisfied, firstly that the applicant has made out a *prima facie* case on the merits. It will then examine whether there is a possibility of serious and irreparable damage to the applicant which gives rise to urgency. Purely financial damage is not generally considered to be grounds for urgency,[5] and suspension of regulations and directives, legislative measures which may affect a wide range of third parties, is rare.

Interim measures may also be granted where this is necessary to maintain the status quo, where the contested measure would otherwise produce a situation which would be very difficult to reverse if the action for annulment was later to succeed.[6]

---

4   One example is Case 105/75 *Giuffrida v Council* [1976] ECR 1395.
5   See, eg Cases C51/90R and 59/90R *Comos Tank v Commission* [1990] ECR I-2167.
6   See, eg Case 56/89R *Publishers Association v Commission* [1989] ECR 1693.

Challenge to Community acts before national courts

The requirements which must be satisfied in a direct action before the Court of Justice, in particular the standing rules for individuals seeking to attack Community acts under Article 173, are strict and many acts will simply be immune from challenge in this way. For most individuals, the appropriate avenue of recourse for challenging a Community act, is by an action in the British courts. The act of a Community institution cannot be attacked directly in an action for judicial review but an action can brought for review of a decision of the British authorities which implements, or applies or is otherwise based upon the Community measure. The legality of the Community measure can then be called into question indirectly.

National courts may confirm the validity of Community measures without seeking the opinion of the Court of Justice but they may not, however, declare a Community measure to be invalid without first making a reference to Luxembourg.[7] If a reference is made, it may be possible to persuade a British court to suspend in the interim the operation of national measures which are based on the contested Community measure. The key elements of a positive decision in this respect are a serious doubt about the validity of the Community measure upon which national measures are based, and an urgent need to prevent serious and irreparable damage to the applicants.[8]

CHALLENGING AN INSTITUTION FOR FAILURE TO ACT

Under Article 175, a Community institution can be compelled to adopt a measure or at least to take a decision defining its position. Such a decision may then be open to challenge under Article 173. The requirements of the action for failure to act have been interpreted strictly by the Court of Justice and successful Article 175 actions are rare.

Like Article 173, Article 175 draws the same distinction between privileged and non-privileged applicants. Private individuals may bring actions where an institution of the Community has failed to address to them any act with binding legal force. The requirement that the act be addressed to them seems to limit private parties to challenging failures to adopt decisions addressed to themselves. Certainly individuals cannot

---

7   Case 314/85 *Foto-Frost Firma v Hauptzollampt Lübeck-Ost* [1987] ECR 4199.
8   Cases C143/88 & C92/89 *Zuckerfabrik Süderdithmarschen v Haumptzollampt Itzehoe* [1991] ECR I-415.

challenge the failure to adopt a regulation and it seems also that they cannot challenge a failure to take a decision addressed to someone else.[9]

Proceedings under Article 175 must be commenced within a reasonable time of the institution demonstrating an intention not to act.[10] Having ascertained this intention, the individual must explicitly call upon the institution to act, following which the institution has three months in which to take a position on the matter. Where no position is taken, the proceedings continue and if they are successful the institution is required to take the necessary measures to comply with the Court's judgment. If the institution does take a position, the Article 175 proceedings must cease and the applicant must start again with an action for annulment.[11]

An important obstacle to Article 173 challenges to an institution's refusal to act is that in order to have standing, an individual must be legally entitled to demand the action in question. Many Commission powers, including those in the field of competition law, and the power to bring enforcement actions against the Member States are, however, discretionary, and individuals cannot compel the Commission to act when it does not wish to.[12]

Problems arose in the past where the Commission took a definite position using a measure, such as an administrative letter or some other form of preliminary act, which did not, in theory, produce legal effects and so could not be legally challenged. In *Automec (No 2)*, however, the Commission conceded that a competition law complainant was entitled to a legally challengeable act in response to a complaint.[13] Provisional opinions on complaints are not legally challengable but if the complainant is not satisfied and insists upon a definitive response, which can be the subject of a legal challenge, then the Commission must produce one. Failure to do so can found an action under Article 175.

INDIRECT CHALLENGES BEFORE THE COURT OF JUSTICE

Article 184, the so-called plea of illegality, allows Community regulations and other general acts to be challenged indirectly, in the course of legal proceedings under some other provision.[14] For example, an individual

---

9   Case 246/81 *Bethell v Commission* [1982] ECR 2277.
10   Case 59/70 *Netherlands v Commission* [1971] ECR 639.
11   Case T28/90 *Asia Motor France v Commission* [1992] ECR II-2285; [1992] 5 CMLR 431.
12   Case 125/78 *GEMA v Commission* [1979] ECR 3173.
13   Case 24/90 *Automec v Commission (No 2)* [1992] ECR II-2223; [1992] 5 CMLR 431.
14   The scope of Art 184 was extended beyond regulations in Case 92/78 *Simmenthal v Commission* [1979] ECR 777.

seeking to challenge a decision based on a regulation which is addressed to him, or by which he is directly and individually concerned, may call into question the validity of the regulation even though he would not have been able to do so under Article 173.

The grounds on which a measure may be challenged indirectly are the same as those discussed above in relation to Article 173. The consequences of a successful indirect challenge differs in that a measure will not be annulled but merely held to be inapplicable in the particular case, but in practice the measure will be treated as invalid by all concerned.

ACTIONS FOR DAMAGES AGAINST THE COMMUNITY

Financial compensation for damage caused by wrongful acts or omissions on the part of the Community institutions or their servants are brought under Article 215. Three different types of damages action may be distinguished.

Ordinary civil wrong

An ordinary tort or delict action can be brought for damage caused by servants of the Community in the course of their duties, although only those acts of its servants which are a necessary extension of tasks entrusted to the institution in question are covered.[15]

Maladministration

Secondly, actions can be brought for damage arising out of wrongful administrative decisions. A notorious example is the *Adams* case in which the Commission disclosed to a pharmaceuticals company the name of one of their employees who had supplied the Commission with evidence that the company was in breach of EC competition rules, as a result of which large fines were imposed upon it. Adams was subsequently seized and imprisoned for industrial espionage and later recovered damages from the Commission.[16]

---

15 Case 9/69 *Sayag v Leduc* [1969] ECR 329.
16 Case 145/83 *Adams v Commission* [1985] ECR 3539. See also Cases 5, 7 and 13-24/66 *Kampffmeyer v Commission* [1967] ECR 245.

Liability for legislation

The third and most common action for damages seeks compensation for loss caused by Community legislation. The action is well-established in Community law but the Court of Justice, no doubt mindful of its consequences for the legislative discretion of the Community institutions and indeed for their financial well-being, has interpreted it very narrowly.

The formula applied by the Court is that in the case of a legislative measure involving a choice of economic policy there will be no liability unless a sufficiently flagrant breach of a superior rule of law for the protection of the individual has occurred.[17] Little weight has been placed on the requirement of a superior rule of law; a breach of any rule of Community law, as under Article 173, seems to suffice, although claims based upon general principles such as equality, proportionality and legitimate expectations appear to have been most successful. That the rule must be for the protection of the individual has also been unimportant, although in a recent case the Court did reject a claim founded upon a breach of a law relating to the division of competence between the institutions of the Community on the grounds that it was not intended to confer rights upon individuals.[18]

The limb of the test on which most claims have floundered is the requirement of sufficiently serious breach. It will only be satisfied in special circumstances, where the institution concerned has manifestly and gravely disregarded the limits on the exercise of its powers.[19] On this view, most illegal measures will not be illegal enough to ground a claim in damages.[20]

Nevertheless, more recent cases have demonstrated that it is possible to win under Article 215 and may signal a revival in damages claims against Community institutions. In *Sofrimport*, for example, the apple importers who established standing and then succeeded in having Commission regulations annulled under Article 173 were also awarded damages. The Commission had breached their legitimate expectations without invoking any overriding reason of the public interest for so doing.[1]

---

17 Case 5/71 *Aktien-Zuckerfabrik Schöppenstedt v Council* [1971] ECR 975.
18 Case C282/90 *Vreugdenkil v Commission* [1992] ECR I-1937.
19 Cases 83, 94/76, 4, 15, 44/77 *Bayerische v Council and Commission* [1978] ECR 1209.
20 See, eg the *Isoglucose* cases: Cases 116 and 124/77 *Amylum and Tunnel Refineries v Council and Commission* [1979] ECR 3497; Case 143/77 *Koninklijke Scholten-Honig v Council and Commission* [1979] ECR 3583.
1   Case C152/88 *Sofrimport v Commission* [1990] ECR I-2477; see also Cases C104/89 and C37/90 *Mulder v Council and Commission* [1992] ECR I-3061.

Common denominators

Certain components are common to the various types of damages action. They are subject to a limitation period of five years and are conditional upon the establishment of a wrongful act. Arguments may be adduced to this effect in the course of the Article 215 proceedings but the illegality may equally have been established earlier, in, for example, an action for annulment or an Article 177 reference. Interim measures, in respect of the act of an institution, can be requested as in an action for annulment under Article 173.

The Court has adopted a restrictive notion of damage. It is unwilling to compensate anticipated profits,[2] and will take account of actual and reasonably possible mitigation of damage,[3] including the extent to which the applicant has been able to spread his losses by, for example, passing them on to customers.[4] Its approach to causation is similarly narrow.[5]

The result of a successful Article 215 claim is a damages award but the Court may state that a measure is illegal whether or not it awards damages. Such a declaration will have the practical effects of an annulment. Bringing a claim in damages may, therefore, enable an individual to avoid the stringent standing criteria and short time limits of the action for annulment, although in recent cases the Court has stressed that a successful applicant should belong to a clearly defined group of economic operators.[6] This in itself introduces informal standing requirements for the damages action.

It should be noted, however, that the appropriate forum for a damages claim will frequently be the British courts. In many cases, the damage will have been caused by a combination of Community legislation and the national authority's acts in implementing it. The Court of Justice has held that in this kind of situation an action before a national court, against the national authority, is to be preferred, where this can provide an effective means of protection for the plaintiff's rights.[7] The *Francovich* decision,[8] establishing that Member States must provide an effective remedy in damages against their breaches of Community law, opens up a range of possibilities in this area which have yet to be clarified.

---

2   Cases 5, 7 and 13-24/66 *Kampffmeyer v Commission* [1967] ECR 245.
3   See, eg Case C37/90 *Mulder v Council and Commission* [1992] ECR I-3061.
4   See, eg Case 256/81 *Pauls Agriculture v Commission and Council* [1983] ECR 1707.
5   Cases 64, 113/76, 167, 239/78, 27, 28, 45/79 *Dumortier Frères v Council* [1979] ECR 3091.
6   Case C152/88 *Sofrimport v Commission* [1990] ECR I-2477; Case C37/90 *Mulder v Council and Commission* [1992] ECR I-3061.
7   Case 175/84 *Krohn v Commission* [1986] ECR 753.
8   Cases C6 and 9/90 *Francovich v Italy* [1991] ECR I-5357.

PROCEDURAL MATTERS

The procedure to be followed by a private party in a direct action before the Court is essentially the same as described in relation to Article 177 references. Certain important differences should be noted, however. Firstly, the client must have an address for service in Luxembourg. Secondly, the written stage of the procedure is more complicated. Rather than each party simply submitting written observations, an initiating writ, or 'Application' is submitted, containing information as to the subject matter of the dispute and the grounds on which the application is based. It must also set out the precise conclusions which are asked of the Court, including conclusions as to costs, and details of the evidence which is relied upon. A Defence, Reply and Rejoinder may follow. A request for interim measures must be made in a separate application. Thirdly, private parties with a special interest may be permitted to intervene in direct actions.

Chapter 5

PROTECTING COMMUNITY LAW RIGHTS: A SUMMARY

THE POSITION IN NATIONAL LAW

In considering the way in which Community law considerations might affect the position in national law, the following series of questions should be gone through:

1 Is there national legislation which purports to implement the Community law obligation?
   If yes, then the national legislation is to be read purposively in a way which gives full and proper effect to Community law.[1]
   If no, then

2 Is there national legislation which has been re-enacted, consolidated or otherwise presented by the national government as implementing the Community law obligation?
   If yes, then again, national law must be given a purposive construction, so as to give full and proper effect to Community law.[2]
   If no, then

3 Is the existing relevant national legislation which is not in implementation of Community law in any way open to interpretation in accordance with the demands of Community law?

---

1 Case 14/83 *Von Colson v Land Nordrhein-Westfalen* [1984] ECR 1891, [1986] 2 CMLR 430. *Litster v Forth Dry Dock & Engineering* [1990] 1 AC 546, [1989] 2 WLR 634, [1989] 1 All ER 1134.
2 Case 80/86 *Officier van Justitie v Kolpinghuis Nijmegen* [1987] ECR 3969, [1989] 2 CMLR 18.

If yes, then any provisions of the national legislation which are open to interpretation are to be given that reading which most favours the full and proper effect of Community law. [3]
If no, then

4   Is the Community provision in question clear, precise and unconditional such as to give rise to direct effect in relation to the parties before the court? It should always be borne in mind at this step that whereas Community law rights derived from articles of the Treaty or from Community regulations may be relied upon against all parties. The Court has insisted, to date, that rights derived from directives can only be pled against public bodies.
If the Community provision is directly effective against the parties to the action, then the Community provision has to be given immediate effect by the national court with the result that all and any rules of national law and procedure which impede the full and proper enjoyment of the rights conferred by it have to be suspended. [4]
If direct effect cannot be relied upon, then there are no further remedies which may be taken against private parties. This does not, however, rule out an action against the State if the conditions set out in the following question are met.

5   Is the Community provision at issue a provision of a directive which confers rights on individuals, the contents of which can be identified from the directive and is there a causal link between the Member State's failure to implement the Community provision and any loss or damage suffered by the claimants?
If yes, then a damages claim may be brought against the State concerned. [5]
If no, then

6   Does the claim concern the breach by the state of another type of provision of Community law, such as a Treaty article or regulation, which has caused identifiable loss or damage to the claimant?
If yes, then a damages claim would appear to be available in principle but the criteria for liability to be applied to such a claim remain to be determined.

---

3   *Webb v EMO Cargo* [1993] 1 CMLR 259.
4   *R v Secretary of State for Transport, ex p Factortame* [1990] 3 WLR 818 at 857-8.
5   Cases C6,9/90 *Francovich and Bonifaci v Italy* [1991] ECR I-5357, [1992] IRLR 84, [1993] 2 CMLR 66.

If no, then the state's breach of Community law can only be dealt with by the European Commission, through negotiation with the state concerned and ultimately through an Article 169 action before the Court of Justice. This is not a matter for national courts and the most that the national lawyer can do in such a situation is to complain to the Commission on behalf of his or her client. Competition law issues raise special considerations. Undertakings concerned about the activities of others may make a complaint to the Commission and request interim protection.

Chapter 6

RESEARCH IN COMMUNITY LAW

INTRODUCTION

The account of the substantive Community law given in this book is intended to be a starting point, a map of the law, rather than a detailed guide. Once it has been established that Community law may have some bearing on a particular matter, further research must be undertaken. This chapter aims to give a brief account of how this might be done.

All law libraries in the United Kingdom now cater, to a greater or lesser extent, to the needs of EC lawyers. The European case reports and major texts are widely available but many official publications of the Community, and notably those containing details of secondary legislation and preparatory acts, are kept only in certain accredited institutions, known as European Documentation Centres.

PRIMARY SOURCES

Legislation

THE TREATIES

The basic texts of the European Community treaties have been produced in various official forms by the Luxembourg based Office for Official Publications of the European Community. These will be found in all European law libraries.

The complete text of all the Treaties relevant to the European Community is produced in Volumes B-I to B-IV of K R Simmonds *Encyclopedia of*

European Community Law (looseleaf) Sweet & Maxwell. The provisions of the main treaties are also reproduced in R Wallace and W Stewart *Butterworths Guide to the European Communities* (2nd edn, 1992) Butterworths, in N Foster *Blackstone's EEC Legislation* (2nd edn, 1992) Blackstone Press and B Rudden and D Wyatt *Basic Community Laws* (4th edn 1993) Clarendon Press. These books also contain some of the Community's most important secondary legislation.

SECONDARY COMMUNITY LEGISLATION

The secondary legislation and related acts promulgated in the Community are published in the *Official Journal of the European Communities* (OJ), a daily gazette composed of two principal series on Community legislation and Community communications respectively. In addition, a *Supplement to the Official Journal* records details of public supply and work contracts and an *Annex to the Official Journal* contains the debates of the European Parliament. An *Index to the Official Journal* is also published separately.

The 'L', for legislation series contains enacted Community legislation. The 'C', for communication, series consists of a variety of other information including proposals for legislation, job vacancies, and, importantly, lists of new actions brought before, and orders and judgments delivered by, the Court of Justice. Issues of the Official Journal are referenced by a year or specific date, a letter and a serial number. The serial number consists of two numbers separated by an oblique dash which indicate the edition number and the page number respectively. It should be noted that the two series of the Official Journal are issued and numbered completely separately.

Thus, the reference OJ 1989 L334/30 18.11.89 means that one should look in the 1989 Official Journal legislation series, edition number 334 at page 30. There will be found the Community Directive on insider dealing, Council Directive 89/592/EEC of 13 November 1989. Note that the date on which a measure is enacted will not usually correspond to the precise date of the edition of the Official Journal in which it is published.

Official translations into English of legislation promulgated in the years 1952-72, before the accession of the United Kingdom, are contained in the *Official Journal Special Edition.*

References to the most important secondary legislation are given in the footnotes of the text of this book. Further references, and importantly, details of amendments to basic measures, may be obtained from the monthly *Index to the Official Journal.* The index is produced in two different classification methods. The first method is called 'alphabetical' and lists Community legislation and communications by their subject matter under reference to keywords or expressions contained in them. The second method is termed 'methodological' and lists regulations, directives and decisions by their individual serial numbers. Like the reference numbers for UK statutory instruments, the serial numbers refer to the year in which the measure was published, its place in the number of like measures published that year, and the Treaty under which the measure was adopted. Thus, Council Directive 79/7/EEC on equal treatment in social security matters was adopted under the European Economic Community Treaty and is the seventh Council Directive published in 1979.

In addition to the index, the Official Journal publishes every six months the *Directory of Community Legislation in Force*. This is in two volumes. The first volume, the analytical register, gives a comprehensive list of Community measures by subject matter and shows which measures are currently in force and whether they have been amended or supplemented. The second volume is a chronological index indicating where measures are to be found in the first volume.

The *Directory* is compiled from the CELEX (*Communitatis Europae Lex*) data base and most European Documentation Centres have on-line access to this database which contains a complete record of Community primary and secondary legislation. CELEX is not an easy system to handle and, given the cost of using it, most of its outlets restrict access to trained personnel. It is also, however, available on CD-ROM, a data retrieval system based on the compact disc. This version is much more user-friendly although at least a few months behind the full index.

Excerpts from the Official Journal of all Community legislation dealing with the completion of the 1992 project of the single European Market have been produced in a looseleaf encyclopedia *Completing the Internal Market of the European Community: 1992 Legislation* (looseleaf) Graham & Trotman and the Office for Official Publications of the European Communities compiled by M Brearley and C Quigley. This collection of legislation extends to almost 20 looseleaf volumes. A companion guide has been produced, M Brearley and C Quigley *1992 Handbook* (2nd edn, 1991) Graham & Trotman in which many of the legislative changes detailed in the encyclopedia are summarised and put in context.

The Sweet & Maxwell *Encyclopedia of European Community Law* contains in Volume C-I to C-X a comprehensive and current compilation of general Community secondary legislation arranged according to subject matter.

The Department of Trade and Industry has recently published a two volume *Euro Manual* (1993) CCH Editions, which seeks to link EC law to UK business functions. The first volume contains general descriptions as to how EC law might affect business functions, for example sales and marketing, human resource management and corporate affairs and refers to the second volume for more detailed description of the potentially relevant law. The second volume is divided into 26 areas of Community policy and summarises the general objectives of Community policy together with the principal legislative measures in those areas. A similar exercise is carried out in Stanbrook & Hooper KPMG European Business Centre *A Business Guide to European Community Legislation* (1993) Chancery Law Publishing.

Butterworths *European Communities Legislation: Current Status 1952-1992* (1993) Butterworths with periodic cumulative supplements is probably the best means of tracing amendments to Community measures, being updated more regularly than the twice yearly *Official Directory*.

DIGESTS AND SUMMARIES

Community law is constantly in flux: regulations are issued, directives adopted, opinions of Advocates-General presented, judgments of both the Court of Justice and of the Court of First Instance produced, all almost on a daily basis. One of the most convenient ways of keeping up to date with this flood of materials is to refer to *European Current Law Monthly Digest* Sweet & Maxwell (monthly, with year-book and annual citators). This contains, *inter alia*, cumulative tables listing and giving the Official Journal references to the following:

- EC Council regulations, both by subject matter and in numerical order;
- draft directives, again by subject matter and in numerical order;
- directives which have been formally adopted but whose implementation date has not yet passed;
- directives which have potentially full force and direct effect in the sense that the date for their implementation has passed;
- EC Commission competition decisions;
- Commission inquiries and proceedings in the matter of anti-dumping.

In addition, the domestic *Current Law Monthly Digest* Sweet & Maxwell/ W Green (monthly, with year-book and annual citators) contain summaries of regulations, directives, decisions, resolutions, conclusions, communications and opinions issued by European Commission and by the Council of Ministers. It also summarises recent decisions of the European Court of Justice and of the Court of First Instance of the

European Communities and lists recently published books and articles on Community matters. *Current Law*, too, contains a particularly useful section listing, in chronological order, UK statutory instruments enforcing EC legislation and it will always be worth checking whether a particular instrument has Community law origins.

Starting from the other end, UK statutory instruments which implement a particular Community directive can be traced through *Butterworths EC Legislation Implementator*, which is regularly updated.

Case Law

Cases before the European Court of Justice are referenced both by name and by number. The first *Factortame* judgment, for example, is referred to as Case C-213/89 *R v Secretary of State for Transport, ex p Factortame (No 1)*. The first figure is a serial number, the second is the year in which the action was brought. Since the advent of the Court of First Instance in 1989, all cases before the Court of Justice are 'C-' cases, the cases of lower court being 'T-' cases. Cases may also be referred to by a shortened name relating to their subject matter. This is particularly the case where the actual name is likely to have occurred in the past, as in Commission versus Member State actions. Therefore, for example, Case 124/81 *Commission v United Kingdom* is generally referred to as *Re UHT Milk*, and Case 40/82 *Commission v United Kingdom* as *Re Newcastle Disease*. These unofficial names are certainly more descriptive, but they are rather unhelpful when it comes to trying to trace the particular case since indexes and citators tend to go by official nomenclature only.

When a case is filed in Luxembourg it will appear in the 'C' Series of the Official Journal and can be referenced accordingly. The opinion of the Court's Advocate General in the case, and later the judgment of the Court itself are published in looseleaf form, and indexed by date. Eventually, but often not for a considerable time, they will appear in bound official reports.

The caselaw of the European Court of Justice is published in English in the official *European Court Reports* (ECR). Since 1990, the ECR has been divided into two parts, Part I dealing with the Court of Justice decisions, Part II with the Court of First Instance. Therefore, *Factortame*, having been decided by the Court of Justice, has the reference [1990] ECR I-2433. Conversely, *SIV v Commission: Re Italian Flat Glass*, a decision of the Court of First Instance is indexed as Joined Cases T-68/69, T-77/89 and T-78/89, and published at [1991] ECR II-1403.

The main problem with the official reporting system is the lengthy, maybe up to two years, delay before publication of cases in English. The first place to look for a case which has not yet appeared in the ECR is in the collection of loose leaf judgments. Judgments of those cases which had English as their original language are published quite promptly. However, cases carried out in other languages require a translation period of several months and in the intervening period, only unofficially translated summaries are available. These summaries may be found in the 'C' Series of the Official Journal, and, in more detail, in the *Weekly Proceedings of the Court of Justice and the Court of First Instance*, which is published without significant delay by the information service of the Court in Luxembourg.

The working language of the Court is French and consequently every case, no matter what its original language, is translated into French at every stage. Accordingly, French language versions of judgments delivered in languages other than English, are available much quicker than their English language counterparts, both in looseleaf form and in the official French Court reports, the *Receuil de Cours* (Rec).

The official reports also suffer from some deficiencies in their indexing system. The reports, and their contents pages (which appear only in the first volume of each year), are arranged chronologically, according to the date when judgment was given by the Court but it should be noted that this bears little relation to the case number, the more usual means of reference. From 1978, the final volume of each year contains more helpful indexes of cases, according to their parties, their subject matter, the legislation to which they refer, and their numbers. The several intermediate volumes (at least six volumes a year are now required for the Court of Justice and three for the Court of First Instance) contain neither contents nor index.

The other, principal European law reports are the *Common Market Law Reports* (CMLR) which constitute another useful but non-comprehensive source of caselaw not only from the European Court of Justice, but also from national courts both within the United Kingdom and from the Continent. A decision of the Court of Justice which has not yet been formally published from Luxembourg may well appear here, although any translation is unofficial. They have the merit of covering some of the more important decisions concerning European law taken in the domestic courts of other Member States. The cases reported in the CMLR are helpfully indexed alphabetically, numerically, by subject matter and according to the Community instruments to which they relate. Other English reports such as the *All England Reports* (All ER) and, in the field of employment law, the *Industrial Relations Law Reports* (IRLR) also cover the most important of Community cases.

European cases, both reported and unreported can be traced through the LEXIS and CELEX databases. Manual research is more difficult as most European Community case citators are incomplete. The *Digest of Community Caselaw* published by the Court provides a record of Court of Justice decisions as well as selected decisions of national courts but at present covers only the period 1977-85; a recently published alphabetical and numerical index, which covers the period up until the end of 1992, is much more helpful. The *European Court of Justice Reporter* is up-to-date, but was first published only in 1982. Sweet & Maxwell's *Gazetteer of European Community Law* covers both decided cases and the decisions of the European Commission on anti-trust matters, is intended ultimately to be comprehensive but presently does not cover part of the 1980s or the 1990s. *Butterworths EC Case Citator and Service* is the most comprehensive non-official reference work and has the considerable advantage of referencing cases also according to their unofficial shortened titles.

SECONDARY SOURCES

The literature currently available in this field is broad and varied, although the majority of texts are directed at students rather than at practitioners. The major publishing houses seems to be catching up in this respect but many of the new publications for practitioners are in the form of looseleaf subscription services which are unlikely to be worthwhile for non-specialists.

In this book, the principal secondary sources in each subject area have been detailed at the end of each chapter. The major student textbooks cover a good deal of the subject matter of this book, albeit from a somewhat different perspective, and are certainly worth consulting. Particularly recommended are D Wyatt and A Dashwood, *European Community Law* (3rd edn, 1993) Sweet & Maxwell; J Steiner *Textbook on EEC Law* (3rd edn, 1992) Blackstones; S Weatherill and P Beaumont *EC Law* (1993) Penguin Books; and N Green, T Hartley and J Usher *The Legal Foundations of the Single European Market* (1991) Oxford University Press. The last mentioned book is restricted to consideration of the areas of free movement of goods, free movement of persons and competition law.

Further bibliographical information can be obtained by consulting Community law bibliographies. The Court of Justice itself publishes an annual *Bibliography of the Court of Justice* covering monographs and other contributions published in periodicals and collective works. The most comprehensive repository of bibliographical information is the Central Documentation Service of the Commission, known as SCAD. Information listing journal articles and other EC documentation is published weekly in the *SCAD Bulletin* but, more usefully, most European Documentation Centres will have access to the SCAD database, either through an on-line link, or on CD-ROM.

Perhaps the most comprehensive account in English of the law which we have described is D Vaughan *Law of the European Communities* (1986) Butterworths which constitutes two volumes of *Halsbury's Laws of England* (and looseleaf updates). British and EC legislation and cases are well indexed in *Vaughan* and its 21 sub-sections of substantive Community law provide a useful starting point for research into any aspect of EC law.

Nevertheless, when confronted with a particular problem which may raise an issue of Community law, it is always worth consulting the major practitioners' texts in the field. The coverage of Community law in these books is uneven but increasingly diligent. Harvey on *Industrial Relations and Employment Law* (looseleaf) Butterworths, for example, whilst addressing its subject matter from a UK law perspective has a reasonably comprehensive account of general Community employment protection legislation and case law in Volume 3, Section P.

The principal English language journals in this field are the *Common Market Law Review* (CMLRev) and the *European Law Review* (ELRev). The majority of general law journals now provide at least some coverage of EC law, notably the *Modern Law Review* (MLR) and the *International Comparative and Law Quarterly* (ICLQ), the latter containing a regular survey of recent developments in various fields of Community activity. The new *European Legal Journals Index* (1993) Legal Information Resources provides an index of legal articles and book reviews dealing with European matters.

A convenient way in which to gather information as to potentially useful books and other secondary sources is to consult the Community itself, through the European Communities Publications Office which publishes a wide variety of reports and studies, many of which contain useful summaries of legislation and case-law applicable in the area under discussion. These are available through HMSO bookshops and through the Commission offices in the United Kingdom which are situated in London, Edinburgh, Cardiff and Belfast. The annual *Directory of EC Information Services* (1993) Euroconfidentiel provides useful names and addresses in relation to Community matters in general.

The Commission's monthly *Bulletin of the European Communities* Office for Official Publications of the European Communities contains useful summaries of, and references in the Official Journal to, the activities of the Commission, Council and Court of the Justice under various general policy headings. Two final, and very useful, sources of up-to-the-minute information, including Court of Justice decisions, are the daily publication *Europe Bulletin Quotidien*, published in English, by the press agency Agence Europe, and *Butterworth's EC Brief.*

FORMS AND PROCEDURE

Butterworths have produced *European Court Practice* (1993) Butterworths which contains essays by practitioners and European Court judges on how to present cases to the Court of Justice and the Court of First Instance as well as the Official Notes for the Guidance of Counsel and relevant Treaty Provision, protocol, rules and forms. The Court of Justice has itself produced *Selected Instruments relating to the Organization, Jurisdiction and Procedure of the Court* (1993) Office for Official Publications of the European Communities which contains, *inter alia*, the Rules of Procedure of both the Court of Justice and the Court of First Instance.

Standard English law forms books such as *Atkins' Court Forms* also contain the important Court of Justice materials relating to the Article 177 reference. *European Community Law in the United Kingdom* (4th edn, 1990) Butterworths by L Collins also contains a useful account of the procedure to be followed in a case which is referred to Luxembourg. Procedural matters before the Court of Justice and the Court of First Instance respectively are dealt with in J Dine, S Douglas-Scott and I Persaud *Procedure and the European Court* (191) Chancery Law Publishing and T Millett *The Court of First Instance of the European Communities* (1990) Butterworths.

Finally as regards getting to grips with Community legal terminology, a short introduction is provided in R P Moore *Glossary of Scottish Legal Terms and Latin Maxims and European Community Legal Terms* (1992) The Law Society of Scotland and Butterworths and a multi-lingual guide is provided in C de Foulay *Glossary of EC Terms and Acronyms* (1992) Butterworths.

Chapter 7

THE INSTITUTIONAL STRUCTURE OF THE EUROPEAN UNION

INTRODUCTION

This chapter describes the formal institutional structure of the European Community, setting out the powers and responsibilities of its various component bodies.

It was noted in Chapter 1 that the foundation treaties of the original European Communities provided only for four central Community institutions: a Parliament, a Council, a Commission and a Court of Justice. The institutional structure of the European Community has, however, evolved over the years and since the conclusion of the Treaty of Maastricht, it has become more fruitful to view the Community and the European Union under four general headings: political, financial, monetary and judicial.

THE POLITICAL INSTITUTIONS OF THE EUROPEAN UNION

Under the heading 'political institutions' are considered those bodies concerned, in various degrees, with the legislative, executive and administrative functioning of the Community and/or the European Union.

The Commission

The European Commission, based in Brussels, is the main executive body of the European Community. It is currently made up of 17 individuals appointed by the Member States with the approval of the European Parliament for a period of 5 years. By convention two individuals from each of the five largest countries in the Community (France,

Germany, Italy, Spain and the United Kingdom) are appointed, while the remaining seven countries (Belgium, Denmark, Greece, Ireland, Luxembourg, the Netherlands and Portugal) have one national each.[1] The Commissioners are, however, independent of the national governments and may take no instructions from any of them, acting instead in the best interests of the Community as a whole. The President and the two Vice-Presidents of the Commission are appointed from amongst the Commissioners by agreement of the governments of the Member States.

Each Commissioner has responsibility for a specific portfolio, assisted by some 15,000 civil servants, based in Brussels and Luxembourg, who are organised into Directorates-General, the equivalent of national government departments.

The Commission's main functions may be summarised as follows:

– The Commission is the guardian of the treaties, charged with ensuring that regulations and directives have been fully implemented by the Member States, and that, in general, Member States meet their obligations under Community law. Any failure by a Member State in this regard may result in the Commission bringing a case against it before the Court of Justice.

– The Commission is an important participant in the legislative process. It has the sole right to initiate Community legislation by submitting proposals to the Council of Ministers. It may also legislate itself, having been given responsibility to implement particular decisions taken by the Council.

– The Commission has important investigative and prosecuting powers in areas such as competition law and unfair international trading practices.

– The Commission represents the European Community in certain international organisations, notably the General Agreement on Tariffs and Trade (GATT).

The European Parliament

The European Parliament consists of representatives (MEPs) directly elected since 1979 by the people of the Member States. The MEPs sit in pan-European party groups. Representation is linked to population size, the Member States with the largest populations having the largest number of seats. Elections to the European Parliament are not co-ordinated with national elections, so the situation can arise whereby the

1   New conventions may develop with the anticipated accession, in January 1995, of Austria, Norway, Sweden and Finland to full membership of the European Union.

majority of a Member State's representatives in the European Parliament are of a different political persuasion to that of their national government.

The Secretariat to the Parliament is located in Luxembourg, but the Parliament's plenary sessions are generally held in Strasbourg, while meetings of its committees are increasingly held in Brussels.

The Parliament has limited legislative powers and plays a consultative and supervisory role closer to the House of Lords than to the House of Commons in the UK system. The Parliament works in tandem with the European Commission, which is the Community institution with the sole right of initiating legislation, and the Council of Ministers, which is the Community institution with final power to enact legislation.

Thus, the Parliament may suggest amendments to draft directives and regulations proposed by the Commission. Where measures have been initiated under the 'co-decision procedure' (Art 189c) the Parliament may, by the votes of an absolute majority of its members, prevent the adoption of a particular measure agreed upon by the Council. Where the 'co-operation procedure' has been followed (Art 189b) Parliament cannot block proposed legislation, but may only require the Council to act unanimously in reaching a decision on the adoption of a particular measure. The procedure to be used in relation to any particular measure is specified in the terms of the Treaty.

Although its role in the legislative process is a relatively minor one, the Parliament has three important powers. Firstly, it may amend, in certain respects, the Community budget which is presented to it after being proposed by the Commission and approved by the Council. It also has the power to reject the proposed budget altogether. Secondly, the Parliament's assent is required for certain types of measures: international co-operation and association agreements between the Community and non-Member States; plans for the enlargement of the Community; any agreed procedure for uniform electoral procedure to the Parliament; measures to facilitate the exercise by citizens of the European Union of their freedom to move and reside throughout the Member States. Thirdly, the Parliament has the power, which has never been used, to dismiss the members of the Commission *en bloc*. It may not, however, require the resignation of individual Commissioners.

The Council of Ministers

The Council of Ministers is the main legislative body within the European Union in the sense that it is primarily responsible for adopting Community legislation such as regulations, directives and decisions (as has been noted, the Commission can, in certain areas, legislate on the basis of power delegated from the Council). The Council acts on proposals from the Commission and cannot, in theory, initiate legislation.

The Council of Ministers is composed of the representatives of the Member States with national ministerial responsibility for the particular issue then under discussion. The Chancellor of the Exchequer represents the United Kingdom in economic affairs, the Minister for Agriculture in agricultural affairs, and so on. The Presidency of the Council of Ministers and so of the Community is held for six months by each of the Member States in turn.

The Council may, in theory. take its decisions by a simple majority of its Members. Normally, however, special voting requirements are specified in the Treaty: these are unanimity or a qualified majority is required by the Treaty. Unanimity is required, for example, when the Council wishes to amend a proposal for legislation put to it by the Commission. Where a qualified majority is required by the Treaty, the votes are weighted for each Member State to reflect their relative size and influence. France, Germany, Italy and the United Kingdom are all given ten votes each. Spain is given eight votes, while Greece, Portugal and the Netherlands have each five votes. Denmark and Ireland have three votes each, and Luxembourg has two votes. This produces a total of 76 votes, of which at least 54 from a minimum of eight Member States must be cast in order to produce a qualified majority.[2] Depending on the provision of the Treaty on which it is relying, the Council may adopt legislation either unilaterally or in conjunction with the European Parliament.

The Council is assisted in its meetings and deliberations by a committee consisting of civil servants and diplomatic staff of each of the Member States' ambassadors (called the Permanent Representatives) to the Community and commonly referred to as 'COREPER'.

The European Council

This is the term for the Summit Meetings of the Heads of Government of the Member States together with the President of the European Commission. Under Article D of the Treaty on European Union the European Council meets twice yearly under the chairmanship of the Member State then heading the Council of Ministers. The European Council is required by Article D to submit a written report after its meetings to the European Parliament and report annually on the progress achieved toward European Union.

2　At the time of writing (March 1994) these provisions on the relative weighting to be accorded each Member State under the qualified majority procedure were the subject of discussion and negotiation in the light of the proposed enlargement of the European Union by the accession of Austria, Finland, Norway and Sweden.

The European Council is used to discuss specific matters affecting the Community and its Member States which have provoked disagreement in the Council of Ministers and matters such as foreign policy which have not been formally transferred to the Community but which are the subject of intergovernmental co-operation. The European Council provides a degree of political impetus for the development of Community policies.

The Economic and Social Committee

The Economic and Social Committee (ECOSOC) is a 189 member consultative committee set up to advise the Council of Ministers and the Commission on proposals in the area of economic and social policy. It consists of individuals appointed by the unanimous decision of the Council for a period of four years. These individuals are intended to represent the various groups making up the economic and social life of the Community. They are appointed from among manufacturers, transport operators and other businessmen, farmers, tradesmen, craftsmen, the liberal professions, trade unionists, consumer groups and the general public. The Committee may issue opinions on its own initiative (Arts 193 to 198). It must be consulted by the Council or Commission whenever specified by the Treaty, but may be consulted on other occasions if thought appropriate by either the Council or the Commission. Its opinions do not, however, bind any of the other institutions of the European Community.

Under the Coal and Steel Treaty there is a separate Consultative Committee to assist the Commission (formerly termed the High Authority) which represents producers, workers, consumers and dealers in the coal and steel industries. These individuals are appointed by the Council for a period of two years.

The Committee of the Regions

This is another consultative committee consisting of representatives of regional and local bodies appointed by the Council acting unanimously on nominations from the respective Member States. The number of representatives from each Member State varies roughly according to the size of their respective populations. Its purpose is to advise the Commissions and Council on matter affecting the regions of the Member States (Arts 198a to 198c). Like the Economic and Social Committee, it must be consulted by the Council or Commission whenever specified by the Treaty, but may be consulted on other occasions if thought appropriate by either the Council or the Commission and may issue opinions on its own initiative. Again, its pronouncements are not binding.

THE FINANCIAL INSTITUTIONS OF THE EUROPEAN UNION

The European Investment Bank

The European Investment Bank (EIB) is owned by the Member States of the Community and is based in Luxembourg. It is headed by a Board of Governors composed of Chairman plus the Finance Ministers from each Member State. Direct management of the activities of the EIB is carried out by a board of 22 directors. Twenty-one of these directors are appointed by the Board of Governors, while the 22nd director is appointed by the European Commission's management committee.

The EIB acts as a borrowing and lending agent. Its task is to contribute to the balanced development of the Community by making finance available to the Community's less developed regions. It raises its funds by issuing public bonds in the capital markets of the worlds stock exchanges. It re-lends the monies so raised on a non profit-making basis to investment projects in the Member States. It also gives guarantees to allow commercial financing for such investment projects (Arts 198d and 198e). It participates in the Community's external development policy through financing and loans to countries of the developing world within the framework of the EC's international co-operation agreements, such as the Lomé Convention.

The Court of Auditors

Despite its title this is not a court or judicial institution but an independent auditing body established in October 1977 to check on the financial activities of the central institutions of the European Communities. It is based in Luxembourg and consists of twelve members appointed for six year terms by the Council of Ministers, after consulting the European Parliament.

The Court of Auditors is charged with ensuring that the financial affairs of the European Community are properly managed and, in particular, that revenue is received and expenditure is incurred in a lawful and regular manner. At the end of each fiscal year it produces a report on the EC Budget and the state of the Community's finances (Art 188a to 188c). It may also submit its observations on specific topics in response to requests from other Community institutions and may draft reports on its own initiative, for example on the financial implications of particular aid programmes or proposed agricultural measures.

THE MONETARY INSTITUTIONS OF THE EUROPEAN UNION

The European Central Bank

The European Central Bank (ECB) was formed under the Maastricht Treaty as a new independent Community institution charged with the administration of the conditions for monetary union within the European Union. The ECB shall have the exclusive right to authorize the issue by national central banks and itself of bank notes within the Union. These banknotes will become the only legal tender within the Union (Art 105a). In the matter of monetary union the ECB has the power to make binding, directly applicable general regulations, to issue non-binding recommendations and opinions and to take specific decisions binding on the parties to whom they are addressed. Failure to comply with obligations imposed by such regulations and decisions may result in an undertaking being fined or penalized (Art 108a). The executive board of the ECB will consist of only six members appointed for a non-renewable term of eight years. The ECB's executive board together with the governors of the national central banks constitute the Governing Council of the ECB (Art 109a) The ECB will be assisted in its tasks by a new advisory and consultative body, the Economic and Financial Committee (Art 109c(ii)).

Prior to the establishment of the ECB, a transitional body preparing the way for full monetary union, the European Monetary Institute (EMI), will perform many of the functions of the future central bank and will seek to strengthen both co-operation between the existing, national central banks and co-ordination of the Member States' monetary policies (Art 109f). During its existence it will be assisted in its tasks by consultation with the Monetary Committee, a body with advisory status (Art 109c(i)).

The European System of Central Banks

The European System of Central Banks (ESCB)will be composed of the European Central Bank and the national central banks. Its basic task will be to define and implement the monetary policy of the European Union and to hold and manage the official foreign reserves of the Member States. Its objectives will be to maintain price stability and to support the general economic policies of the Union in accordance with the principle of an open market economy with free competition (Art 105). No member of the decision making bodies of either the European Central Bank or the national central banks may seek or take instructions from Community institutions or bodies, the governments of Member States or from any other body.

THE JUDICIAL INSTITUTIONS OF THE COMMUNITY

The European Community is currently served by two distinct judicial bodies: the European Court of Justice (Arts 4 and 164-168 of the Treaty of Rome) and the Court of First Instance of the European Communities (Art 168a).

The Court of Justice

The Court of Justice is a collegiate body comprising 13 judges who are assisted by 6 advocates-general. It is charged, under Article 164 of the Treaty with ensuring that 'in the interpretation and application of the Treaty the law is observed'. The judges and advocates-general are appointed for a renewable term of six years. A President of the Court is elected by the appointed judges from among their fellows for a renewable three year term. The Court of Justice is required to sit in plenary session only when a Member State or one of the central European Community institutions which is party to the proceedings so requests (Art 165). It also sits in plenary session in cases which are regarded as particularly complex, important or controversial. Paradoxically, a plenary session does not mean that all 13 judges are sitting. A *petit plenum* can be as few as seven judges and a plenary session may be also constituted by nine or eleven judges. The *grand plenum* is the full complement of 13 judges and is reserved for only the most important of cases. The President of the Court of Justice decides on these matters and otherwise directs the work of the Court and assigns cases to one of the six chambers of the Court consisting of either three or five judges.

The primary task of the Court of Justice is to ensure that a uniform interpretation is given to Community law throughout the European Community by way of the preliminary ruling procedure from national courts under Article 177 of the Treaty. Its other main task is to maintain the institutional balance within the European Community and, to that end, it has exclusive jurisdiction in any actions brought by EC institutions or by the Member States. The Court of Justice has the exclusive competence to hear actions brought by the Member States and the central Community institutions, and to hear and determine questions referred for a preliminary ruling under Article 177 (Art 168a(1)). This position may, however, be changed by subsequent Council decision. The Treaty provides that the decisions of Court of First Instance should be subject to a right of appeal to the Court of Justice. Article 51 of the Statute of the European Court provides that such appeals may be made on points of law only.

In addition to the power to give judgments on Community law in the matters brought before it, the Court of Justice may also issue legally binding opinions on proposed agreements between the Community and third countries (Art 228).

The Court of First Instance

The Court of First Instance of the European Communities was established by a decision of the Council of Ministers in 1988 in response to a request from the Court of Justice for a further judicial body to assist it in its tasks (Art 168a).[3] It is also a collegiate body consisting of 12 judges appointed by the Member States for a renewable term of 6 years. One of these judges is elected by his fellows President of the Court of First Instance. Where necessary in a particular case one of the judges may perform the duties of advocate-general. The Court of First Instance may also sit in plenary session of at least seven judges in cases of difficulty or importance but it normally sits in three or five judge chambers as determined by the President of the Court. The Court of First Instance is prohibited by the Treaty from hearing and determining questions referred for a preliminary ruling under Article 177(Article 168a(1)).

When first set up, the Court of First Instance was given jurisdiction only in Community staff cases and in actions brought against the Commission by undertakings under the Coal and Steel Treaty and by private parties or undertakings as regards the Commission's implementation of the Community rules relating to fair competition. Since late 1993 [4] the Court of First Instance has been given jurisdiction in all annulment actions, actions in respect of failure to act, damages actions, and contractual disputes which have been brought directly to the Court at the instance of private parties. The common factor to the responsibilities transferred to the Court of First Instance is that they are matters which were likely to involve a court in direct investigation of often complex factual situations and which are consequently particularly time-consuming. The Court of First Instance is developing into a specialist legal tribunal entrusted with the task of controlling or checking the acts

3   Decision 88/591, OJ 1988 L319/1 and OJ 1989 L241/4.
4   Decision 93/350, OJ 1993 L144/21.

of administrative authorities of the European Community in so far as their decisions affect individual interests.

The role of the judicial institutions of the Community

The purpose of the judicial institutions of the European Community has been to ensure that the rule of law is respected in the administration and development of the Community.

When producing such legally binding opinions and judgments, the judges of each court sit and speak not individually, but as a college. No dissenting judgments are permitted. In both courts, judgments are drafted by one judge, the *Juge-rapporteur* who is also responsible for preparing a report summarising the facts and the written arguments submitted by the parties and interveners in the case. This draft judgment is discussed, amended and voted on by the judges sitting in the particular case. The majority view becomes the sole judgment of the particular court and is signed by all judges involved in the case. The consequent tendency for judgments to reflect a consensus of the views of all of the judges involved means that judgments are not always internally coherent or consistent with one another. Academic writing commenting on the judgments of the Court of Justice and of the Court of First Instance assumes a particular importance in establishing the development of clear lines of Community legal doctrine.

The judgments of the Court of Justice are generally quite short compared to the judgments produced by courts in the United Kingdom. They have a tendency to repeat formulae or dicta established in previous case law of that Court, while altering the meaning and effect of these phrases by applying them to different factual situations.

The judgments of the Court of Justice and, occasionally also of the Court of First Instance, are preceded by a reasoned opinion delivered in open court by the Advocate-General assigned to the case. In his opinion the Advocate-General may review the relevant case law and academic legal literature, illustrate how a particular doctrine of Community law has been and might be developed and sketch the possible consequences of deciding the case one way or the other. An Opinion will recommend that the Court decide the case in a particular way. The Court is not bound to and does not always follow the course proposed by the Advocate-General, who is excluded from the deliberations on the case. Neither does the Court specify in its judgments whether, how and why it differs from the views of the Advocate-General. The Advocate-General's opinions are nevertheless important in elaborating upon the brief, even terse, judgments ultimately delivered by the Court. The Court's judgments may appear less Delphic when read in the light of the Advocate-General's opinion.

The forms of action before the EC Courts

The Treaty of Rome provides for the following forms of action:

1 Proceedings against a Member State for failure to fulfil an obligation under the Treaty.
   This action may be brought against Member States by the Commission (Art 169) or another Member State (Art 170).

2 Proceedings for annulment of Community acts.
   A Member State, the Council and Commission may bring an action before the Court of Justice to review the legality of any acts of central institutions of the European Community the effect of which is to produce legal effects in relation to third parties (Art 173(1)). The European Parliament and the European Central Bank may also bring actions for annulment before the Court of Justice for the purpose of protecting their respective prerogatives (Art 173(3)). A private party has locus to bring such an annulment action in respect of a Community decision or regulation of direct and individual concern to them (Art 173(4)). The standing requirements are, however, construed strictly.

3 Proceedings against the Council, Commission, European Parliament and European Central Bank for failure to act.
   A Member State and the European Community institutions may bring an action before the Court of Justice alleging an infringement of the Treaty by any of the Council, Commission, European Parliament and European Central Bank in respect of their failure to act (Art 175(1). A private party may also complain to the Court of First Instance under this procedure that a European Community institution has, contrary to the Treaty, failed to address that person by any act, other than by way of a recommendation or opinion (Art 175(3)).

4 Action for damages.
   Actions may be raised against the European Community for financial compensation in respect of damage caused by European Community institutions or servants acting in the performance of

their duties (Arts 178 and 215(2). Compensation has rarely been awarded.

5   Disputes relating to employment matters between the European Community and its employees.
    The Court of First Instance has jurisdiction in any dispute relating to employment matters between the European Community and its employees (Art 179).

6   Disputes involving the European Investment Bank and the European Central Bank (Art 180).
    Actions of annulment may be brought against measures adopted by the Board of Governors (Art 180b) or the Board of Directors (Art 180c) of the European Community Banks. Further, the European Central Bank may bring an action against a national central bank in respect of its failure to fulfil its obligations under the Treaty and the Statute of the European System of Central Banks (Art 180d).

7   Contractual disputes with the European Community.
    The Court of Justice has jurisdiction to give judgment in accordance with any arbitration clause contained in a contract concluded by or on behalf of the European Community (Art 181). Actions brought by natural or legal persons would go to the Court of First Instance.

8   Prorogation of jurisdiction by Member States.
    The jurisdiction of the Court of Justice may be prorogated by special agreement between Member States in disputes between them over matters relating to the Treaty (Art 182).

9   References under international agreements.
    Certain treaties concluded by and within the European Community other than the basic foundation treaties provide for the Court of Justice to have jurisdiction in certain disputes as to the proper interpretation of those treaties. Such treaties include the Brussels and Lugano Conventions on Civil Jurisdiction and Judgments, the Rome Convention on Choice of Law in Contracts, and the Agreement on the setting up of the European Economic Area.

10 References from national courts.
    For the practising lawyer in the United Kingdom, the most significant aspect of the jurisdiction of the Courts of the European Community is that conferred under Article 177 of the Treaty.

National courts of the Member States have power to review the proper administrative implementation of Community law within their jurisdiction. They are also required to uphold and protect and directly effective provisions of Community law which confer rights on European Community nationals.

Questions of the proper interpretation of Community law may accordingly arise before national courts. Where it is necessary to decide on such question in order to give judgment in the case before it the national court may refer the matter to the Court of Justice to enable it to give a ruling on the correct understanding of Community law.

Part II

THE SPECIFIC IMPACT OF COMMUNITY LAW ON THE LEGAL ORDER OF THE UNITED KINGDOM

Chapter 8

AGRICULTURE AND FISHERIES LAW

INTRODUCTION

The highest profile of the Community in popular consciousness is, perhaps, in the area of agriculture and fisheries. Article 38(4) of the Treaty provides that a common policy on agricultural products (which includes fisheries and stock-farming as well as products of the soil) shall be established among the Member States.

The common agricultural policy is the Community's first area of true sovereignty. The Community has taken over a large part of the Member States spending on agriculture. Once the common policy has been decided the Member States play a strictly ancillary role, implementing the decisions reached at the discretion of the Community administration. The legality of a Community provision in the sphere of agriculture can be challenged only if it can be shown that the measure is manifestly inappropriate having regard to its objective.[1]

The Community's common agricultural policy is based on three principles:

- the establishment of a single market for the free movement of agricultural goods within the Community;
- a preference for Community produce whereby priority is given to the sale of Community produce by regulating the flow of imports into and financially supporting exports from the Community, and by subsidising Community agricultural production to make it competitive with goods imported into the Community;

1 Case C-331/88 *R v Minister of Agriculture, Fisheries and Food, ex p Federation Européene de la Santé Animale (FEDESA)* [1990] ECR 4023, [1991] 1 CMLR 507 at para 13.

- financial solidarity whereby all the Member States contribute to a central fund, the European Agricultural Guidance and Guarantee Fund, from which expenditure in pursuit of the aims of this common agricultural policy is made irrespective of the product or the Member State in which it is produced.

The main activity under the common agricultural policy to date has been the implementation of the policy on prices and markets which sought to ensure that market prices for agricultural produce in the Community did not fall below certain minimum levels. These levels were in general greater than world market prices for the products.

Under this price support policy, when supplies were abundant, specialist Community intervention agencies concerned with products ranging from butter and skimmed milk powder to pork, beef and table wine bought in 'surplus' production with a view to returning it to the Community market-place in leaner times or otherwise disposing of it, for example by exports to non-Community countries. With other products, for example sunflower, cotton and rape seed, subsidies were paid to the processing industries to use Community produce. With yet other products, such as flax, hemp and silkworms, flat rate grants on the quantity produced were paid directly to the primary producers.

The consequences of these market intervention mechanisms become notorious. Farmers were given an incentive to greater and more intensive production regardless of the requirements of the marketplace. As a result, in the 1980s wheat production in the Community exceeded consumption by 30 per cent, butter by 34 per cent, skimmed milk powder by 28 per cent, beef by 10 per cent. Some producers regarded the Community intervention agencies as their only customers, and rather than seek new markets, they produced agricultural produce simply with a view to selling it to the intervention agencies at artificially high guaranteed prices. Agricultural over-production has, consequently, been stockpiled indefinitely in warehouses in the form of butter mountains and wine lakes. Spending on this kind of market intervention from the European Agricultural Guidance and Guarantee Fund increased six-fold between 1975 and 1988. Over two-thirds of the total Community budget was spent in agricultural market support. By 1988 the budget of the Agricultural Guidance and Guarantee fund at ECU 27.5 billion was greater than the total national budgets of Ireland or Greece. More than half of this budget was spent on the storage or disposal of surpluses by subsidising exports. The common agricultural policy became an international as well as domestic scandal.

The Commission proposed certain reforms of the common agricultural policy in early 1991 whereby the price support mechanisms would be used only to maintain prices at current world market levels, but the resulting loss of income to smaller farmers would be compensated for by direct payments from the Community. Larger more efficient farmers would be expected to rely to a far greater extent on the open market. These reforms were adopted in part by the Council in 1992. [2] The basic principles of the unity of the market, Community preference and financial solidarity were not, however, changed in these reforms.

Agriculture remains the Community's only truly integrated sector of economic production. Such integration has been achieved by a mass of Community regulations which are directly applicable within the Member States. The institutions and methods of the common agricultural policy no longer serve as examples of how to integrate European industry in post-1992 Europe. The discovery of the principle of subsidiarity means that the favoured methods of integration have been the mutual recognition of national standards and the adoption of Directives, which leave precise methods of implementation to Member States, rather than Community regulations which leave no discretion or room for manoeuvre to the Member States. The centralist interventionist regulatory bias of the common agricultural policy is old-fashioned. This notwithstanding, the achievement of a single internal market in agricultural goods is said, by the Commission, still to require 'common prices, common rules on competition, stable exchange rate in the agricultural sector and the approximation of administrative, public-health and veterinary rules and regulations' [3] with uniform rules applied at the Community's external frontiers. These goals require central management.

Aside from the Community provisions on the general policy to be adopted in the matter of agriculture and fisheries there is a host of Community legislation, both regulations and directives dealing with questions of the health, welfare and hygiene of farmed animals, fish and plants. In addition the Community is concerned to ensure common public health standards throughout the Member States relative to animal and fishery products. These standards fall to be enforced within each Member State so that no further checks need be carried out on such products when they are exported within the Community. The details of this legislation are technical sectoral matters which fall outside the scope of the present work.

Despite the volumes of regulations which are produced by the Community under and in terms of the common agricultural policy, there are surprisingly few publications dealing specifically with the Community law aspects of agriculture and fisheries. The number of reported cases in

---

2   See (1992) 6 *EC Bulletin* 73-74 (paras 1.3.140-1.3.146).
3   European Commission *A Common Agricultural Policy for the 1990s*, (5th edn) European Documentation Periodical 5/1989 at p 16.

the area of the operation of the common agricultural policy is also relatively low.

Where the common agricultural policy has actually required individual producers to restrict their activities, instead simply of subsidizing their continuing over-production or paying them not to produce under the set-aside scheme, there has been a greater impact in the courts. Litigation has resulted from the two main areas of restriction: milk quotas and fishery conservation measures. We shall look at both of these areas in turn.

AGRICULTURE

Milk Quotas

Quota systems as a means of reducing over-production have not been regarded favourably by the European Commission, the body with overall administrative control of the common agricultural policy. Although quotas on production are very efficient in reducing production levels to the desired levels at a stroke, they entail high administrative costs, since quotas have to be allocated, monitored and adjusted to suit varying circumstances. They are regarded as too rigid and they restrict the freedom of farmers to choose to over-produce if they so desire. Accordingly quotas on production are regarded as emergency measures.

A situation requiring such emergency measures occurred in the early 1980s in relation to milk production. The Community was self-sufficient in milk production by 1974. Thereafter production continued to increase at an average rate of 2.6 per cent per annum, while consumption increased by an annual rate of only 0.6 per cent. In 1984 a strict quota arrangement was introduced which sought, in one year, to reduce milk production by 5 per cent. A figure was arrived at for the total production of milk in the Community. This figure was then divided among the Member States whose responsibility it was to apportion their state's share of the milk-production quota among their dairy farmers. Any individual dairy which produced and delivered quantities of milk in excess of its quota was required to pay a levy on the excess quantities. Since production within the quota was still greater than consumption, compensation was offered to farmers not to use up their full quota.

The milk quota scheme was a Community initiative implemented and administered by the appropriate authorities of each Member State.[4] Because of the financial value of the quotas to individual milk producers,

---

4   The Community system of milk quotas has now been codified by Council Regulation 3950/92, 1992 OJ L405/1

the detail of the operation of the scheme has been a continuing source of litigation both before national courts and the Court of Justice. [5]

Of perhaps greater interest than details of the disputes over the precise operation of the milk quota scheme have been the points of general principle which have arisen out of these cases. For example in *Wachauf v Federal Republic of Germany* [6] the Court of Justice held that when Member State authorities adopted or implemented Community legislation, they were required to ensure that the fundamental rights of individuals were respected.

In *Wachauf* the German order which gave effect to the Community scheme of milk quotas and compensation provided that quotas were attached to land rather than to individual milk producers. Tenant farmers could only surrender and receive compensation for the milk quotas which applied to the land they farmed with the consent of his landlord. In Wachauf's case the landlord's consent was withdrawn and so he, as tenant, was unable to claim compensation for the fact that he had ceased milk production. Such a result was held by the Court of Justice to contravene fundamental rights of respect for property and the fruits of an individual's labour. Accordingly, the German court was instructed to look again at the primary Community legislation in the light of human rights considerations set out by the Court of Justice. On receiving this reference back from Luxembourg, the German court came to the conclusion that the relevant section of the German order was void as offending against the principle of equal treatment (between tenant and landowner farmers) and awarded Wachauf compensation. [7]

As a result of the European Court's judgement in *Wachauf*, in 1990 an action was brought in the United Kingdom for the judicial review of the UK Dairy Produce Quotas Regulations 1984. The grounds for the review were that the these regulations, which purported to implement the Community milk quota compensation scheme from 1984 to 1986, were inconsistent with Community law in failing to provide 'compensation to a tenant farmer surrendering his milk quota. A compensation scheme had been introduced in the United Kingdom by the Agriculture Act 1986, but only with effect from September 1986. In *R v Ministry of Agriculture,*

---

5   See eg Case C-314/89 *Rauh v Hauptzollamt Nuernberg-Fuerth* [1991] ECR I-1647 establishing the heritability of milk quotas; Case C-86/90 *O'Brien v Ireland* [1992] ECR I-6251 and Case C-79/91 *Knuefer v Buchmann* [1992] ECR I-6895 on the proper assessment of milk quotas; *R v Ministry of Agriculture, Fisheries and Food, ex p Cox* [1993] 2 CMLR 917, QBD on the requirements for effectual transfer of milk quotas.
6   Case 5/88 *Wachauf v Federal Republic of Germany* [1989] ECR 2609.
7   The German Court decision is reported, in English, as Case 1/2-E 62/85 *Re the Kuechenhof Farm* [1990] 2 CMLR 289.

Fisheries and Food, ex p Bostock [8] the Divisional Court held that, notwithstanding the passage of time since he surrendered his milk quota, compensation might be awarded to Mr Bostock in the light of the interpretation of the Community regulations by the Court of Justice in *Wachauf*. This case, which also has important implications for the application of national time limits to Community rights, was made the subject of an Article 177 reference to the Court of Justice. In his opinion, however, Advocate-General Gulmann effectively suggested that *Wachauf* was wrongly decided and that the Court should find that: [9]

'[N]o duty can be inferred either from the relevant Community regulations or from the fundamental rights applying in the Community legal order for Member States to protect the economic interests of tenants when their tenancies come to an end as regards the milk quotas allocated to them. Such protection must be obtained within the individual Member States' legal systems in accordance with the constitutional rules applying in those States.'

The issue of how far the Court of Justice might scrutinise national legislation for its compatibility with fundamental rights considerations is obviously of great political sensitivity. The judgment of the court in this regard is awaited with interest.

In *Milk Marketing Board of England and Wales v Cricket St Thomas Estate* [10] it was alleged that the requirement of the English Milk Marketing Board that milk producers who were permitted by the Board to market their pasteurized milk direct to the public should nevertheless make compensatory payments to the Board in respect of the business lost to them was contrary to Community law.

This submission was rejected by the Court of Justice who held that such charges, together with further charges as sanction for the independent producer's refusal to supply the Board with the relevant information, were compatible with Community law provided that they were proportionate. On receiving this reply to their reference, the English High Court Queen's Bench Division found the charges to be indeed proportionate. [11]

---

8   *R v Ministry of Agriculture, Fisheries and Food, ex p Bostock*, [1991] 1 CMLR 681, QBD.
9   Case C-2/92 *R v Ministry of Agriculture, Fisheries and Food, ex p Bostock*, notified in OJ 1992 C33/9. See the Advocate-General's opinion of 20 April 1993 at para 36. The judgment of the Court was awaited at the time of writing.
10 Case C-372/88 *Milk Marketing Board v Cricket St Thomas Estate* [1990] ECR I-1345, [1990] 2 CMLR 800.
11 *Milk Marketing Board v Cricket St Thomas Estate* [1991] 3 CMLR 123.

The milk quota cases make it clear that the interpretation and application by national courts of Community legislation or national legislation which implements it, involves more than consideration of the text of the specific Community regulation before it. The interpretation and application of Community law, even in such technical areas as a claim to a milk quota on grounds of exceptional hardship, [12] has to be done in the light of broader considerations, in particular the general principles of Community law, such as the principle of proportionality and respect for human rights.

In other cases, Ministerial decisions which have had the effect of restricting the free movement of agricultural produce throughout the Community contrary to Community law have been the cause of court action, either to reverse such decisions, [13] or for compensation for loss resulting from such decisions. [14] These cases treat agricultural produce as goods, the free movement of which is one of the basic principles of Community law. They do not raise issues peculiar to the common agricultural policy.

FISHERIES

Fishing quotas

The question of the opening up of territorial and other traditional national fishing grounds to the nationals of other Member States is one of great sensitivity in the United Kingdom. In *R v Kirk* [15] a Danish sea captain was found to be fishing in UK waters contrary to measures which the United Kingdom government had passed unilaterally in the face of a deadlock at Community level. The UK measures provided for criminal sanctions in the event of their breach. Captain Kirk was prosecuted under these provisions. The question of the legitimacy of these national provisions under Community law was raised. Community regulations had been passed which sought to give *ex post facto* legitimacy and validity to the UK provisions, which would otherwise have been contrary to the

---

12 See Case C-84/90 *R v Ministry of Agriculture, Fisheries and Food, ex p Dent* [1992] ECR I-2009, [1992] 2 CMLR 597 and *R v Dairy Produce Quota Tribunal for England, ex p Dent*, Unreported, 8 July 1991QBD (Crown Office List), CO/0260/89.

13 Eg *R v Minister of Agriculture, Fisheries and Food, ex p Bell Lines Ltd* [1984] 2 CMLR 502, a judicial review of a Ministerial decision to restrict the import of milk into the United Kingdom to certain specified ports, none of them on the Irish sea.

14 *Bourgoin SA v Ministry of Agriculture Fisheries and Food* [1986] QB 716 and *An Bord Bainne v Milk Marketing Board* [1988] 1 CMLR 605.

15 Case 63/83 *R v Kirk* [1984] ECR 2689, [1984] 3 CMLR 522.

Community's common fisheries policy of open access to fishing waters. The Court of Justice, however, held that these Community regulations were in effect penal provisions which purported to have retroactive effect. They were therefore held to be invalid on human rights grounds. They fell, and with them the national measures which they sought to validate.

The Community's 'Blue Europe' common fisheries policy agreed upon in 1983 was made against a background of the perceived need to conserve fish stocks within the Community waters of the Atlantic Ocean and adjacent seas.[16] With this in mind, total allowable catches were agreed annually for over 100 species of fish. These totals were then apportioned in fixed percentage quotas among the various Member States. The quotas for each Member State were reached after taking into account, among other matters, the size, location, needs and traditional fishing grounds of each Member State's fishing fleet.

In addition to fixing quotas, the common fisheries policy involved the introduction of a new monitoring and inspection regime to enforce quotas and various technical conservation measures which include fixing minimum mesh sizes of nets, specifying the minimum size of landed fish and restricting fishing activities in certain zones.

In 1986 Spain and Portugal joined the Community. The accession of these countries had the result of doubling the number of fishermen and the *per capita* fish consumption in the Community and increased the tonnage of the Community fishing fleet by around 50 per cent.

Quotas were fixed for the large fishing fleets of these new Member States. It soon became apparent, however, that the system of separate quotas for national fishing fleets could be circumvented by vessels owned in and operated from one Member State, for example Spain, re-registering in another Member State, for example the United Kingdom, and so becoming entitled to a share in the UK quota. This practice of 'quota-hopping' was firmly established by 1988 when the UK Parliament passed the Merchant Shipping Act 1988 in order, it was claimed, to implement and enforce the quota system established by the common fisheries policy. [17]

---

16   See Commission of the European Communities *The Common Fisheries Policy* European File CC-AD-91-003-EN-C. See also 'Commission Communication on a Community Framework for Access to Fishing Quotas' OJ 1989 C224/3.

17   See Case C-279/89 *Commission v UK: re fishing licences* ECR I-5785, [1993] 1 CMLR 563 and Case C-280/89 *Commission v Ireland: re British Fishing Boats* [1992] ECR I-6185, [1993] 1 CMLR 273 for earlier attempts by the British and Irish governments, respectively, to deal with the problem of Spanish fisherman sailing under the British flag. Both of these attempts were declared by the Court of Justice to be contrary to Community rules against national discrimination.

The Act, as passed, contained provisions as to British nationality, domicile and residence which had to be satisfied by the owners and operators of vessels before these could be registered in the new Register of British Shipping. Registration was the pre-requisite to obtaining a licence to fish under the quota permitted the United Kingdom by the Community's common fisheries policy. The Act sought to ensure that British registered vessels were operated, managed and controlled from within the United Kingdom. The Act came into force on 1 December 1988 and it was provided by the Merchant Shipping (Registration of Fishing Vessels) Regulations 1988 that the validity of registrations under the previously applicable Merchant Shipping Act 1894 would expire on 31 March 1989.

In *R v Secretary of State for Transport, ex p Factortame* an application was made for the judicial review of the decision of the Secretary of State for Transport not to re-register certain fishing vessels under the new Act. On 10 March 1989 the court at first instance, holding that the matter raised substantive questions of Community law, ordered that a reference be made to the European Court of Justice under Article 177 for a preliminary ruling on these questions of Community law.[18] This was registered with the Court of Justice as Case C-221/89.[19] A second reference to the Court of Justice was made in the case by the House of Lords in July 1989 on the question of the availability under Community law of *interim* relief against the Crown.[20] This was registered as Case C-213/89.[1] On 4 August 1989 the Commission brought an action against the UK Government under Article 169 in respect, inter alia, of the same provisions of the Merchant Shipping Act 1988 as were the subject of the *Factortame* complaint. This case was registered as Case C-246/89.[2] On 10 October 1989 the President of the Court of Justice granted an interim order against the United Kingdom Government in the Article 169 case brought by the Commission.[3] This interim order required the United Kingdom to suspend the application of the nationality requirements contained in s14 of the Merchant Shipping Act 1988.[4]

18 *R v Sec. of State for Transport, ex p Factortame* [1989] 2 CMLR 353, QBD.
19 Case C-221/89 *R v Secretary of State for Transport, ex p Factortame* [1991] ECR I-3905, [1991] 3 CMLR 589.
20 *R v Secretary of State for Transport, ex p Factortame (No 1)* [1990] 2 AC 85.
1 Case C-213/89 *R v Secretary of State for Transport, ex p Factortame* [1990] ECR I-2433, [1990] 3 CMLR 1.
2 Case C-246/89 *Commission v United Kingdom* [1991] ECR I-4585, [1991] 3 CMLR 706.
3 Case C-246/89R *Commission v United Kingdom* [1989] ECR I-3125.
4 As a result of the President's ruling, an Order in Council, the Merchant Shipping Act 1988 (Amendment) Order 1989 (SI 1989/2006) was made which amended Section 14 of the 1988 Act with effect from 2 November 1989 so that the requirements were no

While the various *Factortame* cases were proceeding, the Court of Justice held in *Agegate* [5] and *Jaderow* [6] that Member States were entitled to seek to ensure that vessels fishing against their quota had a genuine economic link with their state, but that this did not justify requirements as to the residence and domicile of a specified percentage of the crew. [7] In its reply to the reference from the Divisional Court judgment on the substantive issues in *Factortame*, [8] the Court of Justice held that the nationality, residence and domicile provisions of s 14 of the 1988 Act, even as amended following the Court's interim order, were contrary to Community law. The Court of Justice held that it was not contrary to Community Law for a Member State to stipulate as a condition for the registration of a fishing vessel in its national register that the vessel in question must be managed and its operations directed and controlled from a port within that Member State since such a requirement was of the essence of establishment. [9] However such a fishing vessel could not lawfully be required to begin its journeys at its port of control or to call there frequently or to land a certain proportion of its catches there or at some other ports within the Member State. The Court confirmed this general position in its judgments in two Article 169 actions [10] brought by the Commission against the United Kingdom and Ireland respectively. As a consequence of the Court of Justice's ruling in *Factortame*, the fishermen affected by the discriminatory provisions of the Merchant Shipping Act 1988 raised an action for damages against the UK Government for its failure to respect Community law in the English High Court which immediately referred the matter to the Court of Justice. [11]

It would appear from these judgments that the Community's common fisheries policy in relation to national fish quotas has been rendered unworkable. The Court of Justice has refused to recognise the legitimacy of the efforts of Member State's seeking to protect the economic interest

longer that a fishing vessel be 'British-owned' but 'Community owned'. However, the Act as amended still retained requirements for qualified EC nationals to be resident and domiciled in the United Kingdom before they could partake in its fishing quotas.
5   Case 3/87 *R v Minister of Agriculture, Fisheries and Food, ex p Agegate Ltd* [1990] ECR 4459, [1990] 1 CMLR 366, [1990] 2 QB 151.
6   Case 216/87 *R v Minister of Agriculture, Fisheries and Food, ex p Jaderow Ltd* [1990] ECR 4509, [1991] 2 CMLR 556, [1990] 2 QB 193.
7   See also Case 223/86 *Pesca Valentia Ltd v Irish Minister for Fisheries and Forestry* [1988] ECR 83, [1988] 1 CMLR 888.
8   Case C-221/89 *R v Sec. of State for Transport, ex p Factortame* [1991] ECR I-3905, [1991] 3 CMLR 589, [1991] 3 All ER 769.
9   See now the Merchant Shipping (Registration, etc) Act 1993.
10   Case 246/89 *Commission v United Kingdom* [1991] ECR I-4585, Case 93/89 *Commission v Ireland* [1991] ECR I-4569.
11   C-48/93 *R v Secretary of State for Transport, ex p Factortame Ltd (No 3)*, notified in OJ 1993 C94/13. The judgment of the Court of Justice was awaited at the time of writing.

of their own traditional fishing industry. The Court refuses to allow Member States effectively to derogate from the general principle of Community law, embodied in Article 6 of the post-Maastricht Treaty of Rome, that there should be no discrimination on grounds of nationality. Doubtless the fear is expressed that if such discrimination was allowed in fishing matters, it might set a precedent for discrimination in other areas and, ultimately lead to the unravelling of the whole supra-nationalist project that is the European Communities. Community law does not, however, prevent 'reverse discrimination' whereby the Member States treats its own nationally registered vessels more strictly than those registered in other Member States. Thus, UK regulations prohibiting British registered vessels from carrying particular types of nets in Scottish waters [12] and regulations requiring British registered vessels to report by radio to their national authorities whenever crossing from one sea area to another have both been upheld by the Court of Justice as not contrary to Community law. [13]

BIBLIOGRAPHY

A Munir *Fisheries after Factortame*(1991) Butterworths.
W Neville and F Mordaunt *A Guide to the Reformed Common Agricultural Policy* (1993) Estates Gazette.
F Snyder *Law of the Common Agricultural Policy* (1985) Sweet & Maxwell.
J Usher *Legal Aspects of Agriculture in the European Community* (1987) Clarendon Press.

---

12 Case 370/88 *Walkingshaw v Marshall* [1990] ECR 4071, [1991] 1 CMLR 419, 1992 SLT 1167.
13 Joined Cases C-251, 252/90 *Procurator Fiscal, Elgin v Wood & Cowie* [1992] ECR I-3467, [1992] 2 CMLR 493.

Chapter 9

BUSINESS LAW

INTRODUCTION

Community company law has its basis in the provisions of the Treaty of Rome which provide for businesses and the self-employed to establish themselves freely throughout the Community. Under Article 58, freedom of establishment extends to companies or firms formed in accordance with the law of a Member State and having their registered office, central administration or principal place of business within the Community. Companies and firms are defined as constituted under civil or commercial law, including co-operative societies, and other legal persons governed by public or private law, save for those which are non-profit making.

Companies do not enjoy the same rights of movement as natural persons and will not do so unless and until other aspects of corporate regulation, such as taxation, can be harmonised throughout the Community.[1] Non-resident companies from other Community states can, nevertheless, claim to be treated on an equal footing with domestic companies in all respects.[2]

Community company law seeks, essentially, to establish a homogeneous legal environment for business operations throughout the Community. Disparities in the regulation of companies in a single market produces market distortions as businesses move to those states whose controls are least stringent. The strategy of the Community has been twofold; firstly, to lay down minimum standards for domestic legal regulation of

---

1   See Case 81/87 *R v HM Treasury and Inland Revenue Comrs, ex p Daily Mail and General Trust plc* [1988] ECR 5483.
2   Case C330/91 *R v IRC ex p, Commerzbank* [1993] ECR I-4017; [1993] 4 All ER 37.

companies; secondly, to establish new forms of corporate structure based almost exclusively on Community law.

Community company law now consists of 13 directives, not all of which have been formally adopted as yet, an amending directive and miscellaneous others setting out minimum regulatory standards as well as a number of instruments dealing with corporate structure.

Community company law has a twofold relevance for the British lawyer. Firstly, it has a direct impact upon domestic company law, an impact which may be felt in all factual situations. There is no need for a transnational element, or 'Community dimension' to establish the relevance of Community law; it must be considered in those purely domestic factual situations which are governed by British legislation which has its origins in Community measures.

Issues of interpretation of that domestic company law which implements Community directives or elaborates Community regulations, may and should be resolved by recourse to the wording, and to the objectives, of the Community provision in question. Resort to the Community legislation may be particularly appropriate where it has introduced novel principles into domestic law. Indeed, it is possible that an examination of the Community measure may reveal deficiencies or ambiguities in the British legislation with regard to the facts of the particular case. In this situation, the provisions of the directive may be given effect, through interpretation, or through direct effect, so as to supplement or displace the national provisions.

Secondly, British practitioners engaged in advising companies which have, or intend to have, dealings in other Member States, should consider the administrative, legal and other advantages of utilising one of the European corporate structures set out in Community legislation.

This chapter outlines the main provisions of the Community company law programme along with details of their implementation in British law. Certain Community proposals which have not yet come to fruition but are likely to do so in the near future will also be mentioned.

DISCLOSURE AND TRANSPARENCY

Disclosure, obligations and nullity

The First Company Law Directive co-ordinates national provisions in three areas.[3] Firstly, Member States must ensure the disclosure of basic documents, such as company statutes, and other information, including

---

3   Directive 68/151 OJ Special Edition, 1968(1), pp 41-45; Companies Act 1985.

transfers of the seat of the company and its winding up and liquidation, by both public and private companies. Secondly, the directive deals with the validity of obligations entered into by companies and, in particular, provides for the force of obligations entered into by the company as regards third parties.[4] Thirdly, the directive governs the circumstances determining, and the legal effect of, a company being declared a 'nullity'. In the United Kingdom, the company's certificate of incorporation is treated as conclusive proof of its formation,[5] and, as such, the concept of nullity is unknown to UK law.

The recent Eleventh Directive governs disclosure requirements of branches of certain types of company.[6] Branches of companies from other states, either within or outside the Community, will henceforth not have to publish separate branch accounts although they will have to publish the annual report and annual accounts of the parent company as required by the state where that company is registered. The directive does not contain a specific definition of a branch but the present UK test is in accordance with the approach adopted in the past by the Court of Justice.[7]

Incorporation and capital of limited liability companies

The Second Directive lays down requirements for the formation of public companies and the management of their capital.[8] It regulates the form and content of the instrument of incorporation of public companies, and matters relating to the share capital of the company. A public limited company must have a minimum capital level, which is £50,000 in the United Kingdom, valued by an independent expert, and there are rules governing increases in and reduction of this capital. The capacity of public companies to buy their own shares is limited and further legislation prevents such a company from using a subsidiary to acquire its own shares without complying with the restrictions of the Second Directive.[9]

4 See s 35(1) and (2) of the Companies Act 1985 which provide that, as regards a person dealing with the company in good faith, all transactions entered into by the directors of the company are deemed to be within the company's capacity.
5 Companies Act 1985, s 13(7)(a).
6 Directive 89/666, OJ 1989 L395/36; (SIs 1992/3178 and 1992/3179).
7 *South India Shipping Corp Ltd v The Export Import Bank of Korea* [1985] BCLC 163; Case 33/78 *Établissements Somafer v Saar-Ferngas* [1978] ECR 2183.
8 Directive 77/91, OJ 1977 L26/1; Companies Act 1985, in particular, ss 23, 143, 162-66, 736.
9 Directive 92/101, 1992 OJ L347/64.

Accounting requirements

The Fourth Directive on annual accounts demands a minimum level of protection of shareholders and creditors by setting out detailed standards relating to the presentation and contents of annual accounts and annual reports.[10] Small and medium sized businesses are subject to less stringent rules than their larger counterparts, being able, for example, to publish abridged accounts.

The Seventh Company Law Directive provides for co-ordination of legislation regarding the production and publication of consolidated accounts, accounts produced by parent companies, which incorporate the dealings of their subsidiaries.[11] Consolidated accounts must be prepared where either the parent company or its subsidiary is established as a limited company. The approach adopted by the directive to the status of subsidiary looks to *de facto* influence by the parent company as well as to the formal, legal position and has required important adjustments to British law.[12]

The Fourth and Seventh Directives were amended in 1990 easing accounting requirements for small and medium sized enterprises (SMEs) but bringing limited partnerships within the accounting requirements.[13] Banks and other financial institutions are subject to special accounting requirements. Uniform accounting requirements have also been extended to include partnerships and unlimited companies where all the members having unlimited liability are limited companies.[14]

The Eighth Company Law Directive on the qualification of auditors concerns the approval of persons responsible for the execution and verification of accounts, reports and audits.[15] The directive prescribes, *inter alia*, qualifying criteria, and requirements of professional integrity and independence for practising auditors.

Proposals

The major outstanding proposals in this field relate to the institutionalisation of employee participation in the running of companies. The United Kingdom has expressed opposition to the Commission's

10 Directive 78/660, OJ 1978 L222/11; Companies Act 1985, Pt VII.
11 Directive 83/349, OJ 1983 L193/1; Companies Act 1989.
12 See Art 1(1) and 1(2) of the Directive; Companies Act 1989, s 21.
13 Directive 90/604, OJ 1990 L317/57; SI 1992/2452.
14 Directive 90/605, OJ 1990 L317/60; SI 1993/1820
15 Directive 84/253/EEC, OJ 1984 L126/20; Companies Act 1989, in particular, ss 119-24.

plans, but at least one of the proposed directives may yet be enacted by majority vote.

MERGERS AND DIVISIONS

The Third Company Law Directive co-ordinates rules relating to the mergers of public limited liability companies within a single Member State, where the assets and liabilities of the acquired company are transferred *in toto* to the acquiring company.[16] Its aim is to ensure the information and protection of shareholders and creditors of merging companies by, for example, extending the disclosure requirements of the First Directive to merger situations.[17] The Sixth Directive on the splitting up of public limited companies seeks to regulate the opposite situation.[18] It provides for the co-ordination of rules relating to division, by acquisition or by creation of a new company, of public limited liability companies.

A further directive has been adopted dealing with notification requirements where a major holding in a listed company is acquired or disposed of.[19] The company concerned must be informed where the size of a person's holding crosses one of a number of thresholds. The company will then notify the appropriate stock exchange.

The Third and Sixth Directives are limited in scope. They do not cover takeovers by one company of another or cross-border transactions, although the Commission has submitted proposals to extend the ambit of Community law in these respects.

CORPORATE STRUCTURE

European economic interest groupings

This is a new form of corporate structure, based on a Community regulation,[20] intended for use by cross-frontier joint ventures. It resembles in some respects a partnership, and in others an unlimited liability company. It is intended to facilitate the operations of its members,

---

16 Directive 78/855/EEC, OJ 1978 L295/36; SIs 1987/1991 and 1987/2118.
17 Employees of companies involved in such transfers are also protected by directive. See Ch 12.
18 Directive 82/891, OJ 1982 L378/1; SIs 1987/1991 and 1987/2118.
19 Directive 88/627, OJ 1988 L348/2. The United Kingdom already had an exacting notification regime, so specific implementation of the directive has not taken place.
20 Regulation 2137/85, OJ 1985 L199/1; SI 1989/638.

through ancillary activities, but not to make profits or otherwise perform the functions of a company itself.

Its main advantage is that, whilst it must be registered in a Member State, it is regulated primarily by the Community provisions, not by domestic company laws. In particular, disclosure requirements are laid down in the Community regulation, there is no minimum capital criterion and no accounts need be made available. The group is limited in size to 500 employees, and is transparent for tax purposes, the profits and losses of the group remaining those of its members. Members of the grouping are jointly and severally liable for its debts and other liabilities incurred.

The European economic interest groupings (EEIG) may be the most appropriate corporate structure for inter-state research and development projects, distribution arrangements and multi-faceted manufacturing or engineering operations, whereby the grouping would have a co-ordinating role. The European Airbus consortium is a prime example of the EEIG in practice.

The European Company

An important part of the Community company law program has not yet become a reality. The project of establishing a European company (*Societas Europae* or SE), has been under discussion for some years but a number of Member States have reservations about its form and legal status. The United Kingdom has objected to two aspects of the proposed company's rules, that company employees must be allowed to participate in its strategic decision-making and that a clear legal distinction be drawn between between managers and supervisors.

Although primarily a Community construct, the SE will be incorporated in one Member State and certain aspects of its activities, including insolvency, governed by the laws of that state. The SE will be taxed in the state of incorporation, but allowed to set-off losses made by branches elsewhere in the Community.

Single-member private limited companies

The Twelfth Directive on Single Member Private Limited Companies, provides for limited liability for sole traders.[1] In return, the trader must comply with safeguards relating to the disclosure of information and the

---

1   Directive 89/667, OJ 1989 L395/40; SI 1992/1699.

protection of creditors. For example, agreements between the company and its sole member must be authorised by the articles of association of the company and formalised in writing.

Structure of public limited companies

The proposed Fifth Directive seeks to establish a distinction between managers and supervisors in the upper echelons of public companies, to institutionalise worker participation in company decision-making, and to harmonise other rules on company administration such as those governing accounts, audits and shareholders' meetings.

EUROPE-WIDE BUSINESS

In addition to the general programme of company law harmonisation, the Community has introduced measures seeking to promote the freedom to provide services and the freedom of establishment across the Community in a number of specific business sectors.

Financial services

Building on the abolition of any remaining national controls on the free movement of capital within the Community in accordance with Article 67 of the Treaty, Community-wide competition is being encouraged in the field of financial services, specifically banking, securities and insurance. The approach of the Community legislation in these areas is to allow firms to provide financial services throughout the Community on the basis of an authorisation or licence granted them by the Member State in which they are primarily based.[2] The 'home' Member State, rather than the host Member State, will have the primary responsibility for controlling and supervising the lawful operation of the firm's activities by ensuring, in particular, that common minimum standards agreed throughout the Community on investor and depositor protection are duly respected. Insider dealing,[3] and money laundering,[4] are also now the

---

2   See eg the Second Banking Coordination Directive 89/646/EEC, OJ 1989 L386/1; SI 1992/3218.
3   Directive 89/592/EEC, OJ 1989 L334/30; SI 1994/188.
4   Directive 91/308/EEC, OJ 1991 L166/77.

subject of specific Community directives and minimum standards have been laid down in respect of listing particulars for securities, disclosure of major shareholdings and public offer prospectuses.

In the field of insurance, recent Community legislation has aimed at allowing insurance companies which have their head office in a Member State to offer their services to potential policyholders throughout the Community without the need to set up a locally established and authorised branch or agency.

Information technology and telecommunications

A truly European marketplace is also sought in the areas of information technology, telecommunications and television. To this end, the Community has adopted legislation designed to encourage competition in the telecommunications market by requiring the Member States to withdraw all special or exclusive rights for the provision of such services and equipment.[5] Instead, new regulatory bodies, independent of the existing providers of telecommunication services, are to be introduced to set standards and issue licences in this sector.[6] Legislation has also been enacted to ensure that Community citizens have access to television broadcasts from other Member States.[7]

Energy supply

With a view to creating a single European market in energy, Community directives have been adopted to make it easier for utilities to transmit both electricity and natural gas across Europe by way of the existing grid networks within the Member States.[8] The aim, ultimately, is to enable consumers to choose their energy suppliers from among companies based all over Europe. There are already rules requiring energy suppliers to ensure the transparency of electricity and gas prices supplied to industrial end users so that an informed choice of energy supplier can be made.[9] The abolition of state monopolies in electricity and gas supply and the introduction of a new system of non-discriminatory licensing for energy suppliers have been proposed.

5   Directive 88/301/EEC, OJ 1988 L131/73.
6   Directive 90/388/EEC, OJ 1990 L192/10.
7   Directive 89/552/EEC, OJ 1989 L298/23.
8   Directive 90/547/EEC, OJ 1990 L313/30; Directive 91/296/EEC, OJ 1991 L147/37.
9   Directive 90/377/EEC, OJ 1990 L185/16.

Pharmaceuticals

The drugs industry in Europe operates in a market still fragmented primarily on national lines. This results from the fact that the production, marketing and sale of products intended to treat or prevent disease has been subject to strict scrutiny and licensing by each of the Member States. Accordingly, there are different licensing authorities in each Member State, each applying its own independently developed standards of control of pharmaceutical products. However, the Commission has proposed a new European Agency for the Evaluation of Medicinal Products. This agency will, in the first instance, introduce a centralised procedure for the assessment and licensing of new medical products resulting from biotechnology and genetic engineering, as well as for certain veterinary products. In addition, the agency will co-ordinate the mutual recognition by the existing drug licensing agencies of the authorisations of particular products by such agencies in other Member States. In the event of disagreements between Member States on licensing decisions, the agency will also provide a framework for the binding arbitration of the disputes.

Legislation has been adopted for the harmonisation of national procedures for the licensing of homoeopathic products, products derived from human blood, radiopharmaceuticals and immunological products. Further directives have been adopted in relation to the pricing, wholesale distribution, manufacturing, classification, labelling and advertising of medical products intended for human and veterinary use.

Industrial manufacturing

In the manufacturing sector, the Community aims to create a single European market by providing for a degree of harmonisation or at least mutual recognition of basic quality and safety requirements for produced goods.

Technical harmonisation of standards at Community level formerly proceeded by way of centrally produced instruments detailing precise standards on a product by product basis. This 'recipe' approach was abandoned in 1985 in favour of an approach based more on mutual recognition throughout the Community of existing national standards. Harmonisation was to be restricted to setting out essential requirements as to health and safety and environmental and consumer protection. These minimum standards have to be adhered to before the products in question can be traded freely throughout the Community.

Three new bodies were formed to set European technical standards for goods: the European Committee for Standardisation (CEN); the European Committee for Electrotechnical Standardisation (CENELEC); and the European Telecommunications Standards Institute (ETSI). These bodies draw up technical specifications for minimum requirements of health and safety and environmental and consumer protection.

The new European technical specifications are, however, voluntary rather than mandatory standards. Where the voluntary standards are complied with, however, the product must be recognised and accepted by each Member State. The product cannot be excluded by a Member State for failing to conform to national technical standards. Harmonisation and mutual recognition of testing and certification standards is also promoted by ensuring the transparency of testing procedures. In addition, the European Standards bodies are engaged in producing a series of common European standards in the field of quality management systems and on the competence of test laboratories and certification bodies.

BIBLIOGRAPHY

J Dine *EC Company Law* (1991) Chancery, with updates.
F Wooldridge *Company Law in the European Community and the United Kingdom* (1991) Athlone Press.
M Anderson *European Economic Interest Groupings* (1990) Butterworths.
N Paul and R Croly *EC Insurance Law* (1991) Chancery.
L Hancher *EC Electricity Law* (1992) Chancery.
P Bogaert *EC Pharmaceutical Law* (1992) Chancery.

Chapter 10

COMPETITION LAW

INTRODUCTION

The creation of a legal regime to promote free competition within the Community is one of the cornerstone objectives of the Treaty. A vigorous competition law system will advance economic growth and ensure that companies cannot erect the sort of artificial barriers to trade which governments are required to abolish.

Community competition law consists, primarily, of Articles 85 and 86 of the Treaty, both of which are directly effective and hence may be considered to form part of domestic law in each Member State. The former article deals with anti-competitive agreements and concerted practices between two or more undertakings, the latter with so-called abuse of dominant position on the market, which may be seen generally as anti-competitive behaviour by a single undertaking. In addition, a recent regulation establishes a Community regime of merger control, and a number of other instruments elaborate Articles 85 and 86 both procedurally and substantively.

WHEN IS COMMUNITY LAW RELEVANT?

British law, through a wide variety of statutory and common law provisions, regulates competition between undertakings in the domestic environment. The first question to be addressed by any national practitioner confronted with a problem of competition law is whether he is required to consider the application of Community law, in addition to that of domestic provisions.

Community competition law is addressed to 'undertakings', a term which is not defined in the Treaty. The term appears to have an economic meaning, encompassing legal persons but also individuals. Associations of undertakings are also expressly included.

The jurisdictional threshold set by both Articles 85 and 86 is that the behaviour in question affects trade between Member States. The effect on inter-state trade may be direct or indirect, actual or potential,[1] and, importantly, it can be found where the behaviour takes place wholly within a single state. This will be the case where, for example, a transaction has the effect of hindering imports into the domestic market from elsewhere in the Community. The fact that an agreement is concluded between British companies and relates solely to the British market does not, then, preclude the application of Community competition law.

It is not only Community undertakings which must have regard to the competition provisions. Undertakings which are situated outside the Community but which 'implement' anti-competitive behaviour within the Community, by means of agents, subsidiaries, or otherwise, may be penalised.[2]

A *de minimis* rule operates to exclude from the ambit of Community law those arrangements producing effects on trade between Member States which are not appreciable.[3] The Commission's Notice on Agreements of Minor Importance clarifies this rule in the context of Article 85: an agreement will not normally fall within Article 85 where the goods or services which it concerns do not represent more than five per cent of the total market in the area of the agreement, and the undertakings involved have an aggregate turnover of less than ECU 200 million.[4] The Notice is not, however, binding on the courts and even if an arrangement falls within its ambit a court could still find on the facts that it has an appreciable effect on the competitive structure of the market-place.

The triggering of Articles 85 or 86 does not automatically exclude the operation of national competition law provisions and the possibility remains that the two regimes may conflict with one another. National rules may not displace, or prejudice the effectiveness of Community law,[5] and behaviour which is prohibited by the latter cannot be sanctioned by national authorities. The position is more complicated where domestic rules are more stringent, and would prohibit an agreement which is inoffensive under Community law. Where behaviour simply does not fall

1   Case 56/65 *Société Technique Minière v Maschinenbau Ulm* [1966] ECR 235.
2   Cases 89, 104, 114, 116-17, 125-29/85 *Re Wood Pulp Cartel: Ahlström v Commission (Jurisdiction)* [1988] ECR 5193.
3   Case 5/69 *Völk v Établissements Vervaecke* [1969] ECR 295.
4   OJ 1986 C231/2.
5   Case 14/68 *Walt Wilhelm v Bundeskartellamt* [1969] ECR 1.

under the restrictions of Articles 85 and 86, national law may be applied, but an agreement which has been exempted from the operation of Article 85(1) because of its pro-competitive nature would, on principle, appear to be immune from national sanction.[6] In Britain, the Director-General of Fair Trading is entitled to decline to act against agreements which have been exempted from the operation of Article 85(1).[7] The issue of conflicts may, however, become academic if, as has been proposed, British competition law is reformulated in the terms of the EEC Treaty.[8]

The borderline between Community and national law is somewhat different in respect of merger control. The Mergers Control Regulation lays down financial thresholds above which the approval of the merger in question is to be a Community prerogative. The combined worldwide turnover of the undertakings concerned must be at least ECU 5 billion, and the aggregate turnover in the Community of at least two of the undertakings must exceed ECU 250 million (Art 1). There are exceptions, however: national authorities may act, regardless of the thresholds, to protect their 'legitimate interests' (Art 21(3)), and the Commission may refer a matter to domestic agencies where a Member State feels that a 'distinct' market within its territory is particularly affected by a proposed concentration (Art 9(3)).

It should be noted, however, that Articles 85 and 86, which have some application to merger control, continue to operate alongside the Merger Regulation. Community law may thus have a relevance even to those proposed mergers which fall short of the turnover thresholds of the regulation.

ARTICLE 85

Article 85(1) prohibits 'all agreements between undertakings, decisions by associations of undertakings and concerted practices, which may affect competition between Member States and which have as their object or effect the prevention, restriction or distortion of competition within the common market'. Certain specific examples of prohibited behaviour, including price fixing, limitation or control of production and market sharing are set out.

---

6 See R Whish *Competition Law* (3rd edn, 1993) Butterworths, pp 39-43.
7 Restrictive Trade Practices Act 1976, s 21(1).
8 *Review of Restrictive Trade Practices Policy* Cm 331 *Opening Markets: New Policy on Restrictive Trade Practices* Cm 727.

Agreements and concerted practices

The provisions of Article 85(1) are intended to act against even the most informal forms of anti-competitive business relationship. The notion of an agreement is broadly interpreted, to include oral contracts and 'gentlemen's agreements'. Examples of agreements which commonly fall to be examined under Article 85 include cartel agreements, specialisation and research and development agreements, joint ventures, exclusive distribution and purchasing agreements, selective distribution and franchising arrangements, price maintenance systems and intellectual property licensing agreements.

More informal arrangements will fall into the ambit of the prohibition on concerted practices, defined as: 'a form of co-operation between undertakings which, without having reached the stage where an agreement properly so called has been concluded, knowingly substitutes practical co-operation between them for the risks of competition.' Each economic operator must determine independently the market policy it intends to adopt.[9]

Clearly, it may be difficult to prove the existence of a concerted practice and the enforcement authorities must be careful to avoid penalising parallel conduct by undertakings which has been provoked, independently, by market conditions and has not resulted from any understanding or arrangement between them.[10] This may particularly be the case in so-called oligopolistic markets, markets which are controlled by a small number of dominant undertakings. The Court of Justice has ruled, for example, that the Commission erred in fining a group of wood pulp producers on the basis of their parallel conduct. The fact that they all announced identical price increases at virtually the same time did not mean that they had concerted with each other. The Community market in wood pulp was said to be transparent and oligopolistic to a high degree and each producer would have known what the others were intending without having to concert with them.[11]

---

9   Case 48/69 *ICI v Commission (Dyestuffs)* [1972] ECR 619, 655; Cases C89, C104, C114, C116-17, C125-29/85 *Re Wood Pulp Cartel: Ahlström v Commission (Merits)* [1993] ECR I-1307; [1993] 4 CMLR 407.
10 See also Case 40/73 *Suiker Unie v Commission* [1975] ECR 1663.
11 Cases C89, C104, C114, C116-17, C125-29/85 *Re Wood Pulp Cartel: Ahlström v Commission (Merits)* [1993] ECR I-1307; [1993] 4 CMLR 407.

Undertakings

The requirement that agreements must be 'between undertakings' is broadly interpreted in most respects. All natural and legal persons involved in some form of economic activity, including individuals such as barristers and inventors, although not employees, are encompassed. However, parent companies and their subsidiaries are generally regarded as a single economic unit and not as separate undertakings.

Restriction of competition

The assessment of whether an agreement, decision or practice has the object or effect of preventing, restricting or distorting competition may be complex. The focus, in the first instance, upon the object of an agreement allows the Commission to take pre-emptive action against anti-competitive behaviour. It also alleviates to some extent the Commission's evidential burden since if an anti-competitive object can be shown, there is no need to analyse the actual effect of the behaviour on the market, and vice versa.

The assessment of anti-competitive effect involves a consideration of a wide range of economic and legal factors. These factors include the nature of the product market, the position of the undertakings concerned in that market, the severity of the restrictions contained within the agreement and whether the agreement forms part of a network of similar agreements.[12] Both horizontal agreements, between competitor undertakings at the same level of the distribution chain, and vertical agreements, such as between manufacturers and dealers, are covered.[13]

Rather than condemning certain terms as automatically and unacceptably restrictive of competition, the Commission has increasingly employed the 'rule of reason' which requires an individualised examination of the objectives of the agreement in question and the necessity of the restrictive terms to these objectives. The Commission will thereby sanction restrictive terms which are essential to the substance of an agreement whose overall aims are pro-competitive or competition-neutral.

12 Case 56/65 *Société Technique Minière v Maschinenbau Ulm* [1966] ECR 235.
13 Cases 56-58/64 *Consten and Grundig v Commission* [1966] ECR 299.

Negative clearance

Undertakings concerned about the possible implications of the Article 85 regime for their proposed behaviour may apply to the Commission for negative clearance, a decision that Article 85(1) is inapplicable. Where clearance is to be granted, the Commission will generally respond with a semi-formal administrative letter, a 'comfort letter'. In addition, the Commission has issued notices setting out its policy on the applicability of Article 85. The most important of these is the Notice on Agreements of Minor Importance, mentioned above. Other notices deal with such matters as joint market research and common certifications of quality, and sub-contracting agreements.

Exemption

The stringent prohibitions of Article 85(1) are mitigated in two ways. Firstly, although all agreements contrary to Article 85(1) are automatically void under Article 85(2), the Court of Justice has held that only individual offending clauses, and not the agreements in their entirety, will be void.[14] United Kingdom courts will apply the 'blue pencil' test: if the severance of the offending clauses would change the character of the agreement, then the whole agreement will fall.[15]

Secondly, the Commission can exempt agreements from the operation of Article 85(1) where, broadly speaking, their beneficial effects outweigh the restrictions which they impose.[16] Exemption may be gained in two ways. Undertakings concerned may notify their agreement to the Commission and apply for exemption, according to Regulation 27/62.[17] In the United Kingdom, the Office of Fair Trading must be notified at the same time, and informed of any exemption or negative clearance granted by the Commission. Decisions of the Commission in this respect are subject to challenge under Article 173(2), although in most cases, as with

---

14 Ibid.
15 *Chemidus Wavin v TERI* [1978] 3 CMLR 514.
16 Article 85(3) provides that Article 85(1) may be declared inapplicable in respect of agreements, decisions and concerted practices which [contribute] to improving the production or distribution of goods or to promoting technical or economic progress, while allowing consumers a fair share of the resulting benefit and which [do] not:
   (a) impose on the undertakings concerned restrictions which are not indispensable to the attainment of these objectives;
   (b) afford such undertakings the possibility of eliminating competition in respect of a substantial part of the products in question.'
17 *OJ Special Edition* 1959-62, p 132. For a detailed account, see C Kerse *Antitrust Procedure* (2nd edn, 1988) European Law Centre.

negative clearance, the Commission sends out administrative letters, which cannot be legally challenged, rather than taking a formal decision.

Alternatively, agreements may be drafted so as to comply with the terms of a relevant 'block exemption' regulation, in which case they need not be notified and are valid and enforceable in their entirety. These regulations provide an element of legal certainty for businesses and, at the same time, serve to reduce the workload of the Commission. Existing block exemption regulations deal with exclusive distribution agreements, exclusive purchasing agreements, patent licences, motor vehicle distribution and servicing agreements, research and development agreements, specialisation agreements, know-how licences, franchise agreements, Liner Conferences, and certain types of agreement in the air transport, and insurance sectors.

The regulations have a similar configuration, each listing certain restrictive terms which are permitted and other provisions which will prevent exemption. Certain block exemptions, including the patent licence and specialisation agreement regulations, also set out 'grey' terms which must examined more carefully. These terms are to be notified to the Commission and will considered to be permitted if the Commission has not opposed them within six months.

It should be noted, however, that agreements which are block exempt may still fall foul of the Article 86 prohibition on abuse of a dominant position in the market.[18]

ARTICLE 86

Article 86 prohibits '[a]ny abuse by one or more undertakings of a dominant position within the common market or a substantial part of it ... in so far as it may affect trade between Member States.' It is aimed essentially at anti-competitive behaviour by a single undertaking although the Court has upheld the application of Article 86 to oligopolies, that is, where the dominant position is shared amongst two or more companies.[19]

Dominant position

The Court has defined a dominant position as 'a position of economic strength enjoyed by an undertaking which enables it to prevent effective

---

18 Case T51/89 *Tetra Pak v Commission* [1990] ECR II-309.
19 Cases T68/69, and T77-78/89 *SIV v Commission (Italian Flat Glass)* [1991] ECR II-1403.

competition being maintained on the relevant market by giving it the power to behave to an appreciable extent independently of its competitors, customers, and ultimately of its consumers.'[20]

Central to the concept of dominance is the definition of the relevant market, which consists of the product market and the geographic market. Two aspects of the product market must be examined. Firstly, the extent to which the allegedly dominant firm's products can be replaced by other, substitute products,[1] and secondly, the extent to which other firms can provide substitute products.[2] The geographic market, which, under Article 86, must consist of at least a substantial part of the Common Market, is fairly easily defined by reference to the selling activities of the undertaking concerned.

Clearly, the narrower the market, the more dominant an undertaking will seem to be and accordingly, the Commission, in penalising dominant undertakings, has generally adopted a restrictive approach to market definition. The actual power of the undertaking within the relevant market will then be determined, not according to a simple market share threshold, as in the United Kingdom, but through examining a variety of factors including the undertaking's market share but incorporating also considerations such as its financial and technological resources and the barriers to entry into the market by other firms.

Abuse

The concept of abuse incorporates both exploitative abuses, where an undertaking seeks to impose oppressive trading conditions on others, and anti-competitive abuses, where damage is not inflicted directly upon individual undertakings, to the detriment of consumers, but more generally, upon the competitive structure of the market as a whole.[3]

Article 86 itself provides a non-exhaustive list of examples of abuses which seem to fall into the former category. These include the imposition of unfair purchase or selling prices or other unfair trading conditions, the tying to agreements of supplementary, unrelated obligations and the application of dissimilar conditions to equivalent transactions thereby placing certain trading partners at a competitive disadvantage. Examples of anti-competitive abuse include predatory pricing, import and export bans and, in certain situations, mergers and takeovers.[4]

20 Case 27/76 *United Brands v Commission* [1978] ECR 207.
1   Ibid.
2   Case 6/72R *Europemballage and Continental Can v Commission* [1972] ECR 157.
3   See, eg, Case 85/76 *Hoffman La Roche v Commission* [1979] ECR 461.
4   Case 6/72R *Europemballage and Continental Can v Commission* [1972] ECR 157.

Undertakings may apply to the Commission for negative clearance in respect of proposed conduct but there is no provision for exemption under Article 86. Instead, the Commission and the Court have exonerated the potentially beneficial behaviour of dominant undertakings by means of the concept of 'objective justification'.

Finally, it should be noted that Article 86 has considerable benefits for British firms in comparison with the equivalent provisions of the Fair Trading Act 1973 and the Competition Act 1980. The latter are discretionary and confer no rights on individuals whereas Article 86 gives rise to both rights and obligations for individuals, and is supported by civil remedies (in national courts) and by the penal sanctions of the Commission.

MERGER CONTROL

The turnover thresholds of the Mergers Regulation dictate that only the largest of proposed mergers, approximately 50 to 60 per year across the Community, will come under Commission, and Community jurisdiction.[4a] For the vast majority of British practitioners, therefore, the substantive provisions of the Mergers Regulation are of little relevance and accordingly, only a brief summary shall be provided.

Mergers which are to be validated by the Commission according to the turnover and other requirements must be notified to the Commission within a week of the decision to merge. The Commission will decide within a month whether to formally investigate the merger, and, if so, has a period of four months after that to come to a final decision. The Commission is required to hear the parties affected at every stage of the investigation and the regulation also provides for interested third parties, notably employees' representatives, to make their views known.

Concentrations which would create or strengthen a dominant position, so significantly impeding effective competition, will be prohibited. In appraising the proposed merger, the Commission will have regard only to competition law, potentially at the expense of industrial and regional policy considerations.[5]

The Mergers Regulation will also apply to 'a joint venture performing on a lasting basis all the functions of an autonomous economic entity, which does not give rise to co-ordination of the competitive behaviour of the parties amongst themselves or between them and the joint venture'.[6]

4a   Reg 4064/89/EEC, OJ 1989 L395/1; OJ 1990 L257/14.
5   See, eg, Decision IV/M/053 *Aerospatiale Alenia/De Havilland* OJ 1991 L334/42; [1992] 4 CMLR M2.
6   Art 3(2). See the Commission's interpretative notice: OJ 1990 C203/10.

Certain difficulties have arisen, however, in the practical application of this provision.[7]

Smaller transactions which lack a Community dimension continue to be governed by Articles 85 and 86. Article 85 does not apply to full mergers, but it may apply to the acquisition of a minority holding in a competing undertaking.[8] An acquisition by a dominant company of a smaller competitor may constitute an abuse within Article 86.[9]

The line between the requirement of validation under the Mergers Regulation and the application of Article 85 may be particularly difficult to draw in the case of joint ventures, whereby independent undertakings contribute resources to a new enterprise which is jointly controlled by them. Joint ventures may be either concentrative and akin to mergers, where the new enterprise is an autonomous economic entity, or co-operative, where the enterprise merely seeks to co-ordinate the activities of the contributing undertakings, or more often, a combination of the two. In general, Article 85 will apply where the agreement contains co-operative elements which are not merely ancillary. Where these elements can be severed, the Mergers Regulation will apply to the concentrative clauses. The distinctions between concentration and co-operation, ancillary and non-ancillary are, however, far from clear-cut.[10]

It should be noted that many joint venture arrangements will fall into the categories of specialisation or research and development agreements which benefit from block exemptions. A more general group exemption for joint venture agreements is in the pipeline.

ENFORCEMENT OF COMPETITION LAW

The European Commission

Under Regulation 17/62,[11] the Commission has broad powers to police the observance by undertakings of the Community competition law regime. It may request all necessary information from Member States and individual undertakings and conduct voluntary or compulsory searches of company premises. It may impose fines where its demands are not met. In the event of a finding that competition law has been

---

7   See W Sibree, 'EEC Merger Control and Joint Ventures' (1992) 17 ELRev 91.
8   Cases 142&156/84 *BAT v Commission* [1986] ECR 1899.
9   Case 6/72R *Europemballage and Continental Can v Commission* [1972] ECR 157.
10   For guidance, see Commission Notice, OJ 1990 C203/5.
11   OJ 1962, L3/204.

breached, the Commission may fine guilty undertakings up to ten per cent of their annual, global turnover in the sector concerned.

In exercising its powers under Regulation 17/62, the Commission is required to observe a variety of procedural safeguards. These safeguards arise partly from the regulation itself but for the most part have been implied by the Court of Justice from general principles of Community law such as the right to a fair hearing and the rights of the defence. Companies under suspicion can, for example, withhold self-incriminating information,[12] and claim privilege for certain types of legal correspondence.[13] The Commission, furthermore, is subject, under the Regulation, to a duty of confidentiality with respect to business secrets,[14] and to a more general duty, arising under Article 214 of the Treaty 'not to disclose information of the kind covered by the obligation of professional secrecy'.[15] The Court has also ruled that information obtained by the Commission under Regulation 17/62 cannot be used against the companies in question by national authorities, who must obtain their evidence independently.[16]

A lawyer confronted with a problem of Community competition law should consider, initially, the role of the Commission. Where the client's proposed behaviour is potentially in breach of competition law, thought should be given to notifying the Commission, and applying for negative clearance, or for individual exemption. Alternatively, the proposed behaviour may be tailored so as to come within Commission notices or block exemption regulations.

Commission decisions in competition law matters can be challenged under Article 173(2) by their addressees before the Court of First Instance, with appeal on points of law to the Court of Justice. It is unclear to what extent less formal measures have legal effects and so are susceptible to challenge; comfort letters have been held to be merely administrative and not susceptible to challenge,[17] but the opposite was held in respect of preliminary letters rejecting complaints about competition law infringement.[18]

Undertakings fined by the Commission are obviously entitled to question the Commission's interpretation of Community competition law. They should, in addition, examine very carefully whether the

---

12 Case 374/87 *Orkem v Commission* [1989] ECR 3283.
13 Case 155/79 *AM&S v Commission* [1982] ECR 1575.
14 Arts 19(2), 20(2) and 21(2); Case 53/85 *AKZO v Commission* [1986] ECR 1965.
15 See Case 145/83 *Adams v Commission* [1985] ECR 3539.
16 Case C67/91 *DGDC v AEB* [1992] ECR I-4785.
17 See, eg, Case 99/79 *Lancôme v ETOS* [1980] ECR 2511.
18 Cases 142 & 156/84 *BAT v Commission* [1986] ECR 1899.

Commission has followed its own procedures, and, furthermore, respected the Community's general principles of administrative justice.

Legal challenges to Commission decisions take on average 18 months to two years to come before the Court of First Instance and during that period interim relief from a Commission decision may be obtained. The addressee must establish a *prima facie* challenge and show that it may suffer serious and irreparable damage in the interim period.[19]

Individuals or companies aggrieved about the behaviour of others may complain to the Commission where they have a 'legitimate interest' in so doing.[20] Individuals and companies who are directly prejudiced by allegedly anti-competitive behaviour are clearly covered.[1]

The Commission is legally obliged to consider the complaints which are submitted to it but the decision to conduct a formal investigation is a discretionary one and cannot be legally challenged. The Commission will only investigate those matters which raise a significant issue at the Community level, preferring to leave other matters to national competition law authorities. As a corollary, the Commission cannot generally be compelled to produce a formal decision, addressed to a third party and published in the Official Journal, in response to a complaint.[2]

When a complaint is made the Commission should issue a preliminary opinion on whether or not it proposes to take action, and inviting further comment from the complainant. These preliminary responses are not susceptible to legal challenge.[3] The Commission conceded in *Automec (No 2)*, however, that it must, if asked, go on to produce a final response to a complaint,[4] which is legally reviewable,[5] and which may then be challenged under Article 173(2) by the complainants themselves,[6] and, in certain circumstances, by other affected parties.[7] If the Commission fails to produce this final opinion, a complainant has grounds for an action under Article 175 for failure to act.

Automec (No 2) also indicates that complainants cannot demand that the Commission issue specific injunctions as to the behaviour of the undertakings involved in the complaint. The Commission could hold that the Treaty had been infringed and order the parties to put an end to the

---

19   See, eg, T29/92R *SPO v Commission* [1992] ECR II-2161.
20   Art 3(2) of Regulation 17/62.
1   See Case 26/76 *Metro v Commission* [1977] ECR 1875.
2   Case 125/78 *GEMA v Commission* [1979] ECR 3173. The exception is where the subject matter of the complaint falls within the Commission's exclusive jurisdiction, such as the withdrawal of an Art 85(3) exemption.
3   Case T64/89 *Automec v Commission (No 1)* [1990] ECR II-367.
4   Case T24/90 *Automec v Commission (No 2)* [1992] ECR II-2223; [1992] 5 CMLR 431.
5   Case 298/83 *CICCE v Commission* [1985] ECR 1105.
6   See Case 26/76 *Metro v Commission* [1977] ECR 1875.
7   Cases 228 and 229/82 *Ford Werke v Commission* [1984] ECR 1129.

infringement but it could not dictate to the parties how this might be achieved.

Complainants may ask the Commission to grant them interim protection during the course of its investigations. The power to grant interim measures was not expressly conferred on the Commission but was nevertheless implied by the Court from the terms of Regulation 17/62.[8] The power has been exercised only rarely, but the decision of the Court of First Instance in *La Cinq* may augur well for future requests. It was held that an applicant for interim measures must establish, firstly, a *prima facie* case and secondly, that it would otherwise suffer grave and irreparable harm. The factor of urgency need not be proved separately but is subsumed within 'grave and irreparable harm' and the latter is to be interpreted more broadly than simply harm which cannot be remedied by future decisions.[9]

Enforcement in national courts

Community competition law is enforced, in addition, by national courts. Articles 85 and 86 are directly effective, both vertically, against the state, and, more importantly, horizontally, against other undertakings.[10] National courts may adjudicate, if necessary, with the help of an Article 177 reference, on virtually all matters relating to the application of these articles, although only the Commission has the power to grant individual exemptions under Article 85(3).

Undertakings whose interests have been prejudiced by the anti-competitive conduct of others should consider bringing an action before a British court. The leading English authority, *Garden Cottage Foods v Milk Marketing Board*,[11] suggests that damages, under the head of breach of statutory duty, are, in principle, available for loss caused by a breach of Article 86 and the same presumably goes for Article 85. It should be noted, however, that in recognising the possibility of a claim in damages arising out of a breach of the competition provisions of the Treaty of Rome *Garden Cottage Foods* reduces the chances of obtaining interlocutory relief.[12]

---

8   Case 792/79R *Camera Care v Commission* [1980] ECR 119.
9   Case T44/90 *La Cinq v Commission* [1992] ECR II-1; [1992] 4 CMLR 449.
10 Case 127/73 *BRT v SABAM* [1974] ECR 51.
11 [1984] AC 130.
12 See the principles stated in *American Cyanamid v Ethicon* [1975] 1 All ER 504. Compare *Cutsforth v Mansfield Inns* [1986] 1 All ER 577.

An action in a British court has the disadvantage that it requires the expenditure of the resources of the private client, rather than those of the Commission. Nevertheless it may prove quicker and more reliable than the often cumbersome enforcement machinery in Brussels. Individuals must also consider that the Commission is primarily concerned with the interest of the Community as a whole and not with the difficulties of those affected by anti-competitive conduct. Specific remedies, such as the granting of court orders to compel companies to resume supplies under dealership agreements can be asked of national courts where they cannot be asked of the Commission and damages and costs, which the Commission has no power to award, may also be available at national level. Faced with an ever increasing workload, the Commission has explicitly encouraged complainants to use their national legal systems where possible and has stated its willingness to provide advice on both procedural and substantive issues to national judges.[13]

Articles 85 and 86 may also be invoked defensively in national courts. A company may, for example, defend an action against it for breach of contract by claiming that the agreement is void by reason of being in breach of Article 85. If a reference has to be made on the point to the Court of Justice, the proceedings may be delayed for up to two years and the implications of 'Euro-defences' for competition litigation strategies are accordingly substantial.

STATE AIDS

Fair competition in the Community is further promoted by Articles 92 to 94 of the Treaty which regulate the subsidies and other forms of aid provided to undertakings by governmental organisations. State aids, which have no exact equivalent in British law, may distort competition by conferring a competitive advantage on a particular producer, or sector of the economy.

As under Articles 85 and 86, Community law will come into operation where trade between Member States may be affected. Special procedures apply to aid schemes whose affect on inter-state trade is minimal.[14]

The concept of 'aid' is interpreted broadly, in terms of its effect, and so incorporates any form of financial or other advantage granted directly or indirectly which furthers the goals of the undertaking. Preferential tax treatment, favourable loans, lower than market prices for resources such

---

13 *Notice on Cooperation between National Courts and the Commission in Applying Article 85 and 86 of the EEC Treaty*, OJ 1993 C39/6, [1993] 5 CMLR 95.
14 Notification of aid scheme of minor importance, OJ 1990 C40/2.

as land and power, and 'sweeteners' provided to encourage privatisation will all come under scrutiny.

Social aid provided to individual consumers and aid to repair the damage caused by natural disasters and other exceptional occurrences are explicitly authorised by the Treaty.[15] Certain other types of aid, including regional aid, to assist underdeveloped areas, and aid to specific industrial sectors, notably shipbuilding and the car industry may also be permitted (Art 92(3)).

The Commission is ultimately responsible for the supervision of state aid schemes. Existing aid schemes are to be kept under constant review and the state may be required to alter or abolish them if they are found to be incompatible with the common market. Proposed new aid schemes must be notified to the Commission and cannot be implemented unless and until they are authorised.[16] Exceptionally, the Council, acting unanimously, may authorise an aid scheme which the Commission considers to be prohibited under Article 92.[17]

The provisions on state aids are directed primarily at the Member States and it is government legal officers who have most need to be aware of the Community regime. Nevertheless, a private practitioner may be confronted with two types of client requiring advice in this area. Firstly, undertakings which have received state aid granted without regard to the procedures for notification and authorisation. The Commission is empowered to require that such aid be repaid to the Member State which provided it. The obligation to repay the aid is virtually absolute and the Member State is constrained even to have the recipient company wound up if this is necessary to recover the money.[18] In the past, several recipient companies have challenged Commission decisions under Article 173(2) requiring repayment of aid, claiming a breach of their legitimate expectations. The Court of Justice has, however, generally been unsympathetic to these arguments.[19]

Of course, recipient companies may suffer financial damage through having to repay aid a considerable time after it has been granted. It is possible, particularly in view of the *Francovich* decision, that such companies may have a remedy in damages against the Member State which illegally provided the aid.[20] However, the state may well argue in

---

15   Art 92(1).
16   Art 93(3).
17   Art 93(2).
18   Case 52/84 *Commission v Belgium* [1986] ECR 89.
19   See, eg, Case 310/85 *Deufil v Commission* [1987] ECR 901. The applicant was successful, however, in Case 223/85 *RSV v Commission* [1987] ECR 4617.
20   Cases C6&9/90 *Francovich v Italy* [1991] ECR I-5357.

its defence that the recipient company was, actually or constructively, aware of the rules on repayment and so brought about its own loss. The efforts of the Commission in recent years to publish its decisions on state aids and the rules on repayment of illegally granted aid would strengthen this argument.[1]

Competitors of companies in receipt of state aids constitute the other group of potential clients who may require advice in this field. Competitors may, firstly, make a complaint to the Commission about aid provided to rival companies. If the Commission fails to act upon the complaint, an action may be brought under Article 175. Any decision taken by the Commission may be challenged under Article 173, within the standard two-month time limit; it has been held that complainant companies, without whose involvement a particular decision would not have come about, have standing to challenge the decision under Article 173(2).[2]

Alternatively, competitors may bring an action against the Member State concerned, in their national courts. The substantive provisions on state aids are not directly effective since their operation is dependent upon the exercise of discretion by Community institutions, but the procedural obligation of Article 93(3), that a Member State may not grant proposed aid until a final decision has emerged from the Commission, may be pleaded before national courts. The Court of Appeal has upheld the standing of a complainant company in this context.[3]

BIBLIOGRAPHY

R Whish *Competition Law* (3rd edn, 1993) Butterworths.
C Bellamy and G Child, *Common Market Law of Competition* (4th edn, 1993) Sweet and Maxwell.
C Kerse *Antitrust Procedure* (2nd edn, 1988) European Law Centre.
D Schina *State Aids under Articles 92-94 of the Treaty of Rome* (1990) ESC.
C Jones, E González-Díaz and C Overbury *The EEC Merger Regulation* (1992) Sweet and Maxwell

---

1   See Commission Communication on the Reimbursement of State Aids Illegally Granted, OJ 1983 C318/3.
2   Case 169/84 *COFAZ v Commission* [1986] ECR 391.
3   *R v A-G, ex p ICI* [1987] 1 CMLR 72.

Chapter 11

CONSUMER PROTECTION LAW

INTRODUCTION

Article 129a of the post-Maastricht Treaty of Rome provides that the Community shall contribute to the attainment of a high level of consumer protection by adopting measures seeking to complete the internal market project. The Community may also take further action, intended to support and supplement policies pursued by the Member States, to protect the health, safety and economic interests of consumers and to provide adequate information to them. Article 129a(3) allows Member States to maintain or introduce more stringent measures for consumer protection than those laid down by the Community, provided always that such measures are compatible with the Treaty and are notified to the Commission.

The Commission's general policy on consumer issues is aimed at promoting five 'fundamental consumer rights'. These are:

- the protection of consumers' health and safety;
- the protection of consumers' economic interests;
- the promotion of consumer information and education;
- the availability of suitable forms of redress for complaints by consumers;
- the right to representation and participation in the Community decision making process as it affects consumer interests.

The whole field of consumer protection in the United Kingdom has become one underpinned by Community law. In particular, the base line for consumer protection in the United Kingdom is now set by Community law. Any UK laws which seek to give a higher degree of protection to the consumer have to be compatible with the general principles as well as the specific legislative provisions of Community law. For example, national consumer protection laws should not constitute a disguised restriction on trade among Member States or otherwise result in arbitrary discrimination among goods.[1] This clearly opens up the possibility of 'Euro-challenges' and 'Euro-defences' in the whole field of the enforcement of consumer protection law in the United Kingdom.

Community consumer protection legislation to date has covered a wide area. Community law has required manufacturers to provide more information on packaging and labels as to ingredients and processes used and to affix, where necessary, appropriate safety warnings on products. Community rules have been laid down in respect of the marketing of products. More recent Community initiatives have aimed at improving consumers' legal redress in case of injury by faulty goods and services or breach of contract by the supplier of the goods. In considering the general field of Community consumer protection law it will be useful to divide the consideration of the legislation into two general areas: consumer health and safety and the protection of consumer's economic interests.

CONSUMER HEALTH AND SAFETY

The Product Liability Directive

Under the 1985 Product Liability Directive[2], the 'producers' of defective products which cause personal injury are liable in damages for such injuries as are attributable to the defect. A product is said to be defective 'when it does not provide the safety which a person is entitled to expect, taking all circumstances into account' (Art 6). 'Producers' are defined very broadly by Article 2 of the Directive as including the manufacturer of a finished product or component part thereof, the producer of the raw material used therein, any person holding himself out by his trade mark or brand as the producer, any person importing the product into the European Community and, where no original producer can be identified, any person supplying the product within the European Community. Liability among the various manufacturers, producers, brand name holders, suppliers and importers is joint and several.

The injured person is required to prove the damage, the defect and the causal relationship between defect and damage. However, the liability of

---

1   See, eg Case 190/87 *Oberkreisdirector v Moormann* [1988] ECR 4689. The Court's case law on what constitutes a measure having an equivalent effect to a quantitive restriction on imports has to be read in the light of Joined Cases C-267, 268/91 *Keck and Mithouard* 24 November [1993] ECR (not yet reported).
2   Directive 85/374/EEC, OJ 1985 L210/29.

'producers' under the directive does not depend on any prior finding of negligence on the part of the producer, nor need there be any contractual relationship between the producer and the injured party.

The producer's liability is not, however, absolute since Article 7 of the directive specifies certain defences, for example that the defect did not exist at the time the product was put into circulation or that the defect resulted from the producer's compliance with mandatory requirements by public authorities. Member States may also provide for a 'state of the art defence' to the effect that the defect could not have been discovered in the light of the then current scientific and technical knowledge.

The producer's liability is in respect of damage caused by death or by personal injuries, and to a limited extent to the private/non-business property of the injured party, other than the defective product itself. This definition of damage is said to be without prejudice to national provisions relating to 'non-material damage'.[3] There is some dispute as to the precise effect of this provision. It may mean that damage which can be claimed under the directive extends only to financial losses and does not include claims in respect of loss of amenity, general damages or *solatium* for pain and suffering or bereavement, loss of expectation of life or any element of punitive damages. Alternatively, it may mean that non-material damage claims may be brought under the directive where such claims are already permitted under the provisions of national law. The latter interpretation would mean that the basis of liability would be harmonised throughout the Community, but that the question of the method of quantification of loss remained within the province of national law. There has been no authoritative ruling from the European Court of Justice on the matter as yet.

Member States are prohibited under the directive from limiting or excluding the producer's liability as regards the injured person and any contractual or other provision which purports so to do will be void. The producer's liability may be reduced by contributory negligence on the part of the injured party, but is not affected by the act or omission of a third party. There is a curiously worded provision in Article 16(1) of the Directive to the effect that Member States may limit the total liability of a producer in respect of 'damage resulting from death or personal injury and caused by identical items with the same defect' to no less than 70 million ECU. It is not clear how this ceiling provision might be applied in practice. It may be that it envisages the possibility of national

---

3   For an account of the differing approaches to the quantification of damages in various European States see D. McIntosh and M Holmes *Personal Injury Awards in EC Countries* (1990) Lloyds of London Press and F Holding and P Kaye *Damages for Personal Injuries: a European Perspective* (1993) Chancery Law Publishing.

jurisdictions allowing for 'class actions' by the group of all those persons injured by the same product defect seeking a pool of damages to be shared out *pro rata* among the group. Alternatively it may mean that the producer is no longer liable for any individual claims brought once the ceiling of damages payouts has been reached. This provisions for a financial cap on damages has not been taken advantage of in the UK's implementing legislation.

IMPLEMENTATION OF THE PRODUCT LIABILITY DIRECTIVE

The directive was implemented in the United Kingdom in Part I of the Consumer Protection Act 1987 which came into force on 1 March 1988. Section 1(1) provides that Part I of the Act:

> 'shall have effect for the purpose of making such provision as is necessary in order to comply with the Product Liability directive and shall be construed accordingly.'

In implementing the directive, the UK Government opted to include a 'state of the art' defence allowed for by Article 7(e) of the directive. Article 7(e) provides that the producer shall not be liable if he proves 'that the state of scientific and technical knowledge at the time when he put the product into circulation was not such as to enable the existence of the defect to be discovered'. This has been translated into s 4(1)(e) of the Act which provides that it shall be a defence in any civil proceedings brought under the Act for a producer to show 'that the state of scientific and technical knowledge at the relevant time was not such that a producer of products of the same description as the product in question might be expected to have discovered the defect if it had existed in his products while they were under his control'.

It is arguable that the UK implementation of the 'state of the art defence' is broader than that allowed in the directive. The UK defence relies not only on the state of scientific and technical knowledge in an absolute sense, but would appear to allow the producer a defence on the basis that the relevant scientific and technical knowledge was not such that a producer of like products might be expected to have known about when the product in question was under his control. This provision of the UK statute might be subject to a Euro-challenge in any national court proceedings in which it is relied upon. At the time of writing, however, there were no reported cases of a successful action taken by a consumer in the United Kingdom on the basis of the supplier's product liability.

Directive on General Product Safety

Whereas the Product Liability directive provides a common European approach to compensation to consumers once accidents have occurred which are attributable to faulty goods, the Directive on General Product Safety[4] seeks to prevent or minimise the danger of such accidents ever occurring. The two directives complement one another.

The Product Safety Directive imposes a broad obligation on 'producers' (defined in similar terms as is contained in the Product Liability Directive) to place only safe products on the market. A product is anything intended or likely to be used by consumers which has been supplied in the course of a commercial activity. A 'safe product' is one which under normal or reasonably foreseeable conditions of use including length of use 'does not present any risk or only the minimum risks compatible with the product's use considered as acceptable and consistent with a high level of protection for the safety and health of persons'.

There is an obligation placed upon producers to supply consumers with such information as is necessary to enable them to assess the risks inherent in the product and an obligation on distributors not to supply products which they knew or ought to have known were unsafe. These duties are conceived in the directives as public duties to be policed and enforced by Member States using such mechanisms as organising checks, requiring information, taking samples and prohibiting or withdrawing unsafe products from the market-place. Action taken under the Product Safety Directive shall not prejudge questions of liability for compensation under the Product Liability Directive.

The Product Safety Directive was adopted on 29 June 1992 and falls to be implemented by 29 June 1994. [5] As regards implementation within the United Kingdom, the provisions of this directive have already largely been anticipated by Part II of the Consumer Protection Act 1987 and by the Food Safety Act 1990. Some amendments of the UK legislation will still be required to bring national provisions totally into line with Community law.

---

4   Directive 92/59/EEC, OJ 1992 L228/24.
5   Note, however, Case C-359/92 *Germany v. Council*, notification in OJ 1992 C288/10 in which the German Government seeks annulment of Art 9 of the Directive in so far as it gives the Commission power to order Member States to take certain measures with regard to the circulation and distribution of products. At the time of writing, judgment had not yet been pronounced in this case.

The liability of suppliers of services: a proposed directive

In October 1990 the Commission proposed a directive on the liability of suppliers of services. The proposal was to the effect that a Community-wide uniform system of civil liability of suppliers of services which have damaged 'the physical integrity of person or property' [6] should be established.

It was proposed as part of this general system that the burden of proof of fault in the supply of services be reversed in favour of the injured party. All that the latter would have to prove was that damage had been caused to him and that there was a causal link between that damage and the service supplied. It would then be up to the supplier of the service to prove that his performance of the service was done without fault or negligence. Fault fell to be assessed in relation to the 'legitimate expectation as to the safety of the service'. In other words the supplier of the service would require to show that he had not failed to exercise the care and skill reasonably to be expected of a supplier of ordinary skill and experience.

The proposal by the Commission was subject to considerable criticism in the European Parliament which suggested a number of radical amendments to the draft including the need on the part of the injured party to prove fault. [7] In response to this criticism the Commission has proposed introducing further special measures in relation to a limited number of sectors, in particular relating to the construction industry and the medical profession, as well as looking again at a new general proposal.

Specific directives relating to consumer safety

Directives have been adopted in a wide number of areas including on the health labelling of tobacco products [8] A directive has also been proposed which will ban tobacco sports sponsorship and all tobacco advertising except at tobacco shops. [9]

The Community's approach to regulation of food has changed from its earlier notorious attempts to lay down recipes setting down the composition

---

6   COM (90) 482 final SYN 308, OJ 1991 C12/8.
7   See the Report of the Committee on Legal Affairs and Citizens' Rights (15 December 1992 A3-0420/92).
8   Directive 89/622/EEC, OJ 1989 L359/1 as amended by Directive 92/41, OJ 1992 L158/30 implemented by the Tobacco Products Labelling (Safety) Regulations 1991 (SI 1991/1530)
9   COM (91) 111, OJ 1991 C167/5.

of particular foodstuffs, attempts which gave rise to tabloid headlines proclaiming a Brussels attack on 'the British sausage', 'British chocolate' or 'British ice-cream'. Instead the modern Community approach to food is to set down minimum standards on matters of health and safety, and consumer protection and fair-trading. These standards are set out in general in framework directives which are then more specifically applied to particular foodstuffs by daughter directives. [10]

PROTECTION OF CONSUMERS' ECONOMIC INTERESTS

Directives on specific consumer problems

There are a number of directives regulating specific problems associated with consumer contracts: for example, misleading advertising, [11] doorstep selling [12] and the provision of consumer credit.[13] A directive has also been adopted in relation to package holidays and travel [14] which sets out the information which must be included in such contracts and the circumstances in which their terms might be altered. There is also a proposed directive regulating the purchase of timeshare properties within the Community, [15] and another proposal dealing with consumer contracts negotiated at a distance from the seller, for example in TV shopping.[15a]

---

10 See, eg the Directive on the classification, packaging and labelling of foodstuffs 79/112/EEC, OJ 1979 L33 as amended by Directive 89/395/EEC, OJ 1989 L186 implemented largely by the Food Safety Act 1990.
11 Directive 84/450/EEC, OJ 1984 L250 implemented by the Control of Misleading Advertisements Regulations 1988 (SI 1988/915). See proposed amendment in COM(91) 147, OJ 1991 C180/14.
12 Directive 85/577/EEC, OJ 1985 L372/31 implemented by the Consumer Protection (Cancellation of Contracts Concluded away from Business Premises) Regulations 1987, SI 1987/2117 as amended. This directive was at the time of writing subject to an Art 177 reference from an Italian court seeking to establish whether or not its provisions might have horizontal effect (Case C-91/92 *Paolo Faccini Dori v Recreb Srl*, notified in OJ 1992 C107/7), Advocate-General's Opinion dated 9 February 1994.
13 Directive 87/102/EEC, OJ 1987 L42/48, the provisions of which were largely anticipated in the United Kingdom by the Consumer Credit Act 1974. There has accordingly been no specific implementation of this directive.
14 Directive 90/314/EEC, OJ 1990 L158/59 implemented by the Package Travel, Package Holidays and Package Tour Regulations 1992 (SI 1992/3288).
15 COM (93) 487 final - SYN 419, OJ 1993 C299/4. This was a proposal sought primarily by the UK Government. See the Timeshare Act 1992 which anticipates much of the proposed directive's provisions.
15a COM (93) 396 final - SYN 411, 1993 C308/18.

These directives all have to be interpreted in a way which insures the protection of consumers. They do not apply as regards relationships among traders or persons in business. [16]

The Unfair Contract Terms Directive

In April 1993 the Council of Ministers adopted the Unfair Contract Terms Directive 93/13. [17] This directive seeks to set out the minimum level of protection which must be accorded to consumers in their contractual dealings by the laws of the Member States.

The directive applies to non-negotiated terms in contracts concluded between a seller or supplier (acting within his trade, business or profession) and a consumer (acting outside his trade, business or profession). Non-negotiated terms of a contract are those which were drafted in advance and over the substance of which the consumer was unable to exercise any influence. The directive applies equally to oral as well as to written pre-formulated standard terms and contracts. The onus is on the seller or supplier claiming that a particular standard term had indeed been individually negotiated to show this or otherwise show that a particular term is not unfair to the consumer. In case of ambiguous terms the interpretation most favourable to the consumer is to be preferred.

The directive does not apply to terms of contracts concluded by parties in the course of business or to any provisions which have been required by statute or regulation of the Member State or which refer to principles of international agreements, particularly in the field of transport, which have been ratified by the Member States or by the Community. [18] It does not apply to employment contracts, to contracts relative to rights and obligations under the law of succession, to the formation and internal organisation of companies or partnerships or to matters of family law.

It does apply to contracts concluded by consumers with sellers or suppliers in the public sector as well as the private sector. Article 3 of the directive defines non-negotiated terms of a standard contract with a consumer as 'unfair' if the term can be said, contrary to the requirements of good faith, to 'cause a significant imbalance in the parties' rights and obligations arising under the contract to the detriment of the consumer.'

'Good faith' is expanded in the preamble to the directive to mean that regard has to be had to 'the strength of the bargaining positions of the parties, whether the consumer had an inducement to agree to the terms

---

16   Case C-361/89 *France v Di Pinto* [1991] ECR I-1189, [1993] 1 CMLR 399. See also Case C-89/91 *Shearson Lehman Hutton v TVB Treuhandgesellschaft Fuer Vermoegensverwaltung und Beteiliging* [1993] ECR I-139 for a definition of 'consumer contract' for the purposes of the Brussels Convention.

17   Directive 93/13/, OJ 1993 L95/29.

18   See the text of the common position on the directive at OJ 1992 C283/1.

and whether goods and services were sold or supplied to the special order of the consumer.' Good faith is said to be satisfied if the seller or supplier had dealt 'fairly and equitably' with the consumer and has taken into account his or her legitimate interests.

The reference to the requirements of good faith thus appears to be akin to the idea of 'reasonableness' already known in the United Kingdom[19] but it may require the development in UK law of a broader concept of fair and open dealing in which difference in bargaining power are not to be abused.

An annex to the directive provides an indicative list of the type of terms of which might be considered to be unfair taking into account the contract as a whole, any other contract upon which it is dependent, the nature of the goods or services and all the circumstances attendant upon the conclusion of the contract.

Such potentially unfair terms include those which purport to exclude or limit the liability for death or personal injury to the consumer resulting from act or omission of the seller or supplier, or which permit unilateral variation of the contract by the supplier or seller without reason. Terms which have the effect of obliging the consumer to fulfil his obligations without a similar requirement on the supplier or seller or which purport to give the seller or supplier the exclusive right to interpret the contract or to determine whether or not goods supplied under the contract are in conformity with its terms are also seen as potentially unfair. Similarly, terms which effectively exclude or limit the consumer's right to seek legal redress or which require the consumer to pay disproportionate penalties or compensation in the event of his or her non-performance under the contract are also regarded as potentially unfair to the consumer.

Given that the list is indicative only, it may be added to or otherwise altered by Member States when implementing the directive, provided that such implementation does not have the effect of lowering the level of consumer protection below that required by the directive.

The directive requires Member States to ensure that terms which are 'unfair' according to the test in the directive will not bind the consumer. Member States are further required to take adequate and effective measures to prevent the continued use of such unfair terms. Sellers and suppliers are required by the directive only to ensure that their standard terms are drafted in plain and intelligible terms and that the consumer has the opportunity to read all the terms.

If collective or representative actions are already permitted within the national jurisdictions then third parties with an interest, for example,

19 *Interfoto Picture Library Ltd v Stiletto Visual Programmes Ltd* [1988] 1 All ER 348 at 353. Cf *Bank of Nova Scotia v Hellenic Mutual War Risks Association (Bermuda) Ltd* [1989] 3 All ER 628.

consumer pressure groups, may raise an action against (associations of) suppliers seeking a declaration from the national courts that particular terms used or recommended are or would be contrary to the provisions of the directive.

Any term of a contract whereby the seller or supplier seeks to designate the law of a non-EC country as the applicable law to the contract will not be given effect to if the contract can be said to have a close connection with the territory of a Member State.

IMPLEMENTATION OF THE UNFAIR CONTRACT TERMS DIRECTIVE

Implementation of the directive in the Member States is required by 31 December 1994. The directive will apply to consumer contracts concluded on or after 1 January 1995.

Despite its title, the UK Unfair Contract Terms Act 1977 was not a code dealing with general terms of contracts which might be described as unfair in the context of the whole contract. Instead the 1977 Act, in a manner which differs as between Scotland and England, dealt only with clauses seeking to limit or to exclude liability. Extensive legislative changes will therefore be required in the United Kingdom to implement the directive to ensure that any contractual term which, in the whole circumstances, offends against principles of good faith and causes a significant imbalance to the detriment of the consumer in his or her contractual rights and obligations will not bind the consumer under national law. In particular, the anomalous special treatment accorded to insurance contracts whereby their terms were excluded from the 1977 legislation will be ended. Insurance contracts will now require to be treated in the same way as any other contracts concluded with consumers. Consumer contract law in the United Kingdom will henceforth have to be understood and applied on European lines.

BIBLIOGRAPHY

T Askham *Consumer Law* (1993) Butterworths European Law Service.
A Geddes, *Product and Service Liability in the EEC: the new strict liability regime* (1992) Sweet & Maxwell.
C Hodges *Product Liability: European Laws and Practice* (1992) Sweet & Maxwell.
F Holding and P Kaye *Damages for Personal Injuries: a European Perspective* (1993) Chancery Law Publishing.
P Kelly and R Attree *European Product Liability* (1992) Butterworths.

C Lister *The Regulation of Food Products by the European Community* (1992) Butterworths.
D McIntosh and M Holmes *Personal Injury Awards in EC Countries* (1990) Lloyds of London Press.
W Pfenningstorf *Personal Injury Compensation* (1993) Lloyds of London Press.

Chapter 12

EMPLOYMENT PROTECTION LAW

INTRODUCTION

Article 118 of the Treaty of Rome provides that the Commission has the task, in conformity with its general objectives and without prejudice to the other provisions of the Treaty, of promoting close co-operation between Member States in the social field, more particularly in matters relating to employment, labour law and working conditions, the right of association and collective bargaining between employers and workers. Community legislation in the area of the rights and interests of employed persons still requires the unanimity of the Member States' representatives in the Council of Ministers.

In December 1989, all Member States of the Community with the exception of the United Kingdom agreed to subscribe to the Community Social Charter.[1] This was a political declaration with no binding legal force or effect, which enumerated a series of social and labour rights for workers. These rights included the following: freedom of movement throughout the Community; freedom to choose and to engage in an occupation and to be fairly remunerated for it; the improvement of living and working conditions of all workers including rights to paid annual leave and weekly breaks; the right to an adequate level of social security benefits; freedom of association in trade unions and the right to strike and to negotiate and conclude collective agreements; access to vocational training; equal treatment between men and women; the right to information, consultation and participation in decisions involving major changes in the workplace and/or the workforce; satisfactory health and safety conditions in the working environment; the protection of children, the young, the elderly and the disabled.

---

1 Community Charter of Fundamental Social Rights of Workers, 9 December 1989, COM (89) 471 final.

During the negotiations regarding the Maastricht Treaty, it was proposed that the substance of rights set out in the Community Social Charter be fully incorporated into Community law and become part of the body of Community law (the *acquis communautaire*) by appropriate amendment of the Treaty of Rome. Such a development was considered politically unacceptable by those negotiating on behalf of the United Kingdom. A compromise was eventually reached whereby all 12 Member States agreed that Community institutions and procedures could be used to produce proposals and legislation to implement the Social Charter agreed by 11 of the Member States, but that any such legislation would not apply to the United Kingdom and the United Kingdom would be excluded from the Community decision-making procedures on these issues. [2] A two-tier Community was thereby created: a Social Europe of 11 States and an anti-Social Europe, consisting solely of the United Kingdom. In order for Community social legislation to apply to the whole of the Community, it needs to be presented under another guise, for example workplace health and safety. Health and safety matters may be adopted by qualified majority voting in the Council and are thus not subject to the veto of any one Member State.

Under these provisions, for example, the Council adopted the Working Time Directive[3] which, in general terms, lays down a 48 hour maximum working week (inclusive of overtime), provides for a minimum of four weeks paid annual leave and regulated night working. This directive is due to be implemented in national law by 23 November 1996.

In the field of employment protection proper, by the end of 1993 there had been only four directives adopted by the Community. These directives related to the following areas: collective redundancies;[4] the rights of workers on the transfer of a business;[5] the protection of workers' rights in the event of their employer's insolvency; [6] and written particulars to be given in employment contracts.[7] A directive on the protection of pregnant workers [8] was adopted by the Council in 1992 under the guise of a health and safety measure. This directive is dealt with in Chapter 17. There is also a directive on the protection of self-employed commercial

---

2   See Protocol 14 to the Maastricht Treaty on Social Policy together with the 'Agreement on Social Policy' concluded among 11 of the Member States of the European Community with the exception of the United Kingdom.
3   Directive 93/104/EC, OJ 1993 L307/18.
4   Directive 75/129/EEC, OJ 1975 L48/29 as amended by Directive 92/56/EEC, OJ 1992 L245/3.
5   Directive 77/187/EEC, OJ 1977 L61/26.
6   Directive 80/987/EEC, OJ 1980 L 283/23 as amended by Directive 87/164/EEC, OJ 1987 L66/11
7   Directive 91/533/EEC, OJ 1991 L288/32.
8   Directive 92/85/EEC, OJ 1992 L348/1.

agents[9] which, although not strictly a matter of employment law as traditionally understood in the United Kingdom, is dealt with in this chapter.

Given the length of time for which the general employment protection directives have existed, the case law of the Court of Justice interpreting these directives is particularly important in establishing the extent of the rights protected under Community law and the degree to which national legislation has correctly implemented them.

COLLECTIVE REDUNDANCIES DIRECTIVE

This directive [10] requires employers to give advance notification of collective redundancies to their workers and/or their representatives and to consult with their workers about the implementation of the proposed redundancies. This directive was originally implemented in the United Kingdom by ss 99 to 107 of the Employment Protection Act 1975, and are now contained in ss 188 to 198 of the Trade Union and Labour Relations (Consolidation) Act 1992. The UK provisions are more stringent than the requirements of the directive in that they require an employer to consult with recognised trade union representatives if even one redundancy is being contemplated.

The original directive was further amended by Directive 92/56 [11] which provided that the directive applies when there are at least five redundancies and that consultation with a view to avoiding or reducing the proposed redundancy will be required as between the employer and the workers' representatives. The employer will be required to provide specific information on the reasons for the redundancies and the workers' representatives will have the right to call upon the services of experts to consider these submissions. The provisions of the directive, as amended, shall apply regardless of whether or not the decision on redundancy was made by the workers' actual employer or by some other undertaking or business controlling the employer. It is thus intended to apply clearly to situation of cross-border corporate re-structuring.

In *R v British Coal Corpn and Secretary of State for Trade and Industry, ex p Vardy* [12] Glidewell LJ stated that he felt there existed a disparity between the provisions of Article 2 of the unamended Directive 75/129 which provide that, when contemplating collective redundancies,

---

9   Directive 86/653/EEC, OJ 1986 L382/17.
10 Directive 75/129/EEC, OJ 1975 L48/29.
11 Directive 92/56/EEC, OJ L 245/3.
12 [1993] IRLR 104 at 116.

an employer should begin consultations on, among other things, ways and means of avoiding collective redundancies or reducing the numbers of workers affected and mitigating the consequences thereof and the provisions of s 188 of the 1992 Act which require consultation only once there has been a definite proposal about redundancies and do not require the employer to consult with a view to avoiding or minimising the proposed redundancies.

In December 1992 the Commission raised an Article 169 action against the United Kingdom for its alleged shortcomings in the implementation of the collective redundancies directive.[13] The Commission claimed inadequacies in implementation in the UK legislation's:

(i) failure to provide for the designation of employee representatives in the absence of a recognised trade union;
(ii) limitation of scope so as to apply to a narrower range of cases of dismissal than envisaged by the directive;
(iii) failure to require an employer considering collective redundancies to consult worker's representatives with a view to reaching agreement in relation to the matters specified in the directive;
(iv) failure to provide effective sanctions against an employer in the case of failure to consult workers' representatives.

In his Opinion of 2 March 1994 the Advocate-General found all four of the Commision's complaints to be well founded. In anticipation of the Article 169 proceedings the Trade Union Reform and Employment Rights Act 1993 amended the principal act such that consultations about the proposed redundancy must include discussion and consultation about ways of avoiding the dismissals altogether. It is clear, however, that the 1992 amendment to the directive will require additional implementing legislation in the United Kingdom and that further amendment to the UK legislation will be required if the present Article 169 enforcement action succeeds against the government. The judgment of the Court was awaited at the time of writing.

ACQUIRED RIGHTS DIRECTIVE

The Acquired Rights directive[14] requires, in broad terms, that all employees who are covered by a Member State's employment protection legislation should also receive the additional protection that a change in the identity of employer will not *ipso facto* mean the termination of their employment.[15] This protection is dependent on proof that the employees can, in some sense, be said to be doing the same job as before the transfer or change.

13 Case C-383/92 *Commission v UK*, notified in 1992 OJ C316/15.
14 Directive 77/187/EEC, OJ 1977 L61/26.
15 Case 237/84 *Commission v Belgium* [1986] ECR 1247.

If the directive applies, then on the transfer of a business the employee's existing terms and conditions of employment and accrued rights (other than as regards occupational pension schemes relating to old age, survivors or invalidity benefits)[16] are automatically transferred from the old employer to the new person running the business, [17] unless the employee objects to his employment being so transferred.

Partial harmonisation

The directive only achieves a partial harmonisation of the laws of the Member States. The directive does not provide for the application of common Community standards of employee protection. Its aim is to ensure that existing Member States' employment protection laws are applied to cover the case of employees affected by a business transfer. Thus, whereas the term 'worker' used in the articles of the Treaty of Rome has a substantive Community meaning and cannot be defined by reference to the national laws of the Member States, [18] the term 'employee' in the context of the Acquired Rights Directive refers only to those persons accepted as employees under the laws of the Member State concerned. [19]

Purposive interpretation

The Court of Justice has consistently held [20] that, within its limitations as a partial harmonisation measure, the directive should be interpreted in the light of its preamble to provide for the protection of employees in the event of a change of employer, in particular, to ensure that their rights are

---

16 See *Perry v Intec Colleges Ltd.* [1993] IRLR 56, and *Walden Engineering Co Ltd v Warrener* [1993] 3 CMLR 179.

17 The French text of the directive uses the phrase *chef d'entreprise* while the English text uses 'employer'.

18 See Ch 15 on migration law and the case law cited there in relation to the free movement of workers.

19 Case 105/84 *Foreningen af Arbejdledere i Danmark ('Mikkelsen') v A/S Danmols Inventar, in liquidation* [1985] ECR 2639 at 2652-3. See also Case 324/86 *Foreningen af Arbejdsledere i Danmark v Daddy's Dance Hall A/S* [1988] ECR 739, [1988] IRLR 315 and Case 209/91 *Rask and Christensen v ISS Kantineservice A/S* [1992] ECR I-5755, [1993] IRLR 133.

20 See Case 135/83 *Abels v The Administrative Board of the Bedrijfsvereniging voor Metaalindustrie en de Electrotechnische Industrie* [1985] ECR 469, [1987] 2 CMLR 406.

safeguarded while maintaining the improvement described in Article 117 [1] of the Treaty.

Article 7 of the directive provides that 'the directive shall not affect the right of Member States to apply or introduce laws, regulations or administrative provisions which are more favourable to employees'. In line with the approach of the directive as only a partial harmonisation measure, this would appear to mean that employees subject to a transfer have to be treated in national law at least as well as other employees, but may be treated in a more favourable manner. What counts as 'more favourable treatment' may, of course, be the subject of some dispute. The aim of the directive has been said to be manifestly social and biased toward labour seeking to safeguard the employee's employment relationship and the social rights by him acquired therein. [2]

A relevant transfer

With a view to ensuring that the rights of employees subject to a business transfer are indeed protected, the Court of Justice has favoured a maximalist interpretation of Article 1(1) of the directive which provides, in its English version, that the directive 'shall apply to the transfer of an undertaking, business or part of a business to another employer as a result of a legal transfer or merger'.

In deciding whether or not there has been a relevant transfer of an undertaking for the purposes of Article 1(1) it has been stated that technical rules are to be avoided and the substance rather than the form of the change of business looked at.[3]

More specific guidance was provided by the Court in *Rask* when it listed the general considerations which a national judge should take into account in determining whether there had been a transfer of an undertaking for the purposes of the directive.[4] These included the type of undertaking or business concerned, whether the business' tangible assets, such as buildings and moveable property were transferred, the value of its intangible assets at the time of the transfer, whether or not the majority of its employees are taken over by the new employer, whether or not its

---

1 Article 117 provides that:
   'Member States agree on the need to promote improved working conditions and an improved standard of living for workers, so as to make possible their harmonization while the improvment is being maintained.'
2 See opinion of Advocate General Van Gerven in Joined Cases C-132,138,139/91 *Katsikas v Konstantinidis* [1992] ECR I-6577, [1993] 1 CMLR 845 [1993] IRLR 179.
3 The opinion of then Advocate-General, now Lord, Slynn in Case 24/85 *Spijkers v Gebroeders Benedik Abattoir CV* [1986] ECR 1119 at 1121, [1986] 2 CMLR 296
4 Case 209/91 *Rask and Christensen v ISS Kantineservice A/S* [1992] ECR I-5755, [1993] IRLR 133 at 136, paras 17-20.

customers are transferred and the degree of similarity between the activities carried on before and after the transfer and the period, if any, for which those activities are suspended. The court noted, however, that all those circumstances were to be regarded as single factors in the overall assessment which must be made and should not be considered in isolation.

The Court has held that the directive might apply, and hence employees' rights under national law should be protected, in the following situations:

- The canteen service of one company was contracted out to another company in return for a fixed fee which was not linked to the profitability of the service but covered the expenses of the day-to-day running of the service including pay, work clothes, management and supervision costs. Materials, general maintenance, hot water and electricity were all provided free of charge. There was no risk of loss. There was no transfer of any tangible assets, goodwill, customers, or indeed any transfer of a business opportunity. It was simply that one function of a company was contracted out to be done by another.[5]
- A local authority ceased the funding of one charitable organisation and transferred the building previously leased from them by that charity to another foundation. There was no transfer of the moveable property from one charity to another and, while the first charity targeted drug addicts of particular ethnic origin and provided them with social and recreation facilities, the second foundation was concerned only with drug dependency in general. The common factor between the two foundations was no more than a general involvement with drug addicts.[6]
- The owner of a tavern which operated only during the summer months took over in the following season the running of the business previously leased by her after the lessee's breach of their leasing agreement. The Court found the directive applied regardless of whether or not the change in ownership of the undertaking was transferred.[7]
- The lease on a factory expired and the business came to an end, with the employees given due notice of dismissal. The owner of the factory premises shortly thereafter sold the building to a third party who commenced a similar business in the factory. The Court

---

5   Case 209/91 *Rask and Christensen v ISS Kantineservice A/S* [1992] ECR I-5755, [1993] IRLR 133 at 136, paras 17-20.
6   Case C-29/91 *Sophie Redmond Stichting v Bartol* [1992] ECR I-3189, IRLR 366 at 369, para 19.
7   Case 287/86 *Landsorganisationen i Danmark v Ny Molle Kro* [1987] ECR 5465 at 5483.

held that there can be said to be a legal transfer whenever there was a change in the identity of the employer.[8]

- The lease to a bar and restaurant was duly terminated and a new lease entered into with a third party who continued the same business without interruption.[9]

It is clear from these cases that a relevant transfer may be constituted by a wide variety of modes. There is no need for any direct link between the transferor and the transferee, since relevant transfers have been constituted by third parties withdrawing funding from one charity and granting to another, or by transferring the lease of premises from one lessee to another. Further, the fact that a particular business has ceased operation and is then re-started by another party does not prevent there being a relevant transfer. Similarly, the absence of any transfer of tangible assets from one party to another does not preclude the applicability of the Directive.[9a]

The very broad interpretation of the concept of a 'relevant transfer' given by the Court of Justice to date leaves open the possibility that the Acquired Rights Directive applies to, and accordingly the existing rights of employees are protected, in situations such as the following: the privatisation of central government operations; market testing within the National Health Service; the compulsory competitive tendering and hiving off of local government services; the re-organisation of the structures of local government.

An undertaking, business or part of a business

It is sometimes argued before courts in the United Kingdom that the directive can have no relevance to a particular situation unless one can identify a discrete business unit both before and after the alleged transfer. The basis for this argument is the statement of the Court of Justice in *Spijkers* [10] to the effect that the aim of the directive is to ensure the continuity of existing employment relationships within the framework of an economic entity, regardless of the change of owner thereof.

It is clear, however, from the Court's subsequent judgments that the retention of business identity test (in contra-distinction to the mere sale

8   Case 101/87 *P Bork International A/S in liquidation v Foreningen af Arbejdsledere i Danmark* [1988] ECR 3057 at para 13.
9   Case 324/86 *Foreningen af Arbejdsledere i Danmark v Daddy's Dance Hall A/S* [1988] ECR 739, [1988] IRLR 315.
9a See Case C-392/92 *Schmidt v Bordesholm Savings and Loan Bank* notified in OJ 1992 C339/9 concerning the applicability of the directive to the transfer of one cleaner. The Opinion of Advocate-General Van Gerven was delivered on 23 February 1994.
10 Case C-24/85 *Spijkers v. Gebroeders Benedik Abattoir CV* [1986] ECR 1119 at 1128, para 15, [1986] 2 CMLR 296.

of assets of a business) is an example of one instance when the directive may be held to apply. Other tests were applied by the Court in both *Rask* and *Sophie Redmond* since in neither of these cases is there any retention of an independent pre-existing business identity. Instead of seeking to identify distinct economic units in order to determine the applicability of the directive, the Court has concentrated on what is done, the carrying on of a particular business or activity. For example, the significant fact, in *Rask*, is that a canteen continues to be operated and, in *Sophie Redmond*, that drug addicts continue to be cared for. The matter is then approached from the point of view of the employee. [11]

Protection from dismissal

Where any employees are dismissed with a view to and before a transfer falling within the directive, their dismissal must be regarded as contrary to Article 4(1) of the Directive.[12] Under the UK implementing legislation the national court is required to provide an effective remedy against such unlawful dismissal.[13] It has recently been held that this remedy may include an award against the original transferor employer who carried out the dismissals, notwithstanding the terms of TUPE Regulation 5 (2) which provides for the automatic assignation of the transferor's rights and liabilities to the transferee.[13a]

Article 4(1) of the Directive provides an exception for dismissals which take place for economic, technical or organisational reasons entailing changes in the work-force. However, this reference to the possibility of justifiable dismissal has been interpreted very strictly by the Court of Justice since it is a derogation from the aim of the directive to protect employees.[14]

On this analysis, any economic, technical or organisational reasons relied upon to justify the dismissal have to be unconnected with the fact of the transfer. If, however, the dismissal or purported dismissal of the employee results from the transfer of the undertaking or business, then it is absolutely prohibited and cannot be justified by reference to these

---

11 See the opinion of Advocate-General Van Gerven in Case C-29/91 *Sophie Redmond Stichting v Bartol* [1992] ECR I-3189, IRLR 366.
12 Case 19/83 *Knud Wendelboe and L J Music* [1985] ECR 457.
13 *Litster v Forth Dry Dock* [1990] 1 AC 546.
13a See *Robert Allen v Stirling District Council* EAT 759/93, Lord Caulsfield's judgment in the Scottish Employment Appeal Tribunal (15 February 1994, unreported).
14 See, in particular, Advocate-General Van Gerven's opinion in Case C-362/89 *D'Urso v Ercole Marelli Elettromeccanica Generale SpA* [1991] ECR I-4105, [1992] IRLR 136 at 1147, para 35.

additional economic, technical or organisational reasons. This is a matter for national courts to determine. [15]

Union recognition and employee representation

Article 5 of the directive provides that if a business preserves its autonomy on transfer, then the status and function of employee representatives as laid down under national law shall be preserved.

Under current UK law, however, union recognition agreements whereby union officials are accepted as the representatives of employees who are members of that union are not legally enforceable. An employer may accordingly unilaterally withdraw his union recognition, and with it the standing of union officials as employee representatives.

Although the Court has been unequivocal in its rejection of suggestions that the directive imposes a uniform level of employee protection throughout the Community, there is still scope for an argument to the effect that, notwithstanding differences in national labour laws, Community law guarantees to workers covered by the directive a minimum standard of employee protection. The Court of Justice seeks to ensure the protection of the fundamental rights contained in the European Convention for the Protection of Human Rights and Fundamental Freedoms and other similar charters. These rights include, in Article 11(1), the right to form and join trade unions for the protection of the individual's interests. According to the case law of the European Court of Human Rights this right does not include a concomitant right to the formal recognition and consultation of such unions by the state and by employers for the purposes of collective bargaining.[16] In Community law, by contrast, in addition to protecting the right of employees to join a particular union where consultation between management and labour is provided for by particular Community legislation (for example, the Acquired Rights and the Collective Redundancies Directives) it has been suggested that there must then be some (legally enforceable) mechanism in the Member State for the compulsory designation or appointment of workers' representatives where employers are not prepared voluntarily to recognise such representatives.[16a]

15   Case 101/87 *P Bork International A/S in liquidation v Foreningen af Arbejdsledere i Danmark* [1988] ECR 3057, [1989] IRLR 41 at 44.
16   See, in particular, *National Union of Belgian Police Case* Series A, Volume 19, Decision 12 April 1975, Judgment 27 October 1975 at para 38, pp 17-18; *Swedish Engine Drivers' Union Case* Series A, Volume 20, Judgment 6 February 1976; *Schmidt and Dahlstroem Case* Series A, Volume 21, Judgment 6 February 1976.
16a   Case C-382/92 *Commission v UK*, Opinion of Advocate-General Van Gerven of 2 March 1994 at para 14. Judgment awaited.

Liquidation, receivership and administration orders

The directive has been held not to apply to transfers which occur in the course of insolvency or bankruptcy proceedings involving the liquidation of a business under the supervision of the national courts,[17] unless Member States have, on their own initiative, decided to apply the principles of the directive to such transfers. [18]

By contrast, transfers in the course of proceedings which do not involve the total liquidation of a company but instead permit its continued trading, for example, under receivership or administration orders, may be covered by the directive.[19]

Waiver of protection and enforcement of rights under the directive

Since the directive has primarily a social purpose, the Court has held that the protection afforded by the directive is mandatory. As a matter of public policy, then, employees are not entitled to waive the rights given them by the directive, for example, as regards continuity of employment. Rights so protected by the directive cannot be restricted, even where the employee has consented to this restriction. Their existence is and is independent of the will of the parties.[20]

However, the directive does not require that an employee be transferred to a new employer against his will. This would be contrary to one of the fundamental rights of an employee, namely to choose whom he works for. [1] Accordingly, an employee otherwise subject to a transfer may object to his individual contract of employment being transferred and thereby fall outside the protection of the directive. If, however, he does not object to the transfer of his employment, he cannot after this transfer seek to enforce rights and obligation arising out of the employment

---

17 Case 135/83 *Abels v The Administrative Board of the Bedrijfsvereniging voor Metaalindustrie en de Electrotechnische Industrie* [1985] ECR 469.
18 Case 186/83 *Arie Botzen v Rotterdamsche Droogdok Maatschappij BV* [1985] ECR 519.
19 Case C-362/89 *D'Urso v Ercole Marelli Elettromeccanica Generale SpA* [1991] ECR I-4105. The situation in *Litster v Forth Dry Dock* [1990] 1 AC 546 was an example of a transfer in the course of a receivership.
20 Case 324/86 *Foreningen af Arbejdsledere i Danmark v Daddy's Dance Hall A/S* [1988] ECR 739, [1988] IRLR 315.
1 Joined Cases C-132,138,139/91 *Katsikas v Konstantinidis* [1992] ECR I-6577, [1993] 1 CMLR 845, [1993] IRLR 179.

relationship against his original employer, unless the Member State has specifically provided for the joint liability of the original and the new employer in this regard. [2]

Implementation in the United Kingdom

Correct implementation of this directive has proved to be particularly problematic for the United Kingdom. The Transfer of Undertakings (Protection of Employment) (TUPE) Regulations 1981[3] were intended to implement the Acquired Rights Directive into UK law. However, the regulations as originally drafted failed to cover one class of employees, namely those who were employed in undertakings which are not in the nature of a commercial venture. The regulations also provided for consultation about a transfer only with any recognised trade unions. Failure so to inform and consult allowed for an order against the employer for payment of an amount of money no greater than two weeks' wages of each employee affected by the transfer. Further, the regulations did not render any dismissal made because of the transfer void, but provided simply that such a dismissal would constitute unfair dismissal for the purposes of the existing employment protection regulations.

In October 1992 the European Commission took the United Kingdom before the European Court of Justice under Article 169 for its failure to fulfil its obligations under the Treaty in respect of its implementation the Acquired Rights Directive.[4] In response to this Article 169 action, the United Kingdom government passed the Trade Union Reform and Employment Rights Act 1993, s 33 of which amends the existing TUPE regulations with a view to bringing them fully into line with the Acquired Rights Directive. Further, following the decision in *Katsikas v Konstantinidis* [5] the UK regulations, which provided originally for the automatic transfer of the rights and obligations arising out of the employment relationship to the transferee employer,[6] were also amended to provide for the employee's right to refuse to be transferred to a new employer. Exercise of this right means, however, the automatic termination of the contract of employment and is not to be treated as either redundancy

2   Joined Cases 144,145/87 *Berg and Busschers v Besselsen* [1988] ECR 2559, [1989] IRLR 447.
3   SI 1981/1794.
4   Case C-382/92 *Commission v United Kingdom* notification in OJ 1992 C306/11. The Opinion of the Advocate-General was delivered on 2 March 1994, but the judgment of the Court was awaited at the time of writing.
5   Joined Cases C-132,138,139/91 *Katsikas v Konstantinidis* [1992] ECR I-6577, [1993] 1 CMLR 845 [1993] IRLR 179.
6   See *Newns v British Airways plc* [1992] IRLR 575.

or unfair dismissal. There is no provision in the Act that any of these amendments should be retrospective.

UK case law on the transfer of undertakings

It is clear from *Litster v Forth Dry Dock* [7] that the House of Lords has accepted that the unamended TUPE Regulations 1981 should be construed even against private parties in the light of European Community directives and relevant case law of the European Court of Justice given that the domestic regulations in question were specifically intended by Parliament to implement the directive.

As noted in Chapter 2, in *Litster* the House of Lords effectively amended and judicially updated the apparently unambiguous provisions of the TUPE Regulations in order to make them comply with the changing case law of Court of Justice on the interpretation of the Directive. In order to ensure that the UK regulations reached the same result as the directive, words were read into the TUPE regulations so that they applied not only to persons 'immediately before the transfer' but also to any individuals who would have been so employed had they not been dismissed beforehand for reasons connected with the transfer. A broader purposive reading was taken of the UK regulations. This was in accordance with the national courts' duty under Article 5 of the Treaty of Rome to ensure the full and effective protection of Community law rights.

However, subsequent case law of the UK courts on the TUPE Regulations, in particular of the Employment Appeal Tribunal, appears to have failed to give sufficient weight to the directive and case law of the European Court of Justice in interpreting and applying the regulations. Thus, in *Expro Services Ltd v Smith* [8] the Employment Appeal Tribunal suggested that the TUPE Regulations be applied only in a case in which it can be said that the undertaking (or part thereof) transferred operated as a 'commercial venture' prior to the transfer. And in *Stirling v Dietsmann Management Systems Ltd* [9] the Employment Appeal Tribunal in Scotland found that the TUPE Regulations did not apply to a situation in which the relevant employers operated a ship manning contract for a fixed fee plus costs, since under the terms of the contract the employers had no possibility of making any trading profit or loss and thus could not be said to be a 'commercial venture'.

7   *Litster v Forth Dry Dock* [1990] 1 AC 546 at 555.
8   *Expro Services Ltd v Smith* [1991] IRLR 156, [1991] ICR 577.
9   *Stirling v Dietsmann Management Systems Limited* [1991] IRLR 368.

In more recent cases[10] the Employment Appeal Tribunal under the chairmanship of Wood J seem to suggest that the applicability or otherwise of the directive to cases involving the privatisation of local authority services is entirely a matter of the particular facts and circumstances. The Tribunal apparently concentrates on the *Spijkers* test of a continuing identifiable economic unit and ignores the concern with the fact of a continuing activity and the protection of employee's rights shown in *Rask* and *Sophie Redmond*. [11]

Notwithstanding that the Employment Appeal Tribunal provides authoritative guidance to the industrial tribunals on matters of law, where the higher tribunal has given insufficient weight to relevant considerations of Community law, then the lower tribunals cannot consider themselves bound by their decisions and should not be regarded as in any way a precedent to be followed by industrial tribunals. [12]

Better guidance has been given to industrial tribunals by the decisions of the High Court in *Kenny v South Manchester College* [13] where it was found in the light of the Community case law (and notwithstanding the non-commercial undertaking exclusion) that the transfer of prison educational services from local authority control to further education corporations following compulsory competitive tendering constituted a transfer covered by the Acquired Right Directive. Citing this case with approval, the court in *Porter and Nanyakkara v Queen's Medical Centre (Nottingham University Hospital)* [14] relied on the direct effect of the directive and found that the transfer of supply of paediatric and neo-natal services from two district health authorities to an NHS Trust constituted a legal transfer for the purposes of Article 1(1) of the Acquired Rights Directive.[15]

The whole matter is obviously one of great political sensitivity in the United Kingdom. If the directive can apply to the privatisation of public services, then the existing rights of persons employed in those services will be protected. This may affect the economising aspects of the present UK Government's policies of privatisation, in particular the compulsory competitive tendering of and for local authority services and the market testing of national health services.

10 See *Wren v Eastbourne Borough Council* [1993] IRLR 425; *Dines v Initial Health Care Services Ltd* [1993] ICR 978. The latter case was, at the time of writing, under appeal to the Court of Appeal.
11 See the Advocate-General's Opinion of 23 February 1994 in Case C-392/92 *Christel Schmidt v Savings and Loan Bank of the Former Bordesholm, Kiel and Cronshagen District*. The judgment of the Court of Justice was still awaited at the time of writing.
12 Case 166/73 *Rheinmühlen-Düsseldorf v Einfuhr- und Vorratsstelle für Getreide und Futtermittel* [1974] ECR 33.
13 *Kenny v South Manchester College* [1993] IRLR 265.
14 [1993] IRLR 486.
15 See also *R v Secretary of State for Education and Science, ex p the National Association of Teachers in Further and Higher Education*, Mann LJ and Leonard J, QBD, 5 October 1992.

As noted in Chapter 2, there is an argument that persons who have been deprived to date of the protection of the directive, or the right to object thereto may have a claim in damages against the UK Government for its failure properly to implement Community law under the general principles established by the Court of Justice's ruling in *Francovich*.[16]

THE DIRECTIVE ON THE PROTECTION OF WORKERS' RIGHTS ON INSOLVENCY

This directive[17] required Member States to establish a guarantee fund to finance the payment of pay which remains due to employees on the insolvency of their employers. In the United Kingdom the directive was implemented by ss 106 and 122 of the Employment Protection (Consolidation) Act 1978 and by the establishment of the State Redundancy Fund contributed to by employers and underwritten by the government. The directive would appear to be insufficiently precise to have direct effect. Notwithstanding this lack of direct effect, it was the Italian Government's failure to implement this directive, despite a successful Article 169 action raised against it by the Commission, which resulted in the *Francovich* judgment. As a result of this ruling the Italian State was found liable to make the appropriate compensation payments to the otherwise unprotected employees.[18]

THE DIRECTIVE ON WRITTEN PARTICULARS IN EMPLOYMENT CONTRACTS

This directive[19] obliges employers to provide employees written details of the principal conditions of their employment within eight weeks of starting work and to be notified in writing of any substantial changes in their contract details. This directive will require only minor changes in the pre-existing UK law on written contract particulars, contained in ss 1-11 of the Employment Protection (Consolidation) Act 1978. The

---

16 Joined Cases C-6,9/90 *Francovich and Bonifaci v Italy* [1991] ECR I-5357, [1992] IRLR 69, [1993] 2 CMLR 66.
17 Directive 80/987/EEC, OJ 1980 L 283/23.
18 See now Case C-334/92 *Teodoro Wagner Miret v Fondo de garantia salarial* ECJ, 16 December [1993] ECR (not yet reported) where the Court held that in providing no protection for senior management of an insolvent company the Spanish Government had failed properly to implement the directive and so left itself open to *Francovich* damages claims from such employees.
19 Directive 91/533/EEC, OJ 1991 L288/32.

appropriate amendments to UK law have been made in Sch 4 of the Trade Union Reform and Employment Rights Act 1993.

THE DIRECTIVE ON THE PROTECTION OF SELF-EMPLOYED COMMERCIAL AGENTS

This directive[20] aims to harmonise national rules on the rights and obligations of commercial agents and their principals. It requires substantial changes in the existing common law of agency in both England and Scotland. Accordingly, both the United Kingdom and Ireland were granted an extended period of time (until January 1994) in which to implement it.[1] The directive governs, in particular, the remuneration of commercial agents and guarantees their right to commission on relevant transactions by the principal both during and, in certain circumstances, even after the termination of the agency contract. Under the directive the agent is entitled to receive full payment in respect of any transaction predominantly attributable to the agent's work during the period of agency (Art 8). Periods of notice are laid down for the due termination of an agency contract concluded for an unlimited period (Art 15). The extent to which restraint of trade clauses might be enforced after the termination of an agency contract is also specified in the directive (Art 20). The agent will generally be entitled to an indemnity or compensation for loss of commission on the termination of his agency (Art 17).

PROPOSALS FOR FUTURE DIRECTIVES

There are numerous proposals from the Commission regarding directives on the establishment of a European Works Council;[2] on worker participation on the boards of companies;[3] on employee participation in profits;[4] on working conditions, social protection and health and safety of part-time, seasonal and temporary workers;[5] on the employment conditions of workers temporarily posted to other Member

20 Directive 86/653/EEC, OJ 1986 L382/17
1   See the Commercial Agents (Council Directive) Regulations 1993 (SI 1993/3053).
2   OJ 1991 C39/10 as amended by OJ C336/11.
3   COM (89) 268. On 27 July 1992 the Council of Ministers adopted a non-legally binding recommendation on employee share ownership.
4   COM (91) 259, OJ 1991 C24.
5   OJ 1990 C224/4/9, OJ 1990 C305/8.

States.[6] Further progress on many of these proposals at the European level depends largely on the agreement of the United Kingdom.

RESTRICTIVE EMPLOYMENT COVENANTS AND COMMUNITY LAW

Given that one of the main principles of the European Community has been free movement of workers and the promotion of free competition, the question arises as to the enforceability under Community law of restrictive covenants which limit or prohibit an individual from working within certain geographical areas and/or business sectors.[7]

The Court of Justice has described free access to employment as 'a fundamental right which the Treaty confers individually on each worker of the Community.'[8] This right is derived from Article 48 of the Treaty which has been found by the Court to be directly effective against both public authorities and private parties.[9] Subject to limitations justified on grounds of public policy, public security or public health, Article 48(3) provides that workers should have the right to accept offers of employment actually made and to move freely within the territory of the Member States for that purpose.

The right to set up business within the Community, the freedom to trade, has also been described by the Court as 'a fundamental right ... of which the Court [of Justice] ensures observance'.[10] This right is derived from Article 52 of the Treaty which has also been found to be directly effective[11] and is to be respected by the state and by private parties.

It is at least arguable on the basis of this fundamental rights jurisprudence that Community law might apply to restrictive covenants which seek to limit taking up employment or starting a business purely within the territory of a Member States.[12] In addition to a social policy which seeks to protect individual employees, the Community is based on the idea of

---

6   OJ 1991 C225/6.
7   In *Morris Angel & Son Ltd. v Hollande* [1993] IRLR 169 the Court of Appeal held that such restrictive covenants could be enforced by the transferee of a business against former employees of the transferor by virtue of the TUPE Regulations. No points of Community law appear to have been argued before the court.
8   Case 222/86 *UNECTEF v Heylens* [1987] ECR 4097 at 4117, para 14.
9   Case 41/74 *Van Duyn v Home Office* [1974] ECR 1337, [1975] Ch 358.
10 Case 240/83 *Procureur de la Republique v ADBHU* [1985] ECR 520 at 531.
11 Case 2/74 *Reyners* [1974] ECR 631.
12 Compare Case 175/78 *R v Saunders* [1979] ECR 1129. See also Case 180/83 *Moser v Land Baden Wurttemburg* [1984] ECR 2539, [1984] 3 CMLR 720 for another example of 'reverse discrimination' against a Member State's own nationals. No cross-border element appeared to have been required in Case 260/89 *Elleniki Radiophonie Tileorasi v Dimotiki Etairia Pliroforissis* [1991] ECR I-2925 for the Court to apply its fundamental rights jurisprudence.

free trade and the need to ensure full and fair competition (see Art 85 and 86 of the Treaty). It may well be that applying such considerations, Community law will come to different conclusions as to the reasonableness of such restrictions.

Finally it should be noted that in the case of self-employed commercial agents, Article 20 of Directive 86/653[13] requires that restraint of trade clauses shall be valid only if concluded in writing and relate to the geographical area and/or group of customers and to the kind of goods covered by his agency under the contract. Such restraint of trade clauses would be valid for no more than two years after the termination of the agency contract.

BIBLIOGRAPHY

Butterworths *Compendium of EC Employment and Social Security Law* (1990) Butterworths.
M Duggan *Business Reorganisations and Employment Law* (1992) Longman.
P Elias and J Bowers *Transfer of Undertakings: the legal pitfalls* (4th edn, 1992) Longman.
Encyclopaedia of Employment Law (looseleaf) Sweet & Maxwell Volume 1, Part 1, Division A, Volume 2, Part 3.
Harvey on Industrial Relations and Employment Law (looseleaf) Butterworths, Volume 3, Section P.
J McMullen *Business Transfers and Employee Rights* (2nd edn, 1992) Butterworths.
F Younson *Employment Law and Business Transfers: a practical guide* (1989) Sweet & Maxwell.

---

13   OJ 1986 L382/17.

Chapter 13

ENVIRONMENTAL PROTECTION AND PLANNING LAW

INTRODUCTION

Environmental law is concerned with the protection of the physical environment for the benefit of the public in general. The first Community directive dealing with environmental protection was adopted in 1975[1] and, despite the lack of any explicit legal provision giving the Community competence in this field, environmental protection was declared by the Court of Justice to be 'one of the Community's essential objectives'.[2] More than 100 Community instruments dealing with environmental protection had been adopted before the Single European Act introduced three new articles into the Treaty of Rome, Articles 130r to 130t, making the achievement of a high level of environmental protection a legitimate end in itself for the Community. Articles 130r to 130t have since been expanded by amendments introduced in the Maastricht Treaty.

Article 130r now sets out the objectives of and principles to be followed by the Community in the area of environmental protection. These include preserving, protecting and improving the quality of the environment; encouraging prudent and rational utilisation of natural resources; protecting human life and promoting international measures where appropriate to deal with transnational environmental problems. The principles to be applied by the Community in the area include that there be a presumption in favour of precautions, that a preventive strategy is to be preferred to a remedial one, that environmental damage should be rectified at source, that the polluter should pay and that the requirements of environmental protection should be wholly integrated

1 Directive 75/439/EEC, OJ 1975 L194/23 on oil waste disposal.
2 Case 240/83 *Procureur de la République v ADBHU* [1985] ECR 531.

into the definition and implementation of other Community policies. Article 130s provides for the procedure to be followed in realizing the objective of the environmental policy as set out in Article 130r.[3] The article also makes it clear that the Community has competence to adopt measures relating to town and country planning and land use matters. Article 130t allows Member States to maintain or introduce more stringent environmental protection measures provided that these are compatible with the Treaty[4] and are duly notified to the Commission.[5]

Other Treaty articles may also form the basis for measures which could result in environmental protection: for example, the regulation of pesticide use under the agricultural provisions of Article 43, the regulation of aircraft noise under the transport provisions of Article 84 and the introduction of an energy tax under the fiscal provisions of Article 99.

There are over 350 Community directives, regulations and decisions concerning environmental matters currently in force. The Community legislation in the area is vast and constantly changing. A full list of the relevant provisions as they have been amended over time is published every six months by the Commission in the *Directory of Community Legislation Currently in Force.*

Rather than attempt any comprehensive survey of the Community's full environmental programme this chapter sets out the main directives in a number of areas which have proved to be fruitful sources of litigation.

WATER

The Community's involvement in setting clean water standards is a particularly sensitive matter in the United Kingdom given the recent

---

3   In Case C-300/89 *Commission v Council* ('Titanium Dioxide') [1991] ECR I-2867 the Court held that whenever a proposed Community measure could be said to promote the establishment and functioning of the internal market then the general procedures laid down in Article 100a rather than the Article 130s procedure should be used. However, the amendments to Article 130s after Maastricht have stated in unequivocal terms the circumstances in which particular procedures may be used in environmental matters. The *Titanium Dioxide* decision is thus probably no longer good law. See now Case C-155/91 *Commission v Council* [1993] ECR I-939 where the Court held that a directive with the main object of protecting the environment was properly adopted under Article 130s procedure.

4   See Case 302/86 *Commission v Denmark* ('Danish Bottles') [1988] ECR 4607 from which it would appear that Member States may only introduce a limited range of measures which might affect the free movement of goods within the Community even when such measures achieve a 'very considerable degree of protection of the environment'.

5   See also Article 100a(4) on notification to and confirmation by the Commission on the application of national provisions on environmental protection among other matters.

privatisation of water utilities in England and Wales and the proposals to hive off responsibility for water in Scotland from local authorities to new independent agencies.

The United Kingdom was recently found to have failed to fulfill its obligations under Community law in that the bathing water in Blackpool, Formby and Southport was found to have fallen short of Community minimum standards.[6]

Community legislation has, firstly, sought to prevent the discharge of dangerous substances into water and, secondly, to set minimum quality standards for the water available to the consumer. Such standards obviously vary depending on how the water is intended to be used (eg for drinking, bathing or eating the fish which swim in it).[7]

With a view to limiting discharge of pollutants into water, a framework directive was adopted in 1976.[8] Daughter directives relating to the discharge of specific chemicals including cadmium, mercury and titanium dioxide were subsequently adopted within the terms of the framework directive. The Ground Water Directive[9] is intended to control pollution of underground water in direct contact with the earth against discharges or seepage into it of certain specified 'dangerous substances'. Appendix 1 of the directive sets out a list of substances, discharges of which should, in general, be banned. Appendix 2 sets out a list of substances, discharges of which should be limited.

WASTE

Current Community legislation

The question of the disposal of waste is also a particularly sensitive matter in the United Kingdom where fears are sometimes expressed by

---

6   Case 56/90 *Commission v UK (Re Blackpool Beaches)* 14 July [1993] ECR I-4109.

7   The Surface Water Directive 75/440/EEC, OJ 1975 L194/26 deals with fresh water from which drinking water is intended to be taken; the Bathing Water Directive 76/160/EEC, OJ 1976 L31/1 applies to sea water as well as to running and still water where bathing is authorised or permitted; The Fresh Water Fish Directive 78/659/EEC, OJ 1978 L222/1 regulates the quality of inland fishing waters; the Shellfish Directive 79/923/EEC, OJ 1979 L281/47 deals with shore water quality; the Drinking Water Directive 80/778/EEC, OJ 1980 L229/11 applies to water intended for human consumption and sets out various parameters (as regards constituent elements, colour, temperature) which constitute the maximum concentrations of each of these which Member States may lawfully permit; the Urban Waste Water Directive 91/271/EEC, OJ 1991 L134/40 sets out detailed requirements regarding the collection and treatment of urban waste water.

8   Directive 76/464/EEC, OJ 1976 L129/23.

9   Directive 80/68/EEC, OJ 1980 20/43.

environmental pressure groups that the present UK Government's commitment to a deregulated free market in all things may lead to the United Kingdom becoming the dustbin of Europe. Waste treatment and disposal is, however, the subject of increasing regulation at the European level.

Under the auspices of the framework Waste Directive 75/442[10] numerous regulations and directives have been adopted regulating toxic and dangerous waste. This original framework directive has been substantially amended by Directive 91/156.[11] The framework applies to the substances set out in Annex I of the Directive (the waste list). Steps are to be taken to minimise the need to dispose of waste by developing clean technologies, as well as new techniques to dispose of dangerous by-products in waste. Member States are encouraged to develop recycling policies. Any waste which unavoidably arises has then safely to be disposed of in a way which does not imperil human or animal health or damage the physical environment. To this end, Member States are required to establish an integrated waste disposal network to dispose of waste as near as possible to the production site. The cost of such waste disposal falls to be borne by the producer of the waste.

Hazardous waste, as specified in the hazardous waste list, is dealt with by Directive 91/689.[12] This directive does not apply to domestic waste, for which a new separate directive is proposed. Periodic inspection of the premises of hazardous waste producers is required under the directive. This directive, which must be implemented by 12 December 1993, is complementary to the framework Waste Directive. A further directive has been proposed in relation to the incineration of hazardous waste.[13]

A directive has been proposed on the disposal of waste by landfill to encourage overall reduction in the use of this method of disposal because of fears of possible contamination of ground-water from leakage.[14] The proposal specified the types of waste which might be used in landfill sites. An operator will be held strictly liable for damage to and impairment of the environment caused by landfill waste. Landfill sites will only be able to be operated under licence. Each operator of a landfill site will be required to provide financial guarantees to cover the cost of closing the site and treating it thereafter. Another proposed directive seeks to encourage re-cycling of packaging.[15]

---

10 Directive 75/442/EEC, OJ 1975 L194/39.
11 Directive 91/156/EEC, OJ 1991 L78/32.
12 Directive 91/689/EEC, OJ 1991 L337/20.
13 COM (93) 296 final - SYN 406, OJ 1993 C190/5.
14 COM (93) 275 final - SYN 335, OJ 1993 C212/33.
15 COM (93) 416 final - SYN 436, OJ 1993 C85/1.

Finally there is now a proposal for a Council regulation on the supervision and control of shipments of waste within, into and out of the European Community.[16] This supplements the existing Directive 84/631[17] on the supervision and control within the Community of the transfrontier shipment of hazardous waste.[18] The declared purpose of this provision is to put an end to 'waste tourism' within the Community as well as the export of Community waste to developing countries.[19]

Civil liability in respect of damage caused by waste: a proposed directive

There was, at the time of writing, a proposal for a Community directive imposing civil liability for environmental damage or injury caused by waste.[20] The directive which applies to all waste (other than nuclear and certain hydrocarbon emissions) generated in the course of commercial activities imposes strict liability (without the need to prove fault) on the producer of the waste. 'Producer' is defined very broadly as 'any person who, in the course of a commercial or industrial activity, produces waste and/or anyone who carried out pre-processing, mixing or other operations resulting in a change in the nature or composition of this waste.' 'Producers' also includes importers into the Community and if the actual producer cannot be identified, any holder of the waste or disposer of the same sat an authorised disposing plant. The producer as so defined will be held liable for death or personal injury to individuals as well as for any significant physical, chemical or biological deterioration of the environment for a period of 30 years from the date when the incident giving rise to the damage occurred. *Locus standi* is explicitly extended to environmental interest or protection groups.

---

16 Council Regulation 259/93 EEC, OJ 1993 L30/1.
17 Directive 84/631/EEC, OJ 1984 L326/31.
18 See Case C-2/90 *Commission v Belgium ('Walloon Waste')* [1992] ECR I-4431, [1993] 1 CMLR 365.
19 COM (92) 121 Bull EC 3-1992, para 1.2.129 and Bull EC 10/1992, para 1.3.99.
20 COM (89) 282, OJ 1989 C 251/3 as amended by OJ 1991 C 192/6. For an ultimately successful attempt to invoke strict liability at common law for pollution from raw materials see *Cambridge Water Co v Eastern Counties Leather plc*, House of Lords, 9 December 1993.

ENVIRONMENTAL IMPACT REPORTS

The Environmental Assessment Directive [1] requires consideration to be given to the effects on the environment of both public and private development projects before planning or development consent may be granted. The appropriate authority with responsibility for development control must consider the environmental impact assessments produced together with any representations from environmental bodies and the general public before determining whether or not consent should be given to the project in question.

The directive fell to be implemented in national law by 3 July 1988. The United Kingdom failed to implement the directive fully by this date and produced a lengthy series of statutory instruments in the course of 1988 and 1989 which were intended to cover the various types of developments encompassed by the directive. These include afforestation, land drainage schemes, salmon farming, the building and extension of harbours, road construction, electricity and pipe-line works as well as general town and country planning developments.

Questions arose before courts in England and Scotland respectively, firstly, as to whether or not the directive could be directly effective and secondly, whether on its proper construction it applied to projects which were already in the pipeline but for which no final approval had been given as at the date of its due implementation.

In *Twyford Parish Council v Secretary of State for Transport* [2] it was held that the directive was unconditional and sufficiently precise to have direct effect after the time limit for its implementation had expired in relation to the types of development set out its in Annex I. It could, therefore, be relied upon to seek an environmental impact report as regards a proposed motorway extension even in the absence of appropriate national regulations. However, it was also held that on a proper construction of the directive any project which had been beyond the initial planning stage as at 3 July 1988 fell outside its scope. No environmental assessment was therefore required in the case of the M 3 motorway extension at Twyford Down.

In *Kincardine and Deeside District Council v Forestry Comrs* [3] Lord Coulsfield, sitting in the Outer House of the Court of Session, held that the same directive could not be directly relied upon in the case of a grant application for an afforestation project. He held that the directive gave Member States a discretion as to whether or not environmental impact

---

1   Directive 85/337/EEC, OJ 1985 L175/40 as amended by Directive 89/428/EEC, OJ 1989 L201/56.
2   [1993] 1 Environmental Law Reports 37, [1992] 1 CMLR 276.
3   1992 SLT 1180, [1993] 1 Environmental Law Reports 151.

assessments were required for the developments listed in Annex II to the directive which included 'initial afforestation where this may lead to adverse ecological changes'. Accordingly, since no implementing national regulations were in force at the time of the initial application for the afforestation grant, there was no obligation to seek an environmental impact report.

These findings both as to direct effect and application to pipeline projects are provisional in the sense that it is the European Court of Justice alone which has final say in interpreting and in determining the direct effect of Community provisions.

ACCESS TO ENVIRONMENTAL INFORMATION

A Community directive[4] provides for public access to environmental information held by public authorities in the Member States. Under the UK regulations implementing this directive the public have a right to information contained on public registers such as the pollution consent registers of Her Majesty's Inspectorate of Pollution, the National Rivers Authority and local authorities. In addition, environmental information not held on the statutory registers is to be made available to the public, subject only to confidentiality based on commercial, personal or national security considerations.

Access to general environmental information and monitoring will be improved also by the European Environmental Agency which was set up by a Community regulation[5] to create an information network, provide a report on the state of the environment every three years and otherwise collate, record and assess environmental data.

THE ECOLABEL SCHEME

Under Council Regulation (EEC) 880/92[6] a voluntary scheme was set up to allow manufacturers to seek official labelling of their products as environmentally friendly. The idea behind the scheme is that consumers will more readily buy such products and so manufacturers will be encouraged to produce ecologically sound goods. The scheme does not apply to food, drink or pharmaceutical products. A total assessment of the products is made, looking not only to their mode of manufacture but

---

4   Directive 90/313/EEC, OJ 1990 L158/56
5   Council Regulation (EEC) 1210/90, OJ 1990 L120/1.
6   OJ 1992 L99/1.

their subsequent life and disposal taking into account impact on soil, water, air, noise, generation of waste, energy efficiency and consumption of resources. The criteria for assessment will be laid down by the Commission while the scheme will be administered by specialist bodies in each Member State. In the case of the United Kingdom the UK Ecolabelling Board was set up in November 1992.

There is also a proposal for a Council regulation[7] setting up an eco-audit scheme whereby business would carry out an environmental review of their industrial sites and set up an environmental management system with the objective of improving their general environmental impact and performance. These eco-friendly sites could then be officially registered and so improve the public profile of the businesses.

IMPLEMENTATION IN THE UNITED KINGDOM

Current implementation by the United Kingdom of the various Community directives has largely been by way of the Control of Pollution Act 1974 and regulations made thereunder. The relevant basic national legislation now includes the Environmental Protection Act 1990, the Water Act 1989 (as amended by the Water Industry Act 1991 and consolidated in the Water Resources Act 1991) and the Water Supply (Water Quality) Regulations 1989 (SI 1989/1147).

THE PROBLEM OF *LOCUS STANDI* AND ENVIRONMENTAL LAW

Environmental law, as opposed to, for example, the law of nuisance, is concerned with the protection of collective rights to the environment. The environment is, by definition, public space. The question arises as to how the environmental rights guaranteed by Community law might be enforced, both against the Member State and private parties. There is little authority directly on the point. In *Commission v Germany* the Advocate-General stated that individuals might rely directly on the minmum quality standards set out in the various anti-pollution/ environmental protection Community measures.[8]

---

7   COM (91) 459 final, OJ 1992 C76/2.
8   Case 361/88 *Commission v Germany: Re Air Pollution* [1991] ECR I-2567, [1993] 3 CMLR 821 the opinion of the Advocate General Mischo at 848.
9   See Ludwig Kraemer 'The Implementation of Community Environmental Directives within Member States: some implications of the direct effect doctrine' (1991) 3 *Journal of Environmental Law*. See also Andrew Geddes '*Locus Standi* and EEC Environmental Measures' (1992) 4 *Journal of Environmental Law* 29.

It has been suggested that where a Community environmental measure can be said to have direct effect in the sense of (i) being precise and unconditional, (ii) leaving no margin of discretion in its performance to the Member States, and (iii) being designed or intended to protect individuals or association or their rights in the field of health and welfare, then any individual affected by the failure of the appropriate authority to enforce such rights will have a right of action under Community law which the national courts require to uphold. These measures might include those which: lay down limit values for concentrations of particular substances in the environment; prohibit certain activities or the use of certain substances; or specify that individuals or interests groups have a right to be informed or consulted.[9]

This reference to the direct effect of environmental norms seems to envisage that they might be enforced in national courts by individuals. In Scots law it is a prerequisite for any court action that a party can show both title to sue in the sense of being a 'party ... to some legal relation which gives them some right which the party against whom he raises the action either infringes or denies'[10] and to have 'a material or sufficient interest'[11] in the outcome of the action. In *Kincardine and Deeside District Council v Forestry Commissioners,* [12] however, the submission that a directive could be enforced by an individual only where it conferred rights on that individual was rejected by the Court. In the English case of *Twyford Parish Council v Secretary of State for Transport* [13] it was suggested by the court that any person actually prejudiced by the failure to respect a directive would have sufficient title to raise an action for its breach.

In any event, a purposive approach has to be taken to the relevant Community provision, whether or not it has direct effect. National legislation requires to be read, as far as possible, in a way which conforms to the result sought by the Community directive. In the case where an emanation of the state is a defending party to an action and the Community provision is suitably precise and unconditional, any provisions of national law contrary to the Community directive may be suspended. Finally, the duty under Article 5 of the Treaty to give full effect to Community law applies not simply to the national courts of the Member States but also to national administrative authorities who are equally required to observe (and give precedence to directly effective) provisions of Community law.[14] Enforcement of this duty might be also be sought directly before national courts.

10 *Dundee Harbour Trustees v Nichol* 1915 SC (HL) 7.
11 *Scottish Old People's Welfare Council, Petitioners* 1987 SLT 179 at 186-7.
12 *Kincardine and Deeside District Council v Forestry Commissioners* 1992 SLT 1180, [1993] 1 Environmental Law Reports 151.
13 [1993] 1 Environmental Law Reports 37, [1992] 1 CMLR 276.
14 Case 103/88 *Fratelli Costanzo v Comune di Milano* [1988] ECR 1839, [1990] 3 CMLR 239.

BIBLIOGRAPHY

N Haigh *Manual of Environmental Policy: the EC and Britain* (Longman 1992 loose-leaf).

D Hughes *Environmental Law* (2nd edn, 1992) Butterworths.

S Johnson and G Corcelle *Environmental Policy of the EEC* (1989) Graham & Trotman.

A Kiss and D Shelton *Manual of European Environmental Law* (1993) Grotius Publications.

L Kraemer *EEC Treaty and Environmental Protection* (1990) Sweet & Maxwell.

L Kraemer *Focus on European Environmental Law* (1992) Sweet & Maxwell.

D Vaughan QC *EC Environmental and Planning Law* (1991) Butterworths.

Chapter 14

INTELLECTUAL PROPERTY

INTRODUCTION

Intellectual property rights, which restrict the exploitation of products on a personal and frequently on a territorial basis, by their very nature tend to inhibit the free movement of goods between Member States, and to distort free and open competition. Further, regulation of intellectual property at a purely national level may increase transaction costs and produce other complications for companies seeking to operate in other Member States. There is, on this basis, a clear case for the application of Community-wide intellectual property principles in the Community-wide market.

WHEN IS COMMUNITY LAW RELEVANT?

The United Kingdom, of course, has its own highly developed body of intellectual property law which in many instances, notably with respect to the doctrine of exhaustion of rights, differs considerably from Community law. The first question to be addressed by a practitioner is, therefore, whether Community law has any relevance to the intellectual property problem with which he has been presented.

The basic rule is that the domestic legal regime will prevail in purely internal scenarios but Community law will supplant UK law in all instances where trade between Member States is involved. Community intellectual property principles fall under the heading either of competition law, or of free movement of goods law. The parameters of the 'Community element' of trade between Member States in these two areas are similar, although not identical, and reference should be had to Chapters 10 and

20. The important point to be noted is that a Community element can be identified in many situations which appear, at first glance, to be purely internal or domestic. A licensing agreement between two British companies in respect of a patent for a product which is made in the United Kingdom, and has only ever been sold in the United Kingdom may nevertheless trigger Community competition rules if, for example, it restricts the export of the product to other parts of the Community.

In addition, a gradual harmonisation of intellectual property rules is under way and will lead eventually to a uniform Community patent and trademark and to analogous copyright protection throughout the Member States. When considering the registration of a patent, therefore, the benefits of the European patent, soon to be replaced by the Community patent, for companies trading elsewhere in the Community should be noted. British trademark and copyright protection has been subject to modification on the basis of Community directives and reference should be made to the Community instrument where the construction of the British implementing legislation is at issue.

INTELLECTUAL PROPERTY RIGHTS AND THE FREE MOVEMENT OF GOODS

Article 36 of the Treaty recognises the protection of 'industrial and commercial property' as a derogation from the principle of free movement of goods,[1] in so far as this does not constitute a means of arbitrary discrimination or a disguised restriction on trade between Member States. Article 222 provides further that the Treaty shall not prejudice national rules governing property ownership. Nevertheless, the clear conflict between the basic goal of market integration and the partitioning of the market which national, territorial, intellectual property protection tends to promote has necessitated the intervention of Community law to limit the effect of national provisions.

The judicial device employed to justify this intervention has been the distinction between the existence of national intellectual property rights, which the Community law cannot question, and their exercise, which the Court of Justice reserves the right to control. The general rule in relation to the exercise of intellectual property rights is that the Court will condone the protection of those rights which constitute the bare essentials, the 'specific subject matter', of the property concerned.

1　The phrase 'industrial and commercial property' has been broadly interpreted. The term 'intellectual property' can readily be substituted.

Exhaustion of rights principle

British law does not regard the exploitation of a product in a state other than the United Kingdom as exhausting the intellectual property rights of its owner. Under Community law, however, once the holder of an intellectual property right markets or consents to the marketing of his product in any Member State of the Community, his rights are exhausted. He may not invoke them subsequently to prevent parallel imports, that is, imports of the product from other Member States into the state(s) where he has marketed, or consented to the marketing of, his product, nor to interfere with the sale or use of the product there. The specific subject matter of property thereby consists only in the guarantee of exclusive rights in respect of the first marketing of the product, whether this marketing is direct, or by means of the grant of licences to third parties.

This principle has been applied to most forms of intellectual property. In *Centrafarm v Sterling Drug*,[2] Sterling held patents for a drug in Britain and Holland. It tried to prevent Centrafarm, a Dutch company, from buying the drug in Britain, where it was appreciably cheaper, and importing it into Holland. The Court held that the function of a patent was to reward the creative effort of the inventor. The specific subject matter of the patent, that is, the attributes which were sufficient to achieve that goal, consisted of the exclusive right to use an invention with a view to manufacturing it and putting it into circulation for the first (but only the first) time.

Patent rights could be used to oppose imports from elsewhere in the Community where the element of consent to marketing was absent. This would be the case where, for example, a product has been manufactured by a third party in another Member State which did not offer patent protection, without the knowledge or consent of the patent holder, or where the original owner of the patent in another Member State was legally and economically independent. There could, however, be no question of a company blocking the import of a product which had been marketed in another Member State with his consent. This would constitute a blatant attempt to partition the Community market on a national basis.

Similarly, the specific subject matter of a trademark has been held to be the exclusive right to use the mark for the purpose of putting products bearing the mark into circulation for the first time. The right holder is entitled to protection against competitors wishing to take advantage of the status and reputation of the trademark by selling products illegally bearing the same mark.[3]

2   Case 15/74, [1974] ECR 1147.
3   Case 16/74 *Centrafarm v Winthrop* [1974] ECR 1183; Case 102/77 *Hoffman-La Roche v Centrafarm* [1978] ECR 1139; Case 3/78 *Centrafarm v American Home Products* [1978] ECR 1823.

The Member States of the Community differ widely in their protection of copyright. The Court has held, nevertheless, that in Community law the essential function of copyright is to protect the moral rights in the work and ensure a reward for creative effort.[4] The specific subject matter of copyright is then a reservation of the exclusive right to reproduce the protected work.[5] The British Copyright, Designs and Patents Act 1988, it should be noted, gives only limited recognition to the moral rights of the author.

The principle of exhaustion of rights, based, more or less uniformly, upon the consent to marketing within the Community, has also been applied to performing rights,[6] industrial designs,[7] and plant breeders' rights.[8] Community law also protects know-how, guaranteeing the right to control the first public disclosure of the protected information and to restrain others from exploiting it until it has been disclosed publicly.

The true basis of the exhaustion of rights principle is not the fact that the patent holder has received the economic reward inherent in having a monopoly in the product in question, but merely that he has consented to the placing on the market of the product in question.[9] The owner must, however, consent in a real sense to the exploitation of his product and the placing of a product on the market by means of a compulsory licence does not, on this basis, exhaust the owner's rights.[10]

The consent doctrine did not, however, prove adequate to define the limits of what the Court regards as the specific subject matter of trademarks. This includes the right to prevent any dealing with the marked product which is likely to impair the guarantee of origin provided by the mark. Accordingly, the Court has qualified its approach in respect of the protection of owners of pharmaceutical trademarks against competitors who import and repackage marked drugs.[11]

4   Case T69/89 *RTE v Commission* [1991] 4 CMLR 586.
5   See also Cases 55 and 57/80 *Musik-Vetrieb Membran v GEMA* [1981] ECR 147.
6   Case 62/79 *Coditel v Ciné Vog Films (No 1)* [1980] ECR 881. Performing rights are generally treated under the heading of free movement of services.
7   Case 144/81 *Keurkoop v Nancy Kean Gifts* [1982] ECR 2853.
8   Case 258/78 *Nungesser v Commission (Maize Seeds)* [1982] ECR 2015.
9   Case 187/80 *Merck v Stephar* [1981] ECR 2063.
10 Case 19/84 *Pharmon v Hoescht* [1985] 3 CMLR 775; Case 341/87 *EMI Electrola v Patricia* [1989] ECR 79. See Cases C235/89 and C30/90 *Commission v United Kingdom and Italy: Re Compulsory Patent Licences* [1992] ECR I-829 on the British provisions for the issue of compulsory patent licences.
11 See *Case 102/77 Hoffman-La Roche v Centrafarm* [1978] ECR 1139; Case 3/78 *Centrafarm v American Home Products* [1978] ECR 1823. Case 1/81 *Pfizer v Eurim-Pharm* [1981] ECR 2913 illustrates that loopholes still exist for the careful parallel importer.

Common origin principle

The Community doctrine of exhaustion is one important way in which Community free movement of goods law restricts the scope of British protection of intellectual property rights. The doctrine of common origin, expounded by the Court in *Van Zuylen v Hag*,[12] was another. The common origin principle would prevent the invocation of trademark rights against goods bearing an identified mark having the same origin. It applied regardless of whether the product in question has been previously marketed in another Member State, and regardless of whether the previous owner consented to the sale of the mark to different owners.

The applicants in *Van Zuylen* had acquired the Hag trademark by way of a Belgian subsidiary of a German company which was appropriated by the Belgian state after the Second World War. There was no question of the German company having consented to the marketing of Hag in Belgium, so when the applicants tried to prevent the import into Belgium of Hag coffee made in Germany, they could not rely upon the exhaustion of rights doctrine. They succeeded, however, because their mark had the same origin as the German Hag trademark. The principle seemed to apply only to trademarks which, given their unlimited duration, have a potentially more serious and enduring effect in partitioning national markets than other forms of intellectual property right.

The Belgian mark was then sold to another company and another case arose when the Belgian company tried to export to Germany. The Court reversed its position reasserting once more the importance of the consent of the trademark owner to the manufacture or marketing elsewhere in the Community goods bearing his mark: *CNL Sucal v Hag*.[13] The common origin principle is, it seems, no more, and a trademark owner can prevent the import of goods bearing the same mark unless he has consented to the marketing of products bearing his mark elsewhere in the Community.

The common origin principle must be distinguished from the situation where a trademark owner tries to prevent the import of products bearing a similar, and thereby confusing, mark. In *Terrapin v Terranova*,[14] the Court allowed Terranova, a German manufacturer of building materials to prevent the registration in Germany of the trade name of the British company, Terrapin, which manufactured similar products, on the basis that it would confuse customers. This principle has also been applied to industrial designs.[15]

---

12 Case 192/73, [1974] ECR 731.
13 Case C10/89, [1990] ECR I-3711.
14 Case 119/75, [1976] ECR 1039.
15 Case 144/81 *Keurkoop v Nancy Kean Gifts* [1982] ECR 2853.

INTELLECTUAL PROPERTY RIGHTS AND
COMPETITION LAW

Intellectual property rights protect their proprietor from competitive pressures as a reward for his input into the product. As such, their protection must be squared with the competition provisions of the Treaty of Rome. Again, the Court has drawn a clear distinction between the existence of intellectual property rights, which cannot infringe Community competition law, and their exercise, which is subject to restriction in the light of Articles 85 and 86.[16]

Intellectual property rights, as above, can only be exercised to the extent of their specific subject matter, in conformity with the doctrine of exhaustion of rights. The protection afforded to the specific subject matter of patents, the guarantee that the patent holder has the exclusive right to use an invention, extends to many forms of patent licensing agreements. The latter may be held to anti-competitive, and in breach of Article 85(1), where, for example, the licensee's marketing activities are restricted. 'Sole' licensing agreements, which prohibit the licensor from appointing further licensees within the territory of the agreement and 'exclusive' licensing agreements, which provide further that the licensor himself shall not exploit the property within the territory have frequently fallen foul of Article 85, but do not automatically do so.

Patent licensing agreements can, however, be exempted under Article 85(3), by individual application, or where they qualify for a block exemption pursuant to Regulation 2349/84.[17] Block exemptions aim to provide guidelines for lawyers. Where an agreement can be drafted in the manner suggested by the regulation it does not need to be notified to the Commission but can be presumed to be exempt from the scope of Article 85. The regulation lists certain provisions which are deemed to be anti-competitive but will nevertheless attract a block exemption (Art 1(1)), such as sole and exclusive licensing terms subject to parallel imports being permitted after the first sale of the patented product and prohibitions on the involvement of a licensee in the territory of other licensees.

The presence of certain provisions in an agreement will not affect the availability of a block exemption (Art 2(1)), such as minimum royalty or minimum production requirements and tie-in clauses which require the licensee to purchase goods or services from the licensor, provided that the goods or services are necessary for the exploitation of the licence. There is also a 'black list' of provisions which will prevent exemption

---

16   See, eg, Case 193/83 *Windsurfing International v Commission* [1986] ECR 611.
17   OJ 1984 L219/15, as amended by Reg 151/93, OJ 1993 L21/8.

(Art 3), including 'no-challenge' clauses whereby the licensee promises not to challenge any of the licensed patents or other intellectual property rights belonging to the licensor and restrictions on the maximum number of products which the licensee may manufacture and sell, or the number of times he may perform a patented process.

The Commission has adopted analogous regulations dealing with the exemption of know-how licensing and franchise agreements.[18]

Where a licensing agreement falls outside the terms of the block exemptions it may still be exempted on an individual basis by application to the Commission. The Commission must be convinced that the agreement has overall benefits for competition which outweigh its restrictions.

Copyright licences may contravene Article 85(1), although in practice they have not often done so. Again, Community law is concerned about the improper exercise of rights and the general principles applicable to patent licensing agreements under Article 85(1), seem to apply here.[19] The Court has sanctioned absolute territorial exclusivity in certain circumstances but ruled against licences which it considers to be excessively long and royalties thought to be out of proportion to the value of the licence. A block exemption regulation has not been adopted in respect of copyright but the regulations on patents and know-how give a very good indication of the Commission's attitude in this area and agreements which conform to those regulations would have a good chance of individual exemption.

Trademark licensing agreements may grant a certain amount of exclusivity to the licensee where this is reasonable,[20] but they cannot be used to partition the market by, for example, preventing parallel imports. Bans on exports outside the licensed territory, bans on active sales and restrictions upon challenges to the validity, although not the ownership, of the licensed mark will usually offend against Article 85.[1] As with copyright, there is no block exemption regulation but the patent and know-how regulations provide considerable guidance.

Article 86, prohibiting the abuse of dominant market positions may also be relevant. The bases of an Article 86 action, the definition of the relevant product and geographical markets, and the notion of abuse which are discussed in greater detail in Chapter 10 have been applied equally to intellectual property matters. One area in which Article 86 has proved important is that of the regulation of collecting societies,

---

18 Commission Regulation (EEC) 556/89, OJ 1989 L61/1 on know-how; Commission Regulation (EEC) 4087/88, OJ 1988 L359/46 on franchises.
19 See *Re GEMA*, JO 1971 L134/15, [1971] CMLR D35, JO 1972 L166/22 (No 2).
20 See, eg *Re Campari Agreement* OJ 1978 L70/69.
1   See also Commission Decision 90/186 *Moosehead v Whitbread* OJ 1990 L100/32, [1991] 4 CMLR 391.

organisations representing individual holders of copyright.[2] Another aspect which has come to prominence in recent years is the situation whereby the exercise of an intellectual right can degenerate into the abuse of a dominant position.

In the *Magill TV Guides* cases, an Irish company which wished to publish a weekly television guide was refused permission by the main television networks to use listings information which they held under copyright. The Court of First Instance found each publisher to be dominant in the relatively narrow product market of advance weekly listings for each network and that they had abused this position by refusing to licence the use of their information. The refusal to licence was not consistent with the essential function of copyright, to protect the moral rights of the author and ensure reward for creative effort, but rather, sought to exclude all competition for the purpose of protecting a monopoly position. The publishers were therefore required to provide the disputed information.[3]

The narrowness of the definition of the relevant product market, and the ease with which a finding of abuse was made in these cases seem to indicate a broad basis for the compulsory licensing of intellectual property rights, in contrast to UK law which requires licences in only limited circumstances. Two of the *Magill* cases are currently on appeal to the Court of Justice which has adopted a much narrower approach to this issue in the area of design rights. It has ruled that the essential subject matter of a design right includes the right to prevent third parties from manufacturing, selling or importing products incorporating the design without the consent of the right holder. Certain features of the exercise of this right, such as the fixing of prices at an unfair level, an arbitrary refusal to supply or the insistence upon an excessively long term for the licence could, however, lead to a finding of abuse.[4]

INTELLECTUAL PROPERTY RIGHTS AND UNFAIR COMPETITION

Many domestic legal systems, including those of the United Kingdom, provide further protection for inventors and producers through provisions

2   Case 127/73 *BRT v SABAM* [1974] ECR 313; see also *Re GEMA* JO 1971 L134/15, [1971] CMLR D35, JO 1972 L166/22 (No 2).
3   Case T69/89 *RTE v Commission*[1991] 4 CMLR 586; Case T70/89 *BBC Enterprises v Commission* [1991] 4 CMLR 669; Case T76/89 *ITV Publications v Commission* [1991] 4 CMLR 745.
4   Case 53/87 *CICRA and Maxicar v Renault* [1988] ECR 6039 and Case 238/87 *Volvo v Veng* [1988] ECR 6211.

on unfair competition. A British manufacturer worried about deliberately imitative goods may, for example, bring an action for passing off. The rights which are protected, which are less tangible than intellectual property rights, are not given special recognition under Community law,[5] although action on a larger scale can be taken by the Commission against counterfeit goods entering the Community from third countries. National laws must, nevertheless, comply with the general Community provisions on measures equivalent to quantitative restrictions on the free movement of goods. Broadly speaking, national laws which directly discriminate against goods from other Member States must be justified under the public policy derogations of Article 36 of the Treaty. Those which apply equally to national and foreign goods but which impose a greater burden upon importers than upon domestic producers and traders must fall within the '*Cassis de Dijon*' principle, being in pursuit of an imperative requirement of the public interest.

THE HARMONISATION OF INTELLECTUAL PROPERTY LAW

Besides acting under the free movement and competition law provisions of the Treaty of Rome, Community law has sought to harmonise national laws concerning the protection of intellectual property rights. The administrative advantages of a Europe-wide system will be appreciated by any practitioner who, in attempting to register an intellectual property right in another European jurisdiction, has had to come to terms with the plethora of existing national and transnational regulatory systems. The harmonisation project has incorporated two strategies, the reform of existing national rules with the aim of standardising legal protection at national level, and the introduction of trans-national rights which are equally valid in the territory of all state parties. It has operated at two distinct levels; within the Community itself, and at a broader international level.

Patents

The European Patent Convention essentially provides a central clearing house to facilitate the process of applying for national patents. A single application is made to the European Patent Office in Munich, and if it is

---

5   See, eg, Case 16/83 *Prantl* [1984] ECR 1299.

successful, a grant is made of a bundle of national patents as specified by the applicant. Successful opposition to a patent grant will, however, result in the revocation of all the national patents.

The European Patent Convention will be replaced, within the Community, by the Community Patent Convention, which is awaiting ratification. Under the Community Patent Convention, applications, grants, revocations, transfers and other patent dealings within the Community can, at the option of the patentor, be deemed to be done on a Community-wide basis. Issues of patent validity will be handled in the central European Patent Office, but matters of infringement shall be dealt with, at first instance, by national courts.

The Community patent will simplify multi-national patent applications and considerably reduce transaction costs. Consistent with the Court's case law, the owner's rights will be exhausted when the product is placed on the market in any of the Member States. National patents will continue to exist, side-by-side with the Community patent.

Trademarks

The Community trademark, valid, and having identical effects throughout the Community, has long been under discussion. As with the Community patent, considerable savings of time and money should accompany the centralised registration system. A further advantage is that a trademark will not be cancelled for lack of use if it has been in use in any of the Member States. National trademarks will co-exist alongside the Community system, however, and will remain the only option for the proprietors of the many marks whose registration will be refused owing to conflict with similar marks in existence in the Community.

The Community has also sought, by means of a directive, to approximate national trademark laws.[6] The directive defines 'trademark' in broad terms: 'any sign capable of being represented graphically, . . . provided that such signs are capable of distinguishing the goods or services of one undertaking from those of other undertakings'. It lists, *inter alia*, the cases where a trademark cannot be registered and the rights conferred by registration, and provides for the revocation of trademark rights where the mark has not, without proper reason, been in genuine use for five years.

Among the changes to UK law necessitated by the directive are the enactment of a unitary standard of distinctiveness in place of the two previous standards, the widening of pre-existing definitions of similarity

---

6   Directive 89/104/EEC, OJ 1989 L40/1.

between marks, and infringement of trademark rights, and the provision for registration of the shape and packaging of goods.

Copyright

The Commission has only recently turned its attention to copyright protection. Measures have been adopted concerning the copyright protection of computer software programs,[7] rental and lending rights,[8] and satellite and cable television broadcasting.[9] A recent directive harmonises the term of copyright protection enjoyed by the author of literary or artistic works to seventy years beyond the life of the author.[10]

Other property forms

Progress has been made at the Community level in two areas in particular. A directive has been adopted which protects the topographical configuration of semi-conductor chips.[11] Also, a directive concerning the granting of patents for biotechnological inventions is imminent.

BIBLIOGRAPHY

P Stone *Copyright Law in the United Kingdom and the European Community* (1990) Athlone Press.
R Whish *Competition Law* (3rd edn, 1993) Butterworths.

7   Directive 91/250/EEC, OJ 1991 L122/42; SI 1992/3223.
8   Directive 92/100/EEC, OJ 1992 L346/1.
9   Directive 93/83/EEC, OJ 1993 L248/15.
10 Directive 93/98/EEC, OJ 1993 L290/9.
11 Directive 87/54/EEC, OJ 1987 L24/36; SI 1993/2497.

Chapter 15

MIGRATION LAW

INTRODUCTION

The right of Community nationals to move freely among the Member States is fundamental to the Community project. The implementation of this right within the United Kingdom has necessitated substantial changes not only to the law governing immigration, so as to permit the entry and residence of those endowed with Community law rights of movement, but also to a diverse range of other rules and regulations, so as to guarantee that Community nationals are treated equally once they have entered the United Kingdom.

This chapter gives a brief account of the broad corpus of Community law governing the free movement of persons. It will cover, principally, the right to enter, reside and work and correlative rights, the right to establish oneself as a self-employed person or business, the right to provide and receive services in other Member States and the right to go elsewhere in the Community for educational purposes.

WHEN IS COMMUNITY LAW RELEVANT?

First and foremost, Community law is concerned only with Community nationals. Nationals of states which are not Member States of the Community cannot directly claim rights under Community law, even if they are lawfully resident within the Community. In order to facilitate freedom of movement, however, Community law grants dependent rights to the family of the person who is primarily entitled to them, regardless of their nationality. Large numbers of non-Community nationals are entitled under Community law on this basis.

Each Member State is entitled to determine the scope of its own nationality laws; under British law, British citizens, British subjects with a right of abode in the United Kingdom and Gibraltarians qualify as British nationals for Community purposes.

As in other areas, the application of Community law principles and policies, or, in many cases, the application of those British regulations inspired by the need to implement Community law within this country, is triggered by the presence of a 'Community element' in the factual situation. This element is generally provided by the crossing of a border. In most cases, a British national, or a member of his family, will be claiming his rights in another Member State, or a national of another Member State will be doing the same in Britain, and Community law is clearly relevant.

Some cases involve, however, a Community national claiming rights against their own government; or, someone with rights dependent upon a Community national arguing against the government of the primary right holder.[1] Community law imposes upon Member States only limited obligations towards their own citizens, and the general rule is that it does not apply to situations which are wholly internal to a Member State. Reverse discrimination, whereby a state treats its own nationals less favourably than it treats those of other Member States, is permissible.

Nevertheless, a Community element may be found in some cases of this type, where the applicant has exercised Treaty rights in moving to another Member State and then returns to his own. Whether a person's movement has been sufficiently substantial to trigger the operation of Community law will be a question of fact in each case. The Court of Justice has ruled in favour of an applicant who emigrated from the UK to Germany for two years,[2] but the High Court has refused to apply Community law on the basis of a four month, non-working stay in Belgium.[3] It is likely that British courts will examine closely the facts of the case, and the motives of the applicants, before sanctioning the avoidance of British immigration rules in this type of situation. Movement to another Member State, however, is a sufficient but not a necessary condition for the establishment of the Community element. The important point is that Community law does not apply to activities all the elements of which are confined within a single Member State; actual physical movement is not required.[4]

---

1 Case 44/84 *Hurd v Jones* [1986] ECR 29; Cases 35-36/82 *Morson v The Netherlands* [1982] ECR 3723.
2 Case C370/90 *R v Immigration Appeal Tribunal and Surinder Singh, ex p Home Secretary* [1992] ECR 1-4265; [1992] 3 CMLR 358.
3 *R v Home Secretary, ex p Ayub* [1983] 3 CMLR 140.
4 Case C153/91 *Petit v Office National des Pensions* [1992] ECR 1-4973.

In summary then, a Community element is present, and Community law must be considered in two main situations. Firstly, where the individual is the national of a Community country other than the one in which he is claiming rights, or derives Community rights from such a person. Secondly, where the individual is a national of the state in which the rights are claimed, here the United Kingdom, or derives Community rights from such a person, and the elements of the factual situation to which the claim relates are not confined within the home state.

It should be noted finally that Community law is relevant not only to legislation and other governmental measures in this field, but also to private rules and practices, such as those of professional bodies.[5]

WHO IS ENTITLED TO FREE MOVEMENT RIGHTS?

Once the *prima facie* relevance of Community law has been established it is necessary to examine in greater detail whether the individual or company in question is entitled to Community free movement rights. The general rule is that the personal scope of the Community rules must be determined by Community law itself and any national provisions which purport to define key Community terms at a national level will be condemned by the Court of Justice.

Article 48 of the Treaty provides for the rights of workers, who are employed persons, to be distinguished from the self-employed who benefit from the freedom of establishment (Art 52) and the freedom to provide services (Art 59). The essence of the employment relationship is that during specified hours, the employee performs services for the employer under his direction and in return for remuneration.[6] This definition is subject to the important qualification that the Community rules cover only the pursuit of effective and genuine activities, and exclude those activities which are on such a small scale as to be purely marginal and ancillary.[7] The scope of the term 'worker' is nevertheless to be interpreted broadly, and the Court of Justice has adopted a liberal view of this latter qualification. Many forms of casual, intermittent, part-time and low-paid jobs have been deemed sufficient to confer the status of worker.[8] Whilst it is clear that in some cases, the individual has taken up small-scale employment precisely in order to claim rights under

---

5 See, eg, Case 36/74 *Walrave and Koch v Union Cycliste Internationale* [1974] ECR 1405.
6 Case 66/85 *Lawrie-Blum v Land Baden-Württemberg* [1986] ECR 2121.
7 Case 53/81 *Levin v Staatssecretaris van Justitie* [1982] ECR 1035.
8 Ibid; Case 139/85 *Kempf v Staatssecretaris van Justitie* [1986] ECR 1741; Case 196/87 *Steymann v Staatssecretaris van Justitie* [1988] ECR 3877.

Community law, the Court has held that the motivation for working is irrelevant for definitional purposes.[9]

The definition of 'worker' also includes those people who are looking for work for the first time in a particular Member State,[10] who are 'between jobs',[11] who are involuntarily unemployed,[12] who are undergoing vocational training relating to their previous field of work,[13] and who have stopped work because they are incapacitated or have retired.[14]

Persons wishing to establish themselves in another Member State, that is, the self-employed and those wishing to set up and manage businesses, benefit under Article 52 of the Treaty. The right of free movement in this context also extends, in some respects, to companies and firms, save for those which are non-profit making (Art 58).

Article 59 of the Treaty provides for the abolition of restrictions on freedom to provide services within the Community. The concept of services in Community law is a broad one. The services provisions of the Treaty are expressly stated to be a catch-all regime, covering all things which are not covered by the provisions on persons, goods and capital. The essence of a 'service' is that it is normally provided for remuneration and this covers a wide range of activities, from insurance broking, to television broadcasting to abortion. Certain services provided by the state, such as education, are not, however, provided for the purpose of obtaining remuneration and so fall outside the Community law regime.[15] Community law confers rights upon self-employed providers of services and companies (Art 60) who benefit also from the freedom of establishment, and also, significantly, upon recipients of services, which category encompasses such broad groups of people as tourists, patients and shoppers.[16]

Free movement rights have also been extended to students, the retired and persons who are not otherwise covered by Community legislation, provided that they are covered by health insurance and/or can otherwise support themselves without resort to the social security system of the host state.[17]

9   Case 53/81 *Levin v Staatssecretaris van Justitie* [1982] ECR 1035.
10   Case C292/89 *R v Home Secretary, ex p Antonissen* [1991] ECR I-745.
11   See *Hoekstra (née Unger) v Bestuur der Bedrijfsvereniging voor Detailhandel en Ambachten* [1964] ECR 177.
12   Directive 68/360/EEC, *JO* 1968 L257/13, Art 7(2).
13   Case C357/89 *Raulin v Minister van Onderwijs en Wetenschappen* [1992] ECR I-1027; [1994] 1 CMLR 227.
14   Regulation 1251/70/EEC, *JO* 1970 L142/24.
15   Case 263/86 *Belgium v Humbel* [1988] ECR 5365.
16   Directive 73/148/EEC, OJ 1973 L171/14, Art 1(1)(b); Cases 286/82 and 26/83 *Luisi and Carbone v Ministero del Tesoro* [1984] ECR 377.
17   See Directive 90/365/EEC, OJ 1990 L180/28 (retired persons); Directive 93/96/EEC, OJ 1993 L317/59 (students); Directive 90/364/EEC, OJ L180/26 (persons not otherwise entitled/persons of independent means).

Finally, as noted above, the family members of those directly entitled to free movement rights are accorded subsidiary or dependent rights.[18] Family members include spouses,[19] dependent children and grandchildren, and dependent relatives in the ascending line (parents, grandparents etc).[20] In the case of students, only spouses and dependent children are covered. The status of dependency is to be determined objectively, by reason of the fact that the worker actually provides support; there is no need to investigate whether the recipient really needs it.[1]

One important qualification to be noted is that a person is classified for Community law purposes according to what they are doing, or have done, in the Member State to which they have travelled. For example, an employed person who goes on holiday in another Member State falls within the Community regime not as a worker but as a tourist and recipient of services and his rights are to be defined accordingly. Persons entitled as family members are, of course, family members at all times.

Having outlined the range of persons who may be entitled to Community rights of free movement, it is now necessary to explain in greater detail what those rights of movement entail.

WORKERS

Immigration rights

The migrant has the right to leave his own country for purposes covered by Community law, primarily, to work in another Member State or to receive services there.[2] He has the right to enter other Member States, on production of a passport or identity card and to obtain a residence permit on proof that he has a job. The permission to stay will be consistent with the migrant's stated purposes; temporary or seasonal workers will acquire a more limited permission. Residence permits must be obtained, but they are merely evidential and the right to reside exists independently

---

18 See Regulation (EEC) 1612/68, *JO* 1968 L257/2, Art 10(1); Directive 73/148/EEC, OJ 1973 L172/14, Art 1(1).

19 On the definition of 'spouse' see Case 267/83 *Diatta v Land Berlin* [1985] ECR 567; Case 59/85 *Netherlands v Reed* [1986] ECR 1283 and *R v Home Secretary, ex p Sandhu* (Court of Appeal) [1983] 3 CMLR 131.

20 Compare Art 10 of Regulation (EEC) 1612/68 (workers), Art 1(1) of Directive 73/148/EEC (self-employed), Art 2(2) of Directives 90/364/EEC, 90/365/EEC, 90/366/EEC (retired, students and others).

1 See Case 316/85 *Centre Public de l'Aide Sociale de Courcelles v Lebon* [1987] ECR 2811.

2 Art 2(1) of Directive 68/360/EEC (workers) and Directive 73/148/EEC (self-employed).

of administrative formalities.[3] People looking for work may enter and stay for a sufficient period to appraise themselves of appropriate job opportunities.[4] Families of migrants may have to acquire an entry visa if they are not nationals of a Member State and must supply proof of the family relationship in order to obtain a residence permit.

Workers may lose their right to reside if they become permanently incapacitated through illness or accident, become voluntarily unemployed,[5] or are absent from the country for more than six months.[6] Involuntary unemployment can provide a basis for restricting the duration of a residence permit when it is renewed for the first time.[7] Family rights, which are subsidiary to the rights of the worker himself, will also be affected in such circumstances.

Regulation 1251/70 provides for the right of the worker and his family to remain in a country after the worker has retired or become incapacitated through illness or accident.[8] Even where the worker dies, his family will usually be able to stay on in their adopted country (Art 3(2)).

Public policy derogations

Member States can withdraw immigration rights from persons otherwise entitled to them under Community law on grounds of public policy, public security or public health. The proviso applies to virtually all aspects of entry and residence under Community law. It covers workers (Art 48(3)), establishment (Art 56) and services (Art 66).

The grounds of derogation are, *prima facie*, vague and potentially broad in application but they are to be interpreted strictly,[9] and the exercise of Member State discretion is further structured by directly effective secondary legislation.[10]

Directive 64/221 lists a series of parameters for the use of the public policy (and public security) limitations. They cannot be invoked to serve economic ends (Art 2(2)). The threat to public policy must stem exclusively from the personal conduct of the individual concerned (Art 3(1)),[11] and

---

3   Case 48/75 *Procureur du Roi v Royer* [1976] ECR 497. See also Art 3(3) of Directive 64/221/EEC, 1964 *JO* 850.
4   Case C292/89 *R v Home Secretary, ex p Antonissen* [1991] ECR I-745.
5   See *Giangregorio v Home Secretary* [1983] 3 CMLR 472.
6   Art 7(1) of Directive 68/360/EEC, *JO* 1968 L257/13.
7   Art 7(2) of Directive 68/360/EEC, *JO* 1968 L257/13.
8   OJ 1970 L142/24.
9   Case 41/74 *Van Duyn v Home Office* [1974] ECR 1337.
10   Directive 64/221/EEC, 1964 JO 850.
11   Case 41/74 *Van Duyn v Home Office* [1974] ECR 1337.

must constitute a genuine and sufficiently serious threat to the fundamental interests of society.[12]

Previous criminal convictions cannot *in themselves* constitute sufficient grounds for derogation (Art 3(2)) but past conduct may constitute a present threat to public policy, where, for example, there is evidence that the individual will offend again, or where the past conduct was particularly grave.[13] Whilst individual deterrence may be an acceptable basis for public policy derogation, in view of the emphasis on personal conduct, the Court has added in this context that a desire on the part of the authorities to deter other people from committing similar crimes is not.[14]

With respect to public health, the directive sets out a list of infectious and contagious diseases, such as tuberculosis and syphilis, which can justify a denial of immigration rights. Once an initial residence permit has been issued, however, subsequent infection with one of the listed diseases cannot justify deportation (Art 4(2)). Drug addiction and mental illness are to be treated under the headings of public policy or public security.

As well as substantive limitations upon the discretion of Member States in operating the public policy derogation, Directive 64/221 also lays down a number of procedural safeguards for individuals seeking immigration rights. Persons must be actually notified of any decision to refuse them entry or residence (Art 7), and provided with 'a precise and comprehensive statement of the grounds for the decision', unless this may prejudice state security (Art 6). Articles 8-9 of the directive, setting out requirements for remedies against immigration decisions, are in general satisfied by the operation of the British Immigration Appeal Tribunal. The only significant grey area is where an immigrant commits a criminal offence and a deportation order is made as part of the sentence of the court.[15] There is a temporary right of residence whilst decisions regarding residence permits are taken (Arts 5(1) and 7).

Rights to equal treatment

Regulation 1612/68 lays down a range of rights to which workers and their families are entitled once they have settled in another Member State.[15a] The worker has the right to work under the same conditions as

---

12 Case 30/77 *R v Bouchereau* [1977] ECR 1999.
13 Ibid. See also *R v Home Secretary, ex p Marchon* [1993] 2 CMLR 132.
14 Case 67/74 *Bonsignore v Oberstadtdirektor der Stadt Köln* [1975] ECR 297.
15 See Case 131/79 *R v Home Secretary, ex p Santillo* [1980] ECR 1585.
15a *JO* 1968 L257/2.

nationals of the host state (Arts 1-6); he may not be discriminated against, directly or indirectly, either with respect to access to employment or with respect to conditions of work, such as pay and dismissal, once he has been employed.[16] Workers are also entitled to equal treatment in respect of trade union activities (Art 8), access to housing, including public housing (Art 9), and access to training in vocational schools and retraining centres (Art 7(3)).

Article 7(2) of the regulation entitles the worker to the same social and tax advantages as national workers, and is one of the most important sources of equal treatment rights. The concept of a social advantage has been given the broadest interpretation by the Court of Justice and includes such benefits as discount railcards, guaranteed minimum incomes, interest free loans following childbirth and some types of student grant.[17] People who are merely looking for work cannot claim social advantages.[18]

As for the rights of families of workers, spouses and children are entitled to work in the host state, seemingly on the same, non-discriminatory conditions as workers themselves (Art 11). The social advantages of Article 7(2) must also be afforded to the worker's family,[19] and the worker's children are entitled to access to educational, apprenticeship and vocational training courses (Art 12).

THE SELF-EMPLOYED AND COMPANIES

The rights of self-employed persons to enter and reside in other Member States, are enacted in terms substantially similar to the provisions on workers.[20] The right of residence for providers and recipients of services, as for temporary workers, is co-extensive with their purposes. The public policy limitations upon immigration rights apply equally in this context.

Regulation 1612/68, which confers various other rights upon workers and their families has no direct parallel in relation to the self-employed. However, the Court of Justice has derived similar principles from the

---

16 On language requirements, see Art 3(1); Case 379/87 *Groener v Minister for Education* [1989] ECR 3967.
17 See, eg, Case 32/75 *Fiorini v SNCF* [1975] ECR 1085; Case 65/81 *Reina v Landeskreditbank Baden-Württemberg* [1982] ECR 33; Case 122/84 *Scrivner v Centre Public d'Aide Sociale de Chastre* [1985] ECR 1027.
18 Case 316/85 *Centre Public de l'Aide Sociale de Courcelles v Lebon* [1987] ECR 2811.
19 See, eg Case 261/83 *Castelli v ONPTS* [1984] ECR 3199.
20 Directive 73/148/EEC, OJ 1973 L172/14, on rights of entry and residence is the counterpart of Directive 68/360/EEC, *JO* 1968 L257/13 and Directive 75/34/EEC, OJ 1975 L14/10 on the right to remain in a Member State after self-employment is equivalent to Regulation 1251/70.

general prohibition of discrimination of Article 6 (formerly 7) of the Treaty, and benefits such as the social advantages of Article 7(2) of the regulation and the right to equal access to housing (Art 9) can be claimed by the self-employed (at any rate those who are established in the state in question) on this basis. The Court has, in general, tried wherever possible to adopt a uniform approach and avoid distinction between the rights of workers and those of the self-employed.

The right to establish

The general rule is that individuals from other Community countries are entitled to establish themselves in and pursue a business under the conditions laid down for its own nationals by the law of the country where they have settled (Art 52). A number of directives specific to particular professions have been issued,[1] although the Court has held that the Treaty right to establish is directly effective and does not depend upon further legislation.[2] Discriminatory rules can, therefore, be challenged in national courts on the basis of Article 52 alone.

Community law prohibits overt or direct discrimination on grounds of nationality,[3] and covert or indirect discrimination, such as that effected by residence requirements, which in practice discriminate against foreigners. Indirect discrimination, however, may be justified on objective grounds.[4] Member States remain free to impose restrictions on economic activities which apply equally to nationals and non-nationals.

Finally, the freedom to establish implies the right to be established in more than one Member State. Rules which require individuals to give up an existing establishment are thereby illegal.[5]

Recognition of qualifications

One of the most important aspects of the freedom to establish in another Member State is the recognition of qualifications. Refusal by states, or their professional bodies, to recognise the equivalence of qualifications acquired or training periods completed in other Community countries

---

1   See *Directory of Community Legislation in Force* sector 06.20.
2   Case 2/74 *Reyners v Belgium* [1974] ECR 631.
3   See, eg, Case C221/89 *R v Secretary of State for Transport, ex p Factortame* [1991] ECR I-3905.
4   See, eg, Case 182/83 *Fearon v Irish Land Commission* [1984] ECR 3677.
5   Case 107/83 *Ordre des Avocats au Barreau de Paris v Klopp* [1984] ECR 2971.

could effectively exclude foreign nationals from certain jobs. The principle of mutual recognition is laid down in the Treaty (Art 57) and 'vertical' directives specific to particular professions were issued in implementation of it.[6] Progress was slow, however, and from 1989, the approach to recognition of qualifications not previously covered by directives is to be horizontal; all qualifications of a particular type are to be recognised by the Member States, subject to further adaptation periods or aptitude tests where they differ significantly from the equivalent qualifications in the host state. Directives have been issued covering all higher education diplomas, secondary education diplomas and periods of professional experience unaccompanied by a formal qualification.[7]

The issue of cross-border legal practice, to take one example, has always been one of considerable political sensitivity. The present situation is that legal qualifications must be recognised under the mutual recognition system but an aptitude test will usually be required before an individual qualified in another Member State is actually admitted to practice. In the United Kingdom the respective professional bodies of the Bar and of solicitors in England and Scotland have devised appropriate 'transfer tests' for qualified lawyers.

Companies

Under the Treaty, the freedom of establishment (and the freedom to provide services) apply equally to companies (Arts 58 and 66) and companies have been able to attack rules which discriminate against them by reason of the fact that they are registered in another Member State.[8] The analogy between natural and legal persons is not, however, complete. Specific policy considerations relating to the regulation of companies dictate that many of the rights which individuals have under secondary legislation, such as the right to leave a Member State in order to establish in another, do not apply to corporate bodies.[9] The reality of free movement for companies will be attained only after the completion of the Community's company law harmonisation program (see Chapter 7).

6   See Directory of Community Legislation in Force sector 06.20.
7   Directive 89/48/EEC, OJ 1989 L19/16; SI 1991/824. Directive 92/51/EEC, OJ 1992 L209/25.
8   See, eg, Case 79/85 *Segers v Bestuur van de Bedrijfsvereniging voor Bank- en Verzekeringswezen Groothandel en Vrije Beroepen* [1986] ECR 2375.
9   Art 1 of Directive 73/148/EEC, OJ 1973 L172/14; Case 81/87 *R v HM Treasury and Commissioners of the Inland Revenue, ex p Daily Mail and General Trust* [1988] ECR 5483.

The right to provide services

Self-employed persons and companies may further benefit from the freedom to provide services within the Community. Service provision in the Community context may occur in a variety of ways; the person providing the service may go to another Member State, the person to whom the service is being provided may travel, or indeed, both parties may remain *in situ*, with the service itself crossing a border, as in the case of broadcasting. Restrictions which may prevent or otherwise obstruct the activities of persons providing services are illegal under Community law (Art 59).

It should be noted at the outset that it may be difficult to distinguish in practice between establishment and service provision, particularly where the latter takes place over a lengthy period, or on a regular basis, but the distinction is of some importance in terms of the applicable law.[10] In borderline cases the implications of both the rules on establishment and those on services should be considered. The decision is to be made on the facts by national judges who should note that the law on services is residual, to be applied where the law on workers and establishment does not.

Community law is concerned with essentially two types of restriction on the freedom to provide services. Firstly, rules which directly discriminate against service providers who are not established in the Member State in question. This discrimination may take the form of a requirement of nationality, or, more commonly, of residence.[11] In this context, national rules do not have to bar completely service provision by foreign residents or nationals to fall foul of the Treaty; it is sufficient that they hinder or restrict such activities by applying different criteria to the non-established.[12]

Secondly, Community law is concerned with measures which are indistinctly applicable, that is, which apply equally to established and non-established service providers, but which nevertheless bear more heavily on the latter. In contrast, it has been noted above that measures relating to the freedom to establish which are not discriminatory on the grounds of nationality or residence cannot be challenged under Community law.

---

10 On the distinction, see Case 205/84 *Commission v Germany: Re Insurance Services* [1986] ECR 3755.

11 Case 33/74 *Van Binsbergen v Bestuur van de Bedrijfsvereniging voor de Metaalnijverheid* [1974] ECR 1229; see also Case 39/75 *Coenen v Sociaal-Economische Raad* [1975] ECR 1547.

12 Case 427/85 *Commission v Germany: Re Lawyers Services* [1988] ECR 1123.

All states regulate the provision of certain services with various valid and important considerations of public policy in mind. However, the need to fulfil regulatory requirements may operate as a considerable discouragement to potential service-providers who are established in other Member States. The Court recognises the need for such measures, but insists that they be objectively justified by considerations of the public interest.[13] It is likely, although by no means certain, that this objective justification must proceed along the same lines as the citation of mandatory requirements of the public interest in the field of free movement of goods.[14] The need to ensure the fairness of commercial transactions, to defend consumers, to safeguard public health and to protect the environment would, on this view, all be sufficient. It is clear, however, that these measures are not justifiable where the service provider is subject to analogous regulatory requirements in his home state. The general requirement that the restrictions imposed by a measure must be proportionate to its objectives also applies.

RECIPIENTS OF SERVICES

The category of recipients of services is immense, potentially encompassing anybody who spends money or wants to spend money in another Member State, but the precise scope of the rights of recipients is unclear. In general, two types of right are involved. Firstly, the right to go to another Member State and avail oneself of a service, without restriction.[15] The notion of restriction clearly includes such matters as barriers to immigration, but may be broadly interpreted so as to include, for example, a right to receive information about the services available in other Member States.[16] Secondly, whilst receiving services in another Member State, a person may be entitled to various corollary rights originating in the principle of non-discrimination. For example, a British tourist who was mugged in Paris was, on this basis, able to obtain French criminal injuries compensation which he had been told was available only to French nationals.[17]

---

13 Case C353/89 *Commission v Netherlands* [1991] ECR I-4069; Case C288/89 *Stichting Collectieve Antennevoorziening Gouda v Commissariaat voor de Media* [1991] ECR I-4007.
14 See '*Cassis de Dijon*', Case 120/78 *Rewe-Zentral v Bundesmonopolverwaltung für Branntwein* [1979] ECR 649. See Ch 20.
15 Cases 286/82 and 26/83 *Luisi and Carbone v Ministero del Tesoro* [1984] ECR 377.
16 Case C362/88 *GB-INNO-BM v Confédération du Commerce Luxembourgeois* [1990] ECR I-667.
17 Case 186/87 *Cowan v Trésor Public* [1989] ECR 195.

THE PUBLIC AUTHORITY EXCEPTION

The rules relating to the free movement of workers do not apply to employment in the public service (Art 48(4)), and Member States can accordingly withhold certain jobs from non-nationals. What does and does not constitute the public service is, however, a matter for Community, not national, law, and the Court of Justice has consistently given as narrow a scope as possible to this concept.

The exception extends to 'posts which involve direct or indirect participation in the exercise of powers conferred by public law and duties designed to safeguard the general interests of the State or of other public authorities.'[18] Such posts presume a special allegiance to the state which can only be provided by nationality. Posts covered by this exception include local authority posts for supervisors, architects, night-watchmen and stock-controllers, managers of public bodies and scientific and technical advisors to the state. Not included are, for example, railway workers, nurses, researchers in public institutions, trainee teachers and teachers in state universities.[19] The exception applies only to conditions of access to public service jobs. It does not justify discrimination against foreigners once they have been appointed.[20]

A similar exception is made in respect of the rules on establishment and services, which do not apply to activities which are connected, even occasionally, with the exercise of official authority (Arts 55 and 66). The Court has interpreted this exception equally narrowly.[1]

STUDENTS

Under the Treaty, the application of Community law in the field of education is limited to the development of a policy for 'vocational training' (Art 128). Through a combination of secondary legislation and judicial policy-making, however, significant rights of access to a wide range of educational facilities across the Community have been developed. This has had a considerable impact on the British university system with large numbers of students from other Community countries applying for

---

18 Case 149/79 *Commission v Belgium* [1980] ECR 3881.
19 Ibid; Case 307/84 *Commission v France* [1986] ECR 1725; Case 225/85 *Commission v Italy* [1987] ECR 2625; Case 66/85 *Lawrie-Blum v Land Baden-Württemberg* [1986] ECR 2121; Case 33/88 *Allue and Coonan v Università degli studi di Venezia* [1989] ECR 1591.
20 Case 152/73 *Sotgiu v Deutsche Bundespost* [1974] ECR 153.
1 Case 2/74 *Reyners v Belgium* [1974] ECR 631.

places and financial support on an equal footing with their British counterparts.

To start with, the term 'vocational training' has been given a broad definition. It extends to any form of education which prepares the student for a qualification for a particular profession, trade or employment, or provides the necessary training and skills for such a profession, trade or employment.[2] University courses fall within this definition so long as they are designed to prepare a person for a career, rather than simply to increase their general knowledge.[3]

In general, three issues arise with respect to the movement of students. Firstly, the right to enter and reside in another Member State for the purpose of taking a course. Secondly, access to places on a course and thirdly, eligibility for grants to cover the costs of a course.

The first problem has been solved in definitive terms by a directive which provides for a right of residence in other Community states for the purposes of pursuing a vocational training course.[4] The student must have sufficient resources to live without resort to the social security system of the host state, and, together with any family members who come with him, must be covered by health insurance. He must prove that he has enrolled as a student in order to obtain a residence permit, which will be limited to the duration of his studies.

As regards the latter two issues, Article 6, the Treaty's general prohibition on discrimination on grounds of nationality, has been held to extend to conditions of access to vocational training.[5] Discriminatory conditions of admission, such as quotas for nationals of other Member States, differential fees, such as previously existed in the United Kingdom, and restricted availability of grants to cover fees can all be challenged by students from other Member States. Maintenance grants, however, are not covered by Article 6, although, as will be discussed below, they may be available under other provisions.

Students may also be entitled to a wide range of free movement rights arising out of their status within another category of Community right-holders.

A Community 'worker' who stops work and takes up a course of study will not lose this status where a connection exists between the course and the worker's previous career.[6] This requirement does not apply where the worker has become involuntarily unemployed. Member States may not

---

2 Case 293/83 *Gravier v Liège* [1985] ECR 593.
3 Case 24/86 *Blaizot v University of Liège* [1988] ECR 379.
4 Directive 93/96/EEC, OJ 1993 C317/59.
5 Case 293/83 *Gravier v Liège* [1985] ECR 593
6 Case 39/86 *Lair v University of Hanover* [1988] ECR 3161.

require an immigrant to work for a certain length of time before qualifying for a grant but people who work as part of the requirements for their course of study are not entitled to the full range of workers' rights, at least in the field of education.[7] As a worker, the student is entitled to the same social and tax advantages as national workers and both fees and maintenance grants have been held to fall within this clause, provided that the course is a vocational one.[8] Workers are also entitled to equality of access to training in vocational schools and retraining centres.[9]

Children of immigrant Community workers are entitled to equal treatment regarding education in the host state.[10] The guarantee applies to general educational and apprenticeship courses as well as to vocational training, and encompasses maintenance grants as well as formal conditions of access to courses and fees.[11] A dependent child of a worker may also be entitled to a grant on the basis that it is an indirect social advantage for the worker himself.[12]

Students attending private sector, non-charitable institutions in other Member States may be able to claim rights as recipients of services and these rights would appear to extend beyond vocational training to other forms of education. Their counterparts in the public sector, however, cannot.[13]

RETIRED PERSONS AND OTHERS

The directives covering retired persons and those not otherwise entitled under Community law confer rights of entry and residence in terms similar to those which are conferred upon workers. Residence permits are to be granted simply on presentation of a valid identity card or passport. As noted above, residence is conditional upon proof of health insurance cover or of sufficient resources to avoid becoming a burden upon the social security system of the host state, in the case of retired persons, and of both in the case of persons not otherwise entitled.

---

7 Case 197/86 *Brown v Secretary of State for Scotland* [1988] ECR 3205.
8 Art 7(2) of Regulation 1612/68, *JO* 1968 L257/2.
9 Art 7(3) of Regulation 1612/68. Grants for university courses are not covered by this provision but do fall within 7(2).
10 Art 12 of Regulation 1612/68.
11 Case 9/74 *Casagrande v Landeshauptstadt München* [1974] ECR 773.
12 Art 7(2); Case C-3/90 *Bernini v Minister van Onderwijs en Wetenschappen* [1992] ECR I-1071.
13 Case 263/86 *Belgium v Humbel* [1988] ECR 5365.

Subsidiary rights to enter and reside and take up employment are granted to spouses and dependent children of persons within this category.

BIBLIOGRAPHY

I MacDonald and N Blake *Immigration Law and Practice in the United Kingdom* (1991) Butterworths Ch 8.
F Burrows *Free Movement in EC Law* (1987) Clarendon Press.
H Adamson *Free Movement of Lawyers* (1992) Butterworths.

Chapter 16

PUBLIC PROCUREMENT

INTRODUCTION

Public procurement, the purchase of goods and services by central, regional and local government, public bodies such as health authorities and public utilities, is one of the newest and fastest growing areas of Community law. The theoretical arguments underpinning the regulation of the award of public contracts are impressive indeed. An estimated 15 per cent of the Community's gross domestic product is spent on government procurement. However, procurement contracts have not traditionally been awarded on the basis of cost and quality alone; other policies, in particular the promotion of national industries, are promoted. As a result, large parts of the Community were protected from the system of fair competition, the 'level playing field', established by Community law.

The exposure of the public procurement market to free and open competition is projected to produce annual savings, from more efficient tendering structures, economies of scale and competitive pricing, of more than £15 billion. Moreover, the European Economic Area Agreement has extended Community procurement rules to the participating EFTA countries, creating a single procurement market of close to £50 billion annually.

What this means in practice is that foreign firms must be given greater access to, and fairer treatment under, British tendering procedures and, conversely, that British firms are now entitled to a range of export opportunities which may not have been open to them previously.

Although the Treaty says nothing specifically about public procurement, certain of its provisions are relevant to the activities of public authorities in this area. Article 6 (formerly 7) prohibits discrimination on the grounds of nationality, Article 52 provides for the abolition of restrictions on the freedom of establishment of nationals, including companies and firms (Art 58(2)), and Article 59 lays down similar rules for the provision of services within the Community. The provisions on the free movement of goods, and in particular Article 30, are also relevant. The bulk of public procurement law is now to be found in secondary legislation but these Treaty articles may all have direct effect under certain circumstances, and so remain important for background argument, and may constitute the sole basis for an action where a procurement matter falls outside the scope of the secondary legislation.

The secondary legislation is in the form of directives which will all ultimately be incorporated into British law, superseding or complementing existing tendering procedures in this country. The directives set (differing) thresholds with respect to the value of the contract up for tender which trigger the application of the Community procedures. In considering the relevance of Community law to a particular contract, it is, therefore, necessary to have regard firstly, to whether it falls within one of the areas of activity covered by the directives, and secondly, to whether its value surpasses the threshold of the relevant directive. Domestic British tendering procedures have, independently of the new Community legislation, recently undergone significant reforms, with the introduction of the compulsory competitive tendering system and it may be necessary in some cases to consider two different procedures and the relationship between them.

SECONDARY LEGISLATION: GENERAL FRAMEWORK

There are four principal, substantive directives to be noted, covering public supply contracts, public works contracts, the public procurement of services and utilities (transport, water, energy and telecommunications). Remedies directives deal with the procedures to be used in their enforcement.

The substantive directives use similar techniques to promote fair competition in the public procurement sector, albeit not in exactly the same terms. Firstly, they attempt to ensure ease of access to the tendering process for all Community companies. Notices of tenders must be advertised promptly in the Official Journal and drawn up in accordance with model notices set out in annexes to the directives. Tenders may not be advertised in the local press before they have been sent for Community-wide publication. Notices of tenders are also available through a computer data-bank known as Tenders Electronic Daily. In addition, public authorities are required to publish in advance their future purchasing requirements.

Secondly, the directives seek to ensure that the selection process is truly competitive by making it as open and as public as possible and preventing public authorities from dealing exclusively with a small number of favoured contractors. Tendering procedures under the directives are of three types: open, where there is no pre-selection of bidders, restricted, where invitations to tender are issued to a limited number of candidates, and negotiated, where the authority consults with a single or a few suppliers. Resort to the negotiated procedure is only allowed under exceptional circumstances and must be justified in a written report. Under the Supplies Directive (93/36/EEC, OJ 1993 L199/54), use of the restricted procedure must be similarly justified, but it enjoys a status equal to the open procedure with respect to works and services.

In open and restricted procedures, no negotiation with candidates or tenderers on fundamental aspects of contracts, and in particular on prices, is permitted.[1] This rule seeks to prevent so called 'sweetheart deals'.

In order to prevent discrimination against firms from other Member States, contracts must be awarded on the basis of either the lowest price, or the 'economically most advantageous offer' and the directives lay down objective criteria which may be considered in relation to the latter. Permitted criteria include quality, technical merit, technical assistance and service, projected delivery date and, of course, price. The criteria to be applied must be listed in the contract notice. Potential contractors may only be eliminated from the tendering process on grounds specified in the directive. These include financial incapacity and lack of professional integrity.

Foreign firms are also protected from indirect discrimination through the insistence by procuring authorities that national technical standards be applied. Subject to limited exceptions, authorities are obliged to have regard to European technical standards, or to national standards implementing European standards, in defining their bids.[1a] In the area of public works contracts the Construction Products Directive, providing for the mutual recognition of certain national standards, supplements existing European standards.[2]

Finally, the directives lay down certain mechanisms which seek to promote the effectiveness of their terms. Under the original public procurement regime, authorities frequently sub-divided contracts in order to circumvent the thresholds above which the provisions of the directives were to apply. Now the value of formally separate contracts awarded at the same time is to be aggregated with reference to financial

---

1 Statement concerning Art 5(4) of Directive 71/305/EEC, OJ 1989 L210/22.
1a See Case 45/87 *Commission v Ireland: Re Dundalk Water Scheme* [1988] ECR 4949.
2 Directive 89/106/EEC, OJ 1989 L40/12; implemented in the United Kingdom by SIs 1991/1620 and 1990/2179.

thresholds. Requirements that authorities report to the Commission on the contracts which they have awarded are intended to secure a general monitoring of compliance with the directives.

It is important to note that the Community regime only applies in situations where the public authority decides to award a contract to perform the required activity. The Community rules can, in some circumstances, legitimately be avoided simply by undertaking the activity in-house. This device is not, however, available to the same extent in Britain since local authorities are now obliged to put a large proportion of the projects they traditionally undertook themselves as a matter of course out to public tender.

The legislative framework must be considered under four headings: public works, public supplies, public services and utilities, which were formerly excluded from the general regime.

PUBLIC SUPPLY CONTRACTS

The Public Supplies Directive applies to contracts 'involving the purchase, lease, rental or hire purchase with or without option to buy of products between a supplier and a public authority'.[3] The contracting authorities covered by the directive are widely defined, including, as well as organs of state, regional and local government, 'other legal persons governed by public law'.[4] The threshold at which the directive comes into force is ECU 200,000 (approximately £140,000).

Procurement of public supplies is complicated somewhat by international regulation under the GATT Government Procurement Code, to which certain agencies of central government are subject.[5] The GATT Code requires non-discriminatory treatment to be accorded to the contractors of all its state parties. Its financial threshold, adjusted annually and published in the Official Journal 'C' series, is substantially lower, approximately £89,000, than that of the Community directive.

PUBLIC WORKS CONTRACTS

The Public Works Contracts Directive applies to contracts for the execution, or both the execution and design, of building and civil

---

3   The legislation governing public supplies contracts has been consolidated in Directive 93/36/EEC, OJ 1993 L199/1; SI 1991/2679.
4   See Annex I to the directive for a full list.
5   See Sch. 1 to the British regulations, SI 1991/2679.

engineering works.[6] The authorities covered are defined in the broad terms of the public supplies directive but a much higher threshold of ECU 5 million, (approximately £3.5 million) is set and in reality only the larger and wealthier arms of the state apparatus will have the need and the resources to undertake projects of this size. The directive covers concession contracts, where consideration for works done consists in whole or in part of the right to exploit them and public authorities are given broad powers to require the involvement of third parties in these contracts.

PUBLIC SERVICES CONTRACTS

The Services Directive defines services as anything which is not covered by its counterpart instruments on public supplies and public works and applies to the same range of public bodies as the directive on public works.[7] Like the Supplies Directive it has a threshold for application of ECU 200,000 (approximately £140,000). The key point to be noted about this directive is that it divides services into two categories, priority and non-priority services. Contracts relating to services in the former category, which includes accounting and auditing, publishing and printing, and cleaning and maintenance services are subject to the full procedures of the directive. Non-priority services, such as legal, educational and health services, are governed only by rules on technical standards and by the obligation to publish details of contract awards.[8]

The directive applies specifically to contracts awarded by private bodies but subsidised by over 50 per cent by a public authority, to defence contracts, subject to Article 223 of the Treaty, the national security escape clause, and to design contests, where a contract is awarded on the basis of a competition which is decided by a jury. It covers the situation where one authority seeks to provide services on behalf of another, but is excluded where the award of a contract is based on an exclusive right conferred by a legal regulation which is compatible with the Treaty.

UTILITIES

The Utilities Directive covers the 'excluded sectors' of transport, water, energy and telecommunications which together account for two-thirds of public procurement turnover in the Community.[9] Certain aspects of these

6 Public works legislation has been consolidated in Directive 93/37/EEC, OJ 1993 L199/54; SI 1991/2680.
7 Directive 92/50/EEC, OJ 1992 L209/1; SI 1993/3228.
8 See Annex I to the directive for a full list.
9 Directive 90/531/EEC, OJ 1990 L297/1; SIs 1992/3279 and 1993/3228.

sectors remain outside the scope of Community regulation, however, notably the purchase of water by water authorities, contracts for the supply of energy, and air and maritime transport.

Significantly, the directive applies not only to public authorities but also to private bodies which operate on the basis of special or exclusive rights granted by public authorities. Privatised utilities such as British Gas, British Telecom and PowerGen are therefore included. The directive has thresholds of ECU 5 million (approximately £3.5 million) for public works, ECU 600,000 (approximately £420,000) for public telecommunications supplies and ECU 400,000 (approximately £280,000) for public supplies in the energy, water and transport sectors.

In general, the directive attempts to ensure a truly competitive tendering process in the 'excluded sectors' in the same way as its counterparts in other areas. An important new departure, however, is the preferential treatment given to Community companies in the eventual selection procedure. Bids from non-Community companies may be rejected unless at least 50 per cent of the products which they incorporate are manufactured in the Community, and a bid from a Community company may prevail over a non-Community bid where it is up to three per cent more expensive.

The Utilities Directive was subsequently amended to include services contracts.[10] The provisions follow closely the pattern in other sectors although one notable difference is that the provision of services 'in-house' in the utilities sector is expressly excluded from the scope of Community rules.

REMEDIES

The main Remedies Directive dealing with the enforcement of the principal public procurement measures reflects a dual approach to compliance.[11] Firstly, the powers of the Commission to supervise fair competition in this sector are strengthened. Aggrieved firms may complain directly to the Commission which will notify the Member State involved so that any infringement can be corrected. If the Commission is not satisfied with the response of the Member State, it may take the matter to the Court of Justice. The Commission will not necessarily act upon complaints, however, and where it does, its effectiveness is frequently dependent upon securing interim relief from the Court.

10 Directive 93/38/EEC, OJ 1993 L199/84.
11 Directive 89/665/EEC, OJ 1989 L395/33. Its terms are covered by other UK implementing legislation.

Secondly, Member States are required to set up 'effective and rapid remedies' to facilitate the domestic enforcement of Community public procurement law by individual tenderers. Review procedures must include the power to suspend the award of contracts in interlocutory proceedings, to set aside contracts unlawfully awarded and to grant damages to persons harmed by the infringement. A firm must prove, however, that it would have been awarded the contract but for the infringement of procurement rules.

The UK regulations expressly state that the duties imposed on the government by the Community secondary legislation are duties which are owed to individual suppliers. Before a contract has been made, the High Court in England, Wales and Northern Ireland and the Court of Session in Scotland have a variety of remedies at their disposal. They may suspend the implementation of the award and then set aside the award of the contract, order the contracting authority to amend relevant documentation and/or award damages. Where a contract has been concluded, however, the only remedy available is in damages. The procedures for awarding the contract cannot be reopened. This restriction does not appear to apply in relation to an in-house award because there is never any contract—an authority does not and cannot contract with itself.

It is debatable indeed whether an in-house award after a tendering procedure can be called an 'award' in the formal sense since this term is defined in the regulations as the acceptance of an offer in relation to a proposed contract, and there is no contract in this context. If this is the case, and the public authority has simply withdrawn the work from open competition, the remedies available to an aggrieved contractor are severely restricted. A purposive interpretation of the regulations would, however, suggest that an award must have taken place.

The Utilities Directive has it own associated Remedies Directive.[12] Most of the comments made in relation to the General Remedies Directive apply here also but the political sensitivities associated with the provision of utilities have necessitated certain changes. For example, review bodies may be empowered to impose fines and take other measures to prevent or punish infringements, instead of suspending or setting aside award procedures. In order to obtain damages, a contractor need only prove that it had a real chance of winning the contract, rather than that it would have won the contract, as under the general Remedies Directive.

The general Community law system of remedies continues to operate alongside the Remedies Directive. Where a directive has not been

---

12 Directive 92/13/EEC, OJ 1992 L76/14; SI 1992/3279.

implemented correctly an individual may be able to rely directly on its terms or require that the national implementing legislation be interpreted in accordance with the terms of the directive. The *Francovich* remedy in damages for breach of Community law may be of particular relevance. It certainly applies where damage has occurred by reason of the non-implementation of one of the Procurement Directives, but it could also be argued that an aggrieved contractor can sue a public authority for breach of Community procurement law, even if it has no right to sue under the national measures implementing the Procurement Remedies Directive.

Where a public contract does not fall within the Community procurement regime, because, for example, it is not valuable enough, or is an exception within the Services Directive, the conduct of the contracting authority may still be challenged on general Community law grounds. The Treaty provisions on free movement of goods and services and freedom of establishment are of particular importance in this respect.

REGIONAL ASPECTS OF PUBLIC PROCUREMENT

Certain of the Member States, including the United Kingdom, operate regional preference systems for the award of some public contracts in order to promote economic growth in underdeveloped areas and so reduce regional disparities. Many of these schemes have remained even after the commencement of the single market although it has been made clear that they must be compatible with the Treaty rules on freedom of movement and non-discrimination.[13]

PUBLIC PROCUREMENT IN THE UNITED KINGDOM

In the United Kingdom, Community public procurement law must be viewed in conjunction with the system of compulsory competitive tendering (CCT) for local authorities and certain other public bodies, first introduced in 1980 and most recently extended in the 1992 Local Government Act. The system intends to ensure that public authorities undertake certain activities only where they can do so efficiently and competitively in relation to the private sector. A wide range of activities which were previously performed 'in-house' as a matter of course must, under CCT, be opened up to public tender.

13   See, eg Case C21/88 *Du Pont de Nemours Italiana Spa v Unità Locale No 2 di Carrara* [1990] ECR I-889; Case 31/87 *Gebroeders Beentjes v Netherlands* [1988] ECR 4635.

Once the decision is taken to offer a contract the Community regime automatically becomes relevant. The result is that there may be two applicable advertising, tendering and selection procedures, the British one and the Community one, and the stricter of the two must be followed.

The first step is to ascertain which of the procurement systems applies, or if they both do. The application of the Community provisions has been discussed above; the subject matter of the contract and its financial value are the crucial variables. The activities subjected to CCT under the Local Government Acts correspond roughly although not exactly to the subject matter of the Public Works and Services Directives. British CCT in general only applies where the gross cost of carrying out the activities in question in the preceeding year exceeded £100,000,[14] substantially less than the threshold under the Public Works Directive and slightly less than that of the Services Directive. Not all authorities will have need to undertake activities of a value which surpasses the Community Public Works threshold of ECU five million, and for them, CCT will be the only system which applies.

The CCT procedures are generally less strict than their Community law counterparts. Specifications of the contract must be given in detail but not according to Community approved technical standards. Advertising need only be in the trade press and a local paper, not Europe-wide. Some overlap in time limits for tendering may occur between the two systems and the greater of the two limits must be followed. The CCT legislation does not lay down specific criteria to be used in evaluating the applicants and selecting the tender,[15] nor does it require that the criteria to be used should be published in advance. The Community directives are much more demanding in this respect and will apply in cases of overlap. Finally, in the matter of remedies, in contrast to the range of options available under the Community regime, CCT provides only for enforcement by the Secretary of State for the Environment who may formally question the activities of particular local authorities and require a new tendering procedure, if necessary without the participation of the local authority's in-house bidder.[16]

---

14 Local Government Act 1988 (Defined Activities) (Exemptions) Order 1988, SI 1988/ 1372.
15 The one exception to this appears to be that under CCT, local authorities are required to consider contractors' race relations records in meeting their obligations under the Race Relations Act 1976, s 71.
16 Local Government Act 1988, ss 13-14.

BIBLIOGRAPHY

P Lee *Public Procurement* (1992) Butterworths.
F Weiss *Public Procurement in European Community Law* (1993) Athlone Press.
A Sparke *The Compulsory Competitive Tendering Guide* (1993) Butterworths.

Chapter 17

SEX DISCRIMINATION LAW

INTRODUCTION

Article 6, formerly 7,[1] of the Treaty of Rome provides that within the scope of the application of that Treaty discrimination by Member States on grounds of nationality is prohibited. Article 48,[2] Article 52[3] and Article 59[4] of the Treaty all provide for equal treatment within the Community for Member States' nationals in the sphere of employment, in establishing a business and in providing services, respectively. All of these Treaty articles have been found by the Court of Justice to have direct effect. They all assert, in a variety of contexts, a right to be treated equally and not to be discriminated against.

From these various articles the Court has concluded that general equality of treatment, that like cases should be treated alike, is one of the basic principles which underlie European Community law.[5] Disparity in treatment by legal provisions and/or by administrative practice must be objectively justified by being shown to rest on legally relevant and significant differences.[6]

---

1   Case 36/74 *Walrave & Koch v Association Union Cycliste Internationale* [1975] ECR 1405.
2   See Case 41/74 *Van Duyn v Home Office* [1974] ECR 1337, [1975] Ch 358.
3   Case 2/74 *Reyners* [1974] ECR 631.
4   Case 33/74 *Van Binsbergen* [1974] ECR 1299.
5   Joined Cases 117/76, 16/77 *Firma Albert Ruckdeschel & Co v Hamburg-DSt Annen ('Quellmehl')* [1977] ECR 1753 at 1769.
6   In Case C-63/89 *Les Assurances de Credit SA and others v Council and Commission* [1991] ECR I-1799, [1991] 2 CMLR 737 it was held that a directive differentiating between the public and private sectors in the matter of export credit guarantees was objectively justified and thus did not offend against the general principle of equal treatment.

Article 119 of the Treaty sets out a context in which sex or gender is to be regarded as an irrelevant or insignificant difference. This article provides that where men and women are carrying out equal work, then they should receive equal pay for it. This article is part of the general social programme of the Community and may be invoked without the need to show its contravention has resulted in any distortion in intra-Community trade. The principle of equal treatment can be relied upon in purely national situations without the need for a cross-border aspect. The Court has characterised the principle of equal treatment of both sexes as 'part of the fundamental rights the observance of which the Court has a duty to ensure'.[7]

Apart from this article on equal pay a number of directives have been adopted by the Community in the field of sex discrimination: the Equal Pay Directive,[8] the Equal Treatment Directive;[9] the Social Security Equal Treatment Directive,[10] the Occupational Pension Directive,[11] and the Self-employed Equal Treatment Directive.[12] Finally, although issued under the second framework directive on health and safety, there is a Directive on Pregnancy and Maternity Leave.[13] The Commission has also adopted a Code of Practice on the Protection of the Dignity of Women and Men at Work which is intended to combat sexual harassment at work. This Code of Practice has been incorporated in a non-legally binding recommendation to the Member States.[14]

ARTICLE 119

Equal pay for equal work

In *Defrenne v Sabena (No 2)* [15] an equal pay case was brought by an air hostess employed in the Belgian national airline. On the basis of Article

---

7   Joined Cases 75, 117/82 *Razzouk & Beydoun v Commission* [1984] ECR 1509 at 1530.
8   Directive 75/117/EEC, OJ 1975 L45/19.
9   Directive 76/207/EEC, OJ 1976 L39/40, applying the principle of equal treatment to access to employment, vocational training and promotion and working conditions.
10   Directive 79/7/EEC, OJ 1979 L6/24.
11   Directive 86/378/EEC, OJ 1986 L225/40.
12   Directive 86/613/EEC, OJ 1986 L359/56.
13   Directive 92/85/EEC, OJ 1992 L348/1 which protects the employment rights of pregnant workers, women workers who have recently given birth and those who are still breast feeding.
14   Commission Recommendation 92/131/EEC, OJ 1992 L49/1. See also the Council Resolution OJ 1990 C157/3 on the protection of the dignity of women and men at work.
15   Case 43/75 *Defrenne v SABENA (No 2)* [1976] ECR 455.

119 of the Treaty the stewardess claimed that she should receive the same pay as male stewards employed by the airline. The Court of Justice held that Article 119 was a sound basis for her claim and could be relied by individuals in each Member State in all Court proceedings against both public and private employers. The ability to use a Community provision against both public and private parties is known as horizontal direct effect. As a directly effective provision, Article 119 can be used both in the absence of domestic legal provisions on equal pay for equal work and over and against any provisions of national law which are inconsistent with this rights as interpreted by the Court.[16]

Pay is defined in the article as being 'the ordinary basic or minimum wage or salary and any other consideration, whether in cash or in kind, which the worker receives, directly or indirectly in respect of his employment from his employer'. The Court of Justice has construed the reference to 'pay' in Article 119 very broadly indeed such that it is held to include the following:

- rights to reduced or free travel on retirement from employment in the state railways;[17]
- payments made by the employer by way of sick pay under national legislation;[18]
- contributions made by an employer to a private pension scheme in the name of his employees[19] (but not payments made by employers into statutory social security schemes);[20]
- severance grant made on the termination of employment under a collective agreement between employer and employees;[1]
- pensions payable from an occupational scheme financed by an employer alone;[2]
- redundancy or pension payments partially replacing the state retirement pension made from a 'contracted out' private occupational pension funds financed by both employer and employees;[3]

16 *McKechnie v UBM Building Supplies (Southern) Ltd* [1991] ICR 710, EAT.
17 Case 12/81 *Garland v British Rail* [1982] ECR 555.
18 Case 171/88 *Rinner-Kuehn v FWW Spezial-Gebaeudereinigung GmbH & Co KG* [1989] ECR 2743, [1989] IRLR 493, [1993] 2 CMLR 932.
19 Case 69/80 *Worringham and Humphreys v Lloyds Bank Ltd* [1981] ECR 767, [1981] IRLR 178, [1981] ICR 558. But compare Case 192/85 *Newstead v Department of Transport* [1987] ECR 4753, [1988] IRLR 66, [1988] ICR 332.
20 Case 80/70 *Defrenne v Belgium* [1971] ECR 445, [1971] 1 CMLR 494.
1 Case C-33/89 *Kowalska v Freie- und Hansestadt Hamburg* [1990] ECR I-2591, [1990] IRLR 447.
2 Case 170/84 *Bilka-Kaufhaus GmbH v Weber von Hartz* [1986] ECR 1607.
3 Case C-262/88 *Barber v Guardian Royal Exchange* [1990] ECR I-1889, [1990] IRLR 240, [1990] ICR 616.

- pensions and benefits paid to the survivors and dependants of employees from a private voluntary scheme financed from contributions made by both employer and employees.[4]

Article 119 has been held also to have direct effect in claims the application by an employer of apparently neutral or gender-blind criteria (eg a lower pay rates between full-time and part-time workers) has in fact resulted in unequal pay between the sexes since the majority of persons employed part-time were women.[5]

Occupational pensions and equal pay

Until the judgment of the Court of Justice in *Barber* it had been generally considered in the United Kingdom that contracted-out private pensions should be considered as a form of social security benefit rather than a form of pay. In matters of social security, Member States had been authorised[6] to defer the compulsory implementation of the principle of equal treatment as regards the determination of the age at which old-age pensions might be paid. Accordingly, contracted-out private pension funds were, in general, managed and paid out on the basis that a woman was entitled to pension at age 60 while a man was only entitled to a pension once he reached 65.

Once private pension payments were re-defined as a form of deferred pay for employment, however, Article 119 required the abolition of conditions which differed according to the sex of the claimant in determining eligibility to a pension. If the judgment in *Barber* were fully retrospective, private pension funds would have been faced with potentially vast claims for back payments of pensions. The Court of Justice, therefore, decided to restrict the effect of its judgment. It held (at paras 44-45) that their finding that private occupational pensions constituted a form of deferred pay which were accordingly covered by Article 119 could not be relied upon in order to claim entitlement to a

---

4   Case C-109/91 *Ten Oever v Stichting Bedrijfspensioenfonds voot her Glazebwassers- en Schoomaakbedrijf* 6 October [1993] ECR (not yet reported), [1993] IRLR 601.

5   Case C-184/89 *Nimz v Freie und Hansestadt Hamburg* [1991] ECR I-297 and Case C-33/89 *Kowalska v Freie- und Hansestadt Hamburg* [1990] ECR I-2591, [1990] IRLR 447. See also Case 170/84 *Bilka-Kaufhaus GmbH v Weber von Hartz* [1986] ECR 1607 and Case 171/88 *Rinner-Kuehn v FWW Spezial-Gebaeudereinigung GmbH & Co KG* [1989] ECR 2743, [1989] IRLR 493, [1993] 2 CMLR 932.

6   See Art 7(1) of Directive 79/7/EEC OJ 1979 L6/24 and Art 9(a) of Directive 86/378/EEC OJ 1986 L359/56.

pension with effect from a date prior to 17 May 1990, except in the case of workers or those claiming under them who had already initiated legal proceedings or raised equivalent claims under national law.

The problem with this limitation of the temporal effect of the judgment was that it appeared to raise more question than it settled. Did the judgment apply to pension rights, both direct and derived, acquired before 19 May 1990? Did it apply to all pensions payable after 19 May 1990 in respect of such pre-existing rights? Did it only to pension rights acquired in respect of service since May 1990? Did it apply only to those workers who became members of and started paying contributions to a pension fund after May 1990? A specific protocol was agreed by the Member States in the Maastricht Treaty specifying that the third interpretation should apply. Various references for clarification of the extent of the retrospectivity were submitted to the Court of Justice. In *Ten Oever* the Court came to the same result as the Maastricht protocol and held that equal pension benefits are required only in relation to benefits payable in respect of periods of employment subsequent to 17 May 1990.[7] In *Neath v Hugh Steeper* [8] the Court further modified this line of case law and departed from the Opinion of the Advocate-General by holding that private companies could continue to calculate pension benefits, in particular transfer values and tax-free lump sum payments, on the basis of actuarial factors which differentiated between men and women.[9]

EQUAL PAY DIRECTIVE

The Equal Pay Directive[10] is intended to eliminate all sex discrimination as regards every aspect of employment remuneration throughout the

---

7 Case C-109/91 *Ten Oever v Stichting Bedrijfspensioenfonds voot her Glazebwassers- en Schoomaakbedrijf* 6 October [1993] ECR (not yet reported), [1993] IRLR 601. At the time of writing, judgment in Case 200/91 *Coloroll Pension Trustees Ltd v Russell*, [1991] IRLIB 431 a UK reference raising similar issues, was still awaited.

8 Case C-152/91 *Neath v Hugh Steeper*, 22 December [1993] ECR (not yet reported), Advocate-General Van Gerven's Opinion 28 April 1993.

9 Case C-132/92 *Roberts v Birds Eye Walls Ltd* 9 February [1993] ECR (not yet reported), [1993] 3 CMLR 822 the Court held that there was no breach of Article 119 when an employer took account of differences in the state retirement scheme to provide for the same overall bridging pension (occupational and state pension combined) for all its former employees regardless of sex, who had been forced to take early retirement due to ill-health.

10 Directive 75/117/EEC, OJ 1975 L45/19.

Member States. It clarifies, and so allows for the better application in practice of, the general principle laid down in Article 119 of the Treaty.[11] It extends Article 119 by providing that the principle of equal pay applies not only to equal or the same work but also to work which may be said to be of equal value. All aspects of employment which might affect pay structure, including job classification are required to be free of any sex discrimination. The directive provides for the abolition of both consensual discriminatory provisions (eg as included in collective agreements or individual contracts of employment) as well as all and any laws, regulations and administrative provisions which run contrary to the principle of equal pay.[12] It has been held by the European Court that in a situation where the employee has produced evidence that women in a particular employment were, in general, paid less than men but that it was unclear whether there was anything about the employer's pay system which was sex discriminatory, the burden of proof of showing the non-discriminatory nature of his pay structure then falls on to the employer.[13]

EQUAL TREATMENT IN EMPLOYMENT DIRECTIVE

The Equal Treatment Directive[14] provides that there should be no discrimination, either direct or indirect, on grounds of sex, or marital or family status in the areas of access to employment, vocational training, working conditions, promotion and dismissal unless it can be shown that sex is a genuine occupational factor.[14a] The directive allows discrimination in favour of women in relation to pregnancy and maternity and permits positive action programmes intended to achieve equality in the workplace.[15]

11 Case 96/80 *Jenkins v Kingsgate (Clothing Productions) Ltd* [1981] ECR 911.
12 This directive was originally held to have been implemented in the United Kingdom by the Equal Pay Act 1975. Following judgment against the United Kingdom for incorrect implementation in Case 61/81 *Commission v United Kingdom* [1982] ECR 2601, [1982] 3 CMLR 284 the Equal Pay (Amendment) Regulations 1983, SI 1983/1794 were passed to ensure that UK equal pay law complied with Community requirements. See *Pickstone v Freemans* [1989] AC 66.
13 Case 109/88 *Danfoss* [1989] ECR 3199, [1989] IRLR 532. This judgment appears to anticipate and rule out the need for the proposed directive on the burden of proof in sex discrimination/equal pay cases COM (88)269, OJ 1988 C176. Adoption of this directive to date has been blocked by UK veto. See also Case 127/92 *Enderby v Frenchay Health Authority* 27 October [1993] ECR (not yet reported), [1993] IRLR 591.
14 Directive 76/207/EEC, OJ L 39/40.
14a Thus, in Case C-345/89 *Stoeckal* [1991] ECR I-4047 the Court held that a national law prohibitng women from working at night was contrary to this directive.
15 In Case C-450/93 *Eckhardt Kalanke v Bremen* notified in OJ 1994 C27/4 the compatibility with the Community principle of equal treatment of an employer's policy to appoint women, other things being equal, has been referred to the Court of Justice. Judgment is awaited at the time of writing.

The Equal Treatment directive was implemented in the United Kingdom by the Sex Discrimination Act as amended by the Sex Discrimination (Amendment) Order 1988, SI 1988/249.

Direct effect of the Equal Treatment Directive

The European Court has held that Article 5 of the directive which prohibits any discrimination on grounds of sex as regards access to and conditions of employment is vertically directly effective.[16] Article 5 of the directive may, therefore, be used in national courts to give directly enforceable rights to individuals who might be said to be employed by 'emanations of the state'[17] but may not be relied upon directly against private employers. Article 6 of the Directive provides that Member States should 'introduce such measures as are necessary to enable all persons who consider themselves wronged by failure to apply the principle of equal treatment ... to pursue their claims by judicial process'. This article has held by the Court to be directly effective in so far as it requires individuals to have access to the courts when alleging sex discrimination.[18] In addition, this same Article 6 of the Directive read with Article 5 of the Treaty has been held to entail that any sanction imposed by national law for unlawful discrimination in terms of the directive should have 'a real deterrent effect on the employer', otherwise real and effective judicial protection of the individual's Community rights would be being denied.[19] In *Marshall 2*[20] the Court of Justice ruled that this sanctions aspect of Article 6 also had (vertical) direct effect. Thus, Article 6 of the directive may be relied upon to as the basis for a claim for adequate compensation, which should include judicial interest at least from the date of any original award.

Child-bearing and the right to equal treatment

The question as to the degree to which the directive prohibits discrimination against women on the grounds of their pregnancy is a vexed one. Some

16 Case 152/84 *Marshall v Southampton and South-West Hampshire Health Teaching Authority* [1986] ECR 723, [1986] IRLR 140, [1986] ICR 335.
17 Case 188/89 *Foster v British Gas* [1990] ECR I-3313, [1991] 2 All ER 705.
18 Case 222/84 *Johnston v Chief Constable of the RUC* [1986] ECR 1651, [1987] QB 129, [1986] IRLR 263.
19 Case 14/83 *Von Colson* [1984] ECR 1891.
20 Case C-271/91 *Marshall v Southampton and South-West Hampshire Health Teaching Authority (No 2)* Advocate General Van Gerven's opinion was delivered on 26 January 1993, the Court's judgment on 2 August 1993.

would argue that if an employer takes any account of a woman's pregnancy in reaching an employment decision then he is guilty of direct sex discrimination since pregnancy has, to date, been a uniquely female phenomenon. Thus, in *Dekker* [1] the Court of Justice held that the refusal to employ a woman on the grounds that she was already pregnant was direct sex discrimination contrary to the directive. On the other hand it might be argued that the law only requires a pregnant woman should be treated in the same way as a man suffering from some medical incapacity for a similar period. Thus, in *Hertz v ALDI Marked K/S* [2] the Court of Justice held that the dismissal of a woman from her employment on medical grounds because of continuing illness after she had given birth would not constitute unlawful sex discrimination if a man who was ill and unfit for work for a similar length of time would have been treated in the same way.

In *Webb v EMO Air Cargo (UK) Ltd* [3] the House of Lords was faced with a situation in which a female employee had been taken on for a specified period to cover another employee's absence on maternity leave. Shortly after beginning her employment the new employee discovered that she was herself pregnant and would, therefore, be unavailable to cover the original employee's maternity leave. She was therefore dismissed from her employment. The question arose as to whether or not such dismissal on the grounds of her pregnancy constituted sex discrimination contrary to the 1976 Equal Treatment Directive. If it did constitute a breach of the directive then the existing UK law in the Sex Discrimination Act 1975 should be interpreted to achieve the same result, in so far as this could be done without distorting the meaning of the statute. Rather then decide whether a positive finding of sex discrimination in such circumstances would distort the meaning of the domestic legislation, their Lordships thought it more appropriate first to make a reference to the European Court of Justice for clarification on the interpretation of the directive.[4] In particular guidance was sought as to whether or not the directive allowed national courts, for the purposes of assessing whether there has been unlawful sex discrimination, to compare the treatment of a pregnant female worker with a hypothetical male colleague suffering some medical incapacity. This, it was hoped, would clarify which of the two possible approaches, as set out in *Dekker* and *Hertz* respectively, should be followed by national courts.

1 Case C-177/88 *Dekker v Stichting Vormingscentrum voor Jong Volwassenen (VJV-Centrum)* [1990] ECR 3941, [1991] IRLR 27.
2 Case 179/88 *Hertz v ALDI Marked K/S* [1990] ECR 3979, [1991] IRLR 31.
3 [1993] 1 CMLR 259, [1993] 1 WLR 49, HL.
4 As Case C-32/93 *Webb v EMO Air Cargo (UK) Ltd* notified in OJ 1993 C75/13.

EQUAL TREATMENT IN SOCIAL SECURITY DIRECTIVE

The Equal Social Security Directive,[5] which applies the principle of equal treatment to statutory social security schemes, is dealt with in Chapter 18.

EQUAL TREATMENT IN OCCUPATIONAL PENSIONS DIRECTIVE

The Equal Pensions Directive[6] is intended to abolish sex discrimination in respect of benefits or access rules to occupational pension schemes run by private employers. Provisions of occupational scheme contravening the principle of equal treatment were to be revised by 1 January 1993. Compulsory application of the principle of equal treatment as regards the determination of pensionable age for the purpose of granting a retirement pension could be deferred until such equality was achieved in statutory schemes or until required by a specific directive. However, this aspect of the directive has in large measure been pre-empted by the decision of the Court of Justice in *Barber v Guardian Royal Exchange* [7] to treat private pensions as a form of deferred pay which are therefore covered by the principle of non-discrimination as set out in Article 119.

As we have seen, as a result of *Barber,* private pension schemes may not discriminate between men and women in relation to retirement ages, regardless of the situation in state schemes. The provisions of the directive may still be relevant in claims of indirect disguised sex discrimination in occupational pensions. The directive fell to be implemented by 30 July 1989 and in the United Kingdom was translated into national law by amendments to the Sex Discrimination Act 1975 introduced by the Social Security Act 1989.

DIRECTIVE ON EQUAL TREATMENT OF THE SELF-EMPLOYED

The self-employed equal treatment directive[8] introduces the principle of equal treatment between men and women engaged in any activity,

---

5   Directive 79/7/EEC on the progressive implementation of the principle of equal treatment for men and women in matters of social security, OJ 1979 L6/24.
6   Directive 86/378/EEC, OJ L225/40.
7   Case 262/88 *Barber v Guardian Royal Exchange* [1990] ECR 1889, [1990] 2 CMLR 513.
8   Directive 86/613/EEC, OJ 1986 L359/56.

including agriculture, in a self-employed capacity. The directive extends protective provisions to self-employed women during pregnancy and maternity. It is intended, *inter alia*, to give protection to married women who participate in the business of their self-employed spouse, but as neither employee or formal partner. It seeks to ensure that these married women working in business with their husbands should have the same access as their spouses to finance and credit, to contributory social security scheme and should equally be able to form companies in connection with their business. In this way will women's contribution to the business be more properly acknowledged.

PROTECTION OF PREGNANT AND NURSING MOTHERS DIRECTIVE

This directive[9] provides that working conditions and working hours of pregnant and nursing mothers have to be adjusted if assessment of the risks involved in their job in their condition reveals a safety or health hazard. Pregnant women may not now be dismissed by their employers for reasons connected with their pregnancy.[10] There is no minimum qualifying period of employment which must be worked before the protection of the directive can be claimed.The duration of maternity leave is set at 14 uninterrupted weeks and during this period the rights of women under their employment contracts are to be maintained (rather than suspended as was previously the case under UK law). In addition the maternity benefits granted to beneficiaries may not be less than those received by a worker stopping work for health reasons. This directive falls to be implemented by 19 October 1994 and has been implemented, in part, in the United Kingdom by the Trade Union Reform and Employment Rights Act 1993.

COMMISSION RECOMMENDATION ON SEXUAL HARASSMENT

Since the decision of the Inner House of the Court of Session in Scotland in *Porcelli v Strathclyde Regional Council* [11] it has been recognised that sexual harassment at work is sexually discriminatory conduct which is covered by the provisions of the UK Sex Discrimination Act 1975. In 1991 the European Commission issued a recommendation on the

9   Directive 92/85/EEC, 1992 OJ L 348.
10   See Case C-177/88 *Dekker* [1991] ECR I-3941, [1991] IRLR 27.
11   [1986] ICR 564, [1986] IRLR 134.

protection of the dignity of employees at work which, among other things, set out criteria for assessing whether or not particular conduct at work could constitute sexual harassment.[12] In *Wadman v Carpenter Farrer Partnership* [13] the Employment Appeal Tribunal under the chairmanship of Wood J instructed industrial tribunals to take into account the contents of this Commission recommendation and Code of Practice in coming to a view as to whether conduct which was the subject of a complaint constituted unacceptable and unlawful sexual harassment.

UNINTENTIONAL INDIRECT SEX DISCRIMINATION IN EMPLOYMENT PRACTICE

Direct sex discrimination, in the sense of an employer treating his employees less favourably on the grounds of their sex than a member of the opposite sex, is clearly contrary to Community law, in the absence of the most compelling reasons of public policy such as national security.[14] However, there may be occasions when an employer treats his employees differently on the basis of grounds other than their sex, for example giving different wage rates or conditions to full-time as opposed to part-time workers. The Court of Justice has held that in certain circumstances difference in treatment of employees on grounds apparently unrelated to their sex may also result in sex discrimination, albeit non-intentional and indirect.

Unintentional indirect sex discrimination in Community law

The Court adopted and adapted from the United States race relations legislation the concept of 'unintentional indirect discrimination' whereby the fact that certain (apparently neutral or gender-blind) criteria required by an employer disproportionately and adversely affect employees of one sex rather than the other is held to establish *prima facie* the existence of sex discrimination, notwithstanding the absence of any evidence of intent to engage in sex discrimination.[15]

---

12 Commission Recommendation 92/131/EEC, OJ 1992 L49/1.
13 *Wadman v Carpenter Farrer Partnership* [1993] IRLR 374.
14 Case 222/84 *Johnston v RUC* [1986] ECR 1651.
15 Case 96/80 *Jenkins v Kingsgate Ltd* [1981] ECR 911, in particular the opinion of Advocate General Warner at 936-7 referring to *Griggs v Duke Power Co* (1971) 401 US 424.

In the face of evidence of a disparate impact between men and women of employment practices or measures, the onus is placed on the party seeking to uphold the validity of those measures to justify them. In the case of an allegedly discriminatory practice by an individual employer the Court has stated that objective justification of employment practices with disparate impact will be established if the measures can be said to be appropriately and necessarily aimed at meeting some 'real need on the part of the undertaking', unrelated to any discrimination on the grounds of sex.[16] Failure of the party seeking to uphold measures to adduce evidence justifying the measures to the satisfaction of the court will lead to the Court to conclude that the measures are a form of disguised sex discrimination which must be declared to be unlawful.[17]

Unintentional indirect sex discrimination in UK law

The concept of indirect sex discrimination was introduced into United Kingdom law by the Sex Discrimination Act 1975. Section 1(1)(b) of the Act is in the following terms:

> '1(1) A person discriminates against a women in any circumstances relevant for the purposes of this Act if— ...
> (b) he applies to her a requirement or condition which applies or would apply equally to a man but—
>> (i)   which is such that the proportion of women who can comply with it is considerably smaller than the proportion of men who can comply with it, and
>> (ii)   which he cannot show to be justified irrespective of the sex of the person to whom it is applied, and
>> (iii) which is to her detriment because she cannot comply with it.

This provision was the subject of litigation on the question as to whether or not it accurately reflected the Court of Justice's concept of unintentional indirect discrimination, at least as applicable to claims of equal pay for work of equal value.

---

16 See Case 170/84 *Bilka-Kaufhaus GmbH v Weber von Hartz* [1986] ECR 1607, para 30 at 1627.
17 See also the decision of the House of Lords in *Rainey v Greater Glasgow Health Board*, 1987 SLT 146.
18 Case C-127/92 *Enderby v Frenchay Health Authority* 27 October [1993] ECR (not yet reported), [1993] IRLR 591.

The Court has ruled that, in order to avoid a finding of indirect sex discrimination, the onus is on the employer to show that statistically significant pay differences between primarily female jobs and primarily male jobs of equal value were objectively justifiable.[18] It was not enough for the employer to show that these differences originally arose for non-discriminatory reasons, neither was the plea of market forces to be regarded as a complete defence for the employer. Further, there was no onus on the employee to identify any particular continuing discriminatory practice or policy which is responsible for these pay differences.[19]

UNINTENTIONAL INDIRECT SEX DISCRIMINATION IN MEMBER STATE'S LEGISLATION

The Court of Justice has extended the notion of unintentional indirect sex discrimination so that it is held applicable not only to the practices of individual employers, but also to the provisions of national legislation of Member States.[20]

However, the Court has consistently stated that the question of whether or not a measure is objectively justified according to the criteria set out by it is a matter of fact for national courts to establish.[1] National judges are therefore required under Community law to consider whether or not national legislative provisions which can be shown to have a disparate impact as between men and women can or cannot be justified on the basis of some national social policy. Further, the judges then have to assess the utility, necessity and appropriateness of such national legislation in achieving that policy.[2]

The presumption in Community law is that the legislation of a Member State having disparate impact will be held to be invalid unless shown to be justified by national policy. The onus is on the governing authorities to appear before the national court to defend the legislation and specify what policy it is aimed at.[3]

---

19 See also *Barber v NCR (Manufacturing) Ltd* [1993] IRLR 95. Compare with *Financial Times Ltd v Byrne (No 2)* [1992] IRLR 163 and *Calder v Rowntree Mackintosh Confectionery Ltd* [1992] IRLR 165.
20 Case C-171/88 *Rinner-Kuehn v FWV Spezial Gebaudereinigung GmbH & Co KG* [1989] ECR 2743, [1989] IRLR 493, [1993] 2 CMLR 932.
1   Case 170/84 *Bilka-Kaufhaus GmbH v Weber von Hartz* [1986] ECR 1607.
2   See *R v Secretary of State for Employment, ex p Schaffter* [1987] IRLR 53 at paras 21 and 37, pp 56-7.
3   See *R v Secretary of State for Employment, ex p the Equal Opportunities Commission* [1992] 1 All ER 545, QBD and [1993] IRLR 7, CA for an attempt to challenge, by way of judicial review, the distinctions made in existing UK employment protection

THE APPLICATION OF COMMUNITY SEX DISCRIMINATION LAW IN THE UNITED KINGDOM

In situations where the Community law right to be treated equally regardless of sex is directly applicable, the Community law concepts of both direct and unintentional indirect sex discrimination will prevail over national law. Community sex discrimination law is directly effective against all parties in the case of equal pay claims under Article 119 and against public sector employers[4] in claims to equal pay and equal treatment under the two Directives 75/117/EEC and 76/207/EEC respectively.[5]

In other situations, for example, a claim to equal treatment under the directive against a private sector employer, the principles of indirect effect[6] and the obligation to interpret national law in line with Community law[7] will apply.

It is now generally accepted that industrial tribunals have jurisdiction in relation to Community law claims,[8] but the question of the precise procedures to be applied to such claims remains a matter of some controversy.

In *Livingstone v Hepworth Refractories*[9] the Employment Appeal Tribunal found that in the absence of domestic procedural rules covering free-standing claims under Community law, claims to direct sex discrimination contrary to Community law should be governed by the procedures of national law under the Sex Discrimination Act 1975. And in *Cannon v Barnsley Metropolitan Borough Council*[10] the Employment Appeal Tribunal suggested that time limits drawn from the provisions of

legislation between full and part-time workers on the grounds of its alleged disparate impact on women and consequent breach of the Community concept of indirect sex discrimination. The House of Lords' judgment was issued on 3 March 1994. See Chapter 2 for a further discussion.

4 Case C-188/89 *Foster v British Gas plc* [1990] ECR 3313 where it was made clear by the European Court that any body which is under the control of the state and is given special powers thereby and made responsible by statute for the provision of a public service may be regarded as an 'emanation of the State' regardless of its particular legal form. See the Court of Appeal judgment in *Doughty v Rolls Royce plc* [1992] IRLR 126.

5 Case 152/84 *Marshall v Southampton and South West Hampshire Area Health Authority* [1986] ECR 723.

6 Case 79/83 *Harz v Deutsche Tradax* [1984] ECR 1921.

7 Case 106/89 *Marleasing SA v La Comercial Internacional de Alimentacion* [1990] ECR I-4135, [1992] 1 CMLR 305.

8 See *Stevens v Bexley Health Authority* [1989] IRLR 240 and *McKechnie v UBM Building Supplies (Southern) Ltd* [1991] IRLR 283.

9 [1992] IRLR 63.

10 [1992] IRLR 474, *Griffin v London Pension Fund Authority* [1993] 2 CMLR 571, EAT.

the Employment Protection (Consolidation) Act, could be applied to claims for non-discriminatory redundancy payments.

In *Rankin v British Coal Corporation* [11] the Scottish Employment Appeal Tribunal found that time limits on the assertion of rights guaranteed under Community directives but not yet properly implemented in the United Kingdom should start to run only once the relevant implementing provisions of national law came into force [12] since it was from this time that it could be said to be reasonably clear to the applicant that they might have existing rights under Community law previously denied them under national law. Citing the Community principle of legal certainty it was suggested by the Employment Appeal Tribunal that a three to six month time limit thereafter would not be unreasonable, given the statutory time limits which applied to analogous claims under national law.

All of these matters as to the correct procedure and time limits to be applied in the case of free-standing claims under Community law may be subject to further clarification, either by the higher courts or by the legislature.

BIBLIOGRAPHY

N Bamforth 'The Changing Concept of Sex Discrimination' (1993) 56 *Modern Law Review* 872.

E Ellis *European Community Sex Equality Law* (1991) Clarendon Press.

Jaques and Lewis *Sex Discrimination and Occupational Pension Schemes* (1993) Butterworths.

C McCrudden *Women, Employment and European Equality Law* (1987) Eclipse Publications.

Nicolson Graham & Jones *EC Pensions Law* (1992, looseleaf) Chancery.

S Prechal and N Burrows *Gender Discrimination Law of the European Community* (1990) Gower.

M Verwilghen *Equality in Law between Men and Women in the European Community* (1987) Presse Universitaires de Louvain.

---

11 [1993] IRLR 69.
12 Following Case C-208/90 *Emmott v Minister for Social Welfare* [1991] ECR I-4269, [1991] IRLR 387, [1991] 3 CMLR 894.

Chapter 18

SOCIAL SECURITY LAW

INTRODUCTION

Article 118 of the Treaty provides that the Commission shall have the task of promoting closer co-operation between Member States in the social field, including the area of social security. Article 51 provides that the Council of Ministers shall, acting unanimously, adopt such measures in the field of social security as are necessary to provide freedom of movement for workers.

There is no specific Community social security system. Instead, Community involvement in the field of social security has been concerned with two separate areas: firstly, making it easier to move from one Member State to another without losing rights to benefits; and secondly, to ensure that the social security systems operated by Member States treat men and women equally.

SOCIAL SECURITY AND THE FREE MOVEMENT OF PERSONS

Community regulation of social security benefits is clearly of considerable importance for the movement of persons between Member States. People may be discouraged from working in other Member States if by so doing they forfeit their social security entitlements. Accordingly, Community law seeks to co-ordinate national social security systems, so as to ensure that no disadvantage as regards social security ensues from exercising the right of free movement.

Community law does not provide for uniform rates and conditions for benefit. Instead, questions of the structure and range of benefits, which benefit to provide to whom and under what conditions are all matters left to the Member States' existing social security systems. Article 51 of the Treaty and secondary legislation issued thereunder apply social security rules to Community nationals as well as to stateless persons and refugees who are permanently resident in one of the Member States.

The Community legislation in this area is in the form of regulations.[1] In accordance with Article 189 these regulations are directly applicable and must accordingly be applied by courts, tribunals and other authorities concerned with the administration of the social security system, where necessary in preference to the requirements of national law.[2]

Individuals must have been insured as employed or self-employed persons under the national insurance scheme of a Member State in order to be covered by the Community regulations. In addition, the dependents of such persons or any survivors of them who are also citizens of the Community are covered by the regulations. Any person with such insurance moving from one Member State to another is covered whether or not he or she has moved for the purpose of employment.[3] 'Member of the family' is defined according to national legislation under which the benefits are provided or claimed (art. 1(f)). A broader, Community definition, has, however, been applied in some cases.[4]

Given that students were granted a right of residence in other Member States with effect from 1 July 1992, the Commission proposed in December 1991 that the existing Community social security regulations be extended to students and their families if they reside in the same Member State.

The categories of benefit covered by Community law are sickness and maternity benefits, invalidity benefits, old-age benefits, survivors' benefits, benefits in respect of accidents at work and occupational diseases, death grants, unemployment benefits and family benefits (Art 4(1)). All general and special schemes, whether contributory or non-contributory are covered (Art 4(2)).

---

1 Council Regulation (EEC) 1408/71, OJ 1971 L149/2 and Council Regulation (EEC) 1390/81 OJ 1981 L143/1. The latter, in general, extends the provisions of the former to cover self-employed persons. Regulation 1408/71 has been subject to codification and much amendment over the years. See most recently Council Regulation (EEC) 1247/92, OJ 1992 L136/1. The procedure for implementing Regulation 1408/71 is laid down in Council Regulation (EEC) 574/72, OJ L74/1 which has also been the subject of much amendment.

2 See *Re a Holiday in Italy* [1975] 1 CMLR 184 and *Re Medical Expenses incurred in France* [1977] 2 CMLR 317.

3 Case 44/65 *Hessische Knappschaft v Maison Singer* [1965] ECR 965.

4 See, eg Case 139/82 *Piscitello v INPS* [1983] ECR 1427. Note that the basic regulation has been amended to provide a standard Community definition of the family with respect to benefits for disabled persons: Council Regulation (EEC) 1247/92, OJ 1992 L136/1.

Certain types of benefit are excluded, the most important of which is 'social assistance', that is, welfare benefits as opposed to social security benefits (Art 4(4)), although the importance of this exception has been reduced considerably by the Court of Justice,[5] and now by legislation.[6] Many benefits have been held by the Court to have both a welfare and a social security function and thereby have been assimilated to social security benefits.[7] Others have been characterised as social security benefits through a broad, teleological interpretation of the Treaty and secondary legislation.[8] The category of welfare benefits seems to be restricted to those benefits whose conferral is contingent upon a discretionary assessment of need or personal circumstances.[9] Furthermore, it has emerged in the case law that what remains of the category of social assistance benefits can be claimed by migrants in the host state as social advantages under Article 7(2) of Regulation 1612/68.[10]

The detailed Community rules on social security co-ordination are founded upon a number of general principles. The overarching consideration is that individuals should not suffer disadvantage in social security terms through exercising their rights of free movement.[11] Thus, a worker moving from one Member State to another is not to lose such rights as he would enjoy under national law alone. However, the basic conditions of affiliation to schemes and entitlement to benefit, and the amount of benefit to be paid remain matters of national law and the Community system will not intervene to help migrants in respect of these matters.[12]

Two principles are founded in the express wording of the Treaty of Rome. The first is that eligibility for and amount of benefit is to be assessed only after aggregating all the periods in which entitlement was acquired under the laws of the various Community countries (Art 51(a)). Entitlements earned in other Member States must be treated as if they had

---

5   See,eg Case 88/88 *Commission v. France* [1990] ECR 3163
6   Council Regulation (EEC) 1247/92, Arts 4-5, extend the scope of Community law to include a variety of non-contributory social security benefits.
7   Case 1/72 *Frilli v Belgium* [1972] ECR 457 (non-contributory, guaranteed minimum income).
8   Case 7/75 *Mr and Mrs F v Belgium* [1975] ECR 679 (special grant for physically disabled persons).
9   See, eg Case 79/76 *Fossi v Bundesknappschaft* [1977] ECR 667.
10 See Case 65/81 *Reina v Landeskreditbank Baden-Wurttemburg* [1982] ECR 33, [1982] 1 CMLR 744 and Case 122/84 *Scrivner and Cole v Centre d'aide social de Chastre* [1985] ECR 1027, [1987] 3 CMLR 638.
11 See, eg Case 24/75 *Petroni v ONPTS* [1975] ECR 1149; Case C10/90 *Masgio v Bundesknappschaft* [1991] ECR I-1119.
12 See, eg Case 110/79 *Coonan v Insurance Officer* [1980] ECR 1445; Case 70/80 *Vigier v Bundesversicherungsanstalt für Angestellte* [1981] ECR 229.

been earned in the state which is calculating the benefit. Secondly, benefits should be exportable, that is, they are to paid in full regardless of where the recipient happens to be living in the Community (Art 51(b)). Article 10(1) of Regulation 1408/71 explicitly applies this principle to invalidity, old-age or survivors' cash benefits, pensions for accidents at work or occupational diseases and death grants. Sickness benefits, family benefits and unemployment benefits are subject to more specific provisions.[13] In the case of unemployed workers migrating in order to seek work, the Court of Justice has ruled that a person who has never worked in the Member State in which he is claiming unemployment benefit is entitled to claim unemployment from that state. The paying state is then entitled to reclaim its payments from the state in which the worker was last employed. There is no general right to unemployment benefit conferred on workers who have never worked in the state in which such benefit is being claimed.[14]

One of the most clearly apparent and widely used of the improvements brought by Community law, the provision of free or low cost medical care whilst on holiday or short business trips in other Member States, was prompted by the principle of exportability.[15] It should be noted, however, that social advantages under Article 7(2) are, *prima facie*, not exportable, except where national law provides otherwise.[16]

Consistent with general principles of Community law, migrants may not suffer discrimination, direct or indirect, on grounds of nationality; they shall be subject to the same obligations and entitled to the same benefits as nationals of the host state (Art 3(1)). In contrast to the general free movement rules, 'reverse discrimination', that is the less favourable treatment of national workers, does not seem to be permitted in the context of social security.[17]

Benefits cannot overlap—migrants cannot be entitled to more than one benefit for the same period of insurance (Art 12(1)). In cases of potential overlap, the 'competent state' (see below) pays the benefit in the largest amount to which the migrant may have been entitled. Any difference between this amount and the amount which the competent state would have paid out under its own legislation is made up by the more generous state.

---

13 Art 19(1) (sickness benefits), Art 73(1) (family benefits) and Arts 67-69 (unemployment benefit). Unemployment benefit, for example, can be paid for up to three months whilst the individual is looking for a job in another Member State.

14 Case C-272/90 *Van Noorden v Association pur l'Emploi dans l'Industrie et Commerce de l'ardeche et de la Drome* [1991] ECR I-2543, [1993] 2 CMLR 732.

15 These benefits can be obtained with the British E111 form.

16 Case C-308/89 *Di Leo v Land Berlin* [1990] ECR I-4185.

17 Case 1/78 *Kenny v Insurance Officer* [1978] ECR 1489.

The final important principle to be noted is that the burden of paying substantial or long-term benefits such as old-age pensions will be apportioned, *pro rata*, between the states where the individual has contributed during his working life (Art 46). An individual cannot, however, lose out under this system: the total sum received may not be less than that which they would have been paid having regard only to the laws of the state of residence (Art 50).

Community social security regulation aims to co-ordinate, rather than to harmonise the various, autonomous national systems and accordingly, the kind of benefits to be provided in each state and the criteria of eligibility for them are a matter for national law. Moreover, each individual can be subject to the social security legislation of only one state (Art 13), generally the state where he works (Art 13(2)(a)).[18] This state, 'the competent state', is ultimately responsible for aggregating and paying for benefits; the Member States settle accounts between themselves at a later stage.[19]

THE DIRECTIVE ON EQUAL TREATMENT IN SOCIAL SECURITY

While the regulations described above require a cross-border element, namely movement from one Member State to another, the directive on equal treatment in social security[20] is applicable in all situations including those purely internal to the Member State.

This directive applies the principle of equal treatment for men and women to statutory social security schemes relating to sickness, invalidity, old age, accidents at work and occupational diseases, unemployment and 'social assistance' so far as intended to supplement or replace any of the other enumerated benefits. It does not apply to provisions concerning survivors' benefits or, in general terms, to family benefits. The principle of equal treatment does not affect provisions relating to the protection of women on the grounds of maternity. It does mean that the entitlement and contribution to, as well as the rate and the duration of statutory social benefits, should be the same as between men and women regardless of, in particular, their marital or family status,[1] in so far as the claimants of

---

18 Exceptions are made for temporary workers, workers employed in two or more Member States and frontier workers (Art 14).
19 Administrative procedures are laid down by Council Regulation (EEC) 574/72, OJ Special Edition 1972 (I), p 160.
20 Directive 79/7/EEC, OJ 1979 L6/24.
1 For example, widows should have the same rights as widowers to elect to receive benefits in respect of thier incapacity for work: Case C-337/91 *AM van Gemart-Darks v Bestuur von de Nieuwe Industriele Badrifs-vereniging* 27 October [1993] ECR (not yet reported).

these benefits can properly be regarded as part of the 'working population'.[1a]

Translating the Community categories into UK social security terms, it would seem that any sex discrimination in the claims of workers for severe disablement allowance, invalidity benefit, disability living allowance, attendance allowance, invalidity care allowance,[2] sickness benefit, industrial injury benefit or retirement pensions is prohibited under Community law.

In relation to retirement pensions, it should be borne in mind that Article 7(1)(a) of the directive does allows Member States to maintain discrimination in the determination of pensionable age for the purposes of granting old-age and retirement pensions. However, general means tested benefits such as income support[3] or housing benefit[4] designed to cover the basic social needs of persons with insufficient resources and unconnected with any of the foregoing benefits do not fall within the directive.[5] In addition, widow's benefit, child benefit, guardians' allowance and maternity benefit are not covered by the principle of equal treatment.

The directive prohibits both direct sex discrimination, whereby sex is made one of the criteria or prerequisites regarding entitlement to or rate of a particular benefit, and indirect sex discrimination.[6] Indirect discrimination may arise when a practice or criterion applied in relation to a benefit has a disproportionate impact on one sex and no objective justification can be offered for this practice which is unconnected with discrimination on grounds of sex.[7] It may also arise when a new apparently non-directly discriminatory benefit is operated so as to continue discriminatory criteria contained in an earlier benefit, for example in the changeover from the clearly discriminatory

1a   See Cases 48, 106, 107/88 *Achterberg-te-Riele v Sociale Verzeberingsbank, Amsterdam* [1989] ECR 1963.
2   See Case 150/85 *Drake v Chief Adjudication Officer* [1986] ECR 1995.
3   Joined Cases C-63/91 and C-64/91 *Jackson & Cresswell v Chief Adjudication Officer* [1992] ECR I-4737, [1992] 3 CMLR 389.
4   Case C-243/90 *R v Secretary of State for Social Security, ex p Smithson* [1992] ECR I-467, [1992] 1 CMLR 1061.
5   See Case 102/88 *Ruzius-Wilbrink v Bedrijfsvereniging voor Overheidsdiensten* [1989] ECR 4311, [1991] 2 CMLR 202 confirming the application of the directive to supplementary benefits related to previous income paid in the event of incapacity for work.
6   Case 30/85 *Teuling v Bedrijfsvereniging voor de Chemische Industrie* [1987] ECR 2497; Case 102/88 *Ruzius-Wilbrink v Bedrijfsvereniging voor Overheidsdiensten* [1989] ECR 4311, [1991] 2 CMLR 202; Case C-229/89 *Commission v Belgium: re unemployed heads of households* [1991] ECR I-2205, [1993] 2 CMLR 403, [1991] IRLR 393.
7   *R v Secretary of State for Employment, ex p Schaffter* [1987] IRLR 53 at paras 21 and 37, pp 56-7.

housewife non-contributory invalidity pension to severe disablement allowance.[8]

Any discriminatory elements in statutory benefits covered by the directive had to be abolished by 23 December 1984.[9] Following that date, the provisions of the directive became directly effective and thus might now be invoked by individuals directly before their national courts to set aside any national provisions regarding entitlement to or amount of benefit which involve an element which can be said to be sex discriminatory.[10]

As has been noted above, the directive allows Member States to exclude from its scope 'the determination of pensionable age for the purposes of granting old-age and retirement pensions and the possible consequence thereof for other benefits.'[11] Thus, Member States which maintain state pension schemes which discriminate as between men and women for example, by having a different retirement age are not acting in contravention of this directive. Employers' voluntary early retirement schemes linked to this difference in state pension ages have been held acceptable within Community law by virtue of this provision of the Social Security Directive[12] but compulsory retirement schemes on the same basis have been held to offend against the general principle of equal treatment in employment.[13]

In *R v Secretary of State for Social Security, ex parte the Equal Opportunities Commission* [14] the Court of Justice held that the United Kingdom's preservation of different pension ages for men and women was not contrary to the directive, notwithstanding the fact that Article 4(1) of the directive provides that there should be no sex discrimination as regards the obligation to contribute and the calculation of contributions to state pension scheme whereas under UK law men were required to continue to pay national insurance contributions for five years longer

---

8   Case 31/90 *Johnson v Chief Adjudication Officer* [1991] ECR I-3723, [1991] 3 CMLR 917.

9   Case 384/85 *Clarke v Chief Adjudication Officer* [1987] ECR 2865.

10 See Case 286/85 *McDermott & Cotter v Minister for Social Welfare* [1987] ECR 1453, [1987] 2 CMLR 607 and Case 31/90 *Johnson v Chief Adjudication Officer* [1991] ECR I-3723, [1991] 3 CMLR 917.

11 In Case 328/91 *Thomas v Adjudication Officer and Secretary of State for Social Security* [1993] ECR I-1247 the Court of Justice held that discriminatory linkages to other social security benefits whereby the attainment of pensionable age triggers a loss of entitlement to, for example, invalidity or invalid care allowance could not be justified in relation to women who chose to work beyond the state pensionable age.

12 Case 19/81 *Burton v British Railways Board* [1982] ECR 555.

13 Case 152/84 *Marshall v Southampton Area Health Authority (Marshall I)* [1986] ECR 723, [1986] 1 CMLR 688.

14 See Case 9/91 [1992] ECR I-4297, [1992] IRLR 376, [1992] 3 CMLR 233.

than-women and yet still to receive the same basic pension. The Court held that to 'de-couple' pensionable age from pension contribution in the manner suggested by the Equal Opportunities Commission would disrupt the complex financial equilibrium of the state pension system. Where, however, a Member State has introduced a common retirement age for men and women, then that state is precluded from maintaining any difference based on sex in the method of calculating the pension.[15]

EQUAL TREATMENT AND PRIVATE OCCUPATIONAL PENSIONS

The Fourth Equal Treatment Directive[16] extends the prohibition of sex discrimination to occupational social security schemes which seek to supplement or to replace the benefits provided by statutory social security schemes. The Court of Justice treats the matter of private pensions primarily as one of employment law covered not only by this Occupational Social Security Scheme Directive prohibiting indirect discrimination, but also by the Equal Treatment in Employment Directive[17] and, indeed, Article 119 of the Treaty.[18]

By contrast, the statutory retirement pensions provided wholly by the state are not to be considered as pay. Contribution to a compulsory state pension scheme is governed not by agreement in the context of an employment relationship, but by legal requirements governed by considerations of general social policy. The Community provisions which govern the application of and derogation from the principle of equal treatment in relation to such public social security scheme are to be found only in the Social Security Directive and no other Community provisions.[19]

If it is possible, however, to argue that benefits received under a state sponsored scheme are in fact a form of pay, even if payable only after the termination of employment, then the broader provisions of Article 119 and the Equal Treatment Directive apply to prevent unequal treatment allied to pensionable age. In *Commission v Belgium: re redundant*

---

15 Case C154/92 *Van Cant v Rijksdienst voor Pensioenen* ECJ, 1 July [1993] ECR I-3811, [1994] IRLR 000.
16 Directive 86/378/EEC, OJ 1986 L225/40.
17 Directive 76/207/EEC, OJ 1976 L39/40.
18 Case 262/88 *Barber v Guardian Royal Exchange Group* [1989] ECR 1889, [1990] 2 CMLR 513. See Ch 17 for a full discussion of this case.
19 See Case 80/70 *Defrenne v Belgium* [1971] ECR 445, [1974] 1 CMLR 494, applied by the EAT in *Griffin v London Pensions Fund Authority* [1993] 2 CMLR 571.

women employees [20] the Court held that a supplementary allowance paid by former employers to employees made redundant between the ages of 60 and 65 to top up their unemployment benefit to their net reference wage contravened Article 119 of the Treaty in that no such benefit was available to women employees since they would be in receipt of an old age pension rather than unemployment benefit during the relevant period.

BIBLIOGRAPHY

E Eichenhofer 'Co-ordination of Social Security and Equal Treatment of Men and Women in Employment: recent social security judgments of the European Court of Justice' (1993) 30 *Common Market Law Review* 1021.
E Ellis 'Recent Case Law of the Court of Justice on the Equal Treatment of Men and Women' (1994) 31 *Common Market Law Review* 43.
Ogus & Barendt *The Law of Social Security* (3rd edn, 1988) Butterworths.
Watson *Social Security Law of the European Communities* (1980) Mansell.

---

20 Case C-173/91 *Commission v Belgium: re redundant women employees* 17 February [1993] ECR (not yet reported), [1993] 2 CMLR 165

Chapter 19

TAXATION LAW

INTRODUCTION

Community competence in matters of taxation is set out in Articles 95 to 99 of the Treaty of Rome. Article 99 provides that the Council of Ministers acting unanimously 'shall . . . adopt provisions for the harmonization of legislation concerning turnover taxes, excise duties and other forms of indirect taxation to the extent that such harmonization is necessary to ensure the establishment and the functioning of the internal market'. The tax harmonisation sought by the Commission is avowedly aimed at an approximisation, rather than a complete standardisation of national legislation. National tax regimes are to be mutually compatible, without necessarily being uniform in all their details, such as to lead to 'the creation of a common area without internal frontiers in which people, goods, services and capital can move around freely.'[1]

VALUE ADDED TAX

The turnover tax which the Member States were required to adopt was value added tax (VAT). VAT is a tax paid at all stages of the production or distribution of goods and services, but the ultimate burden of which is borne by the end user. It is characterised by its simplicity from the point of view of national administrations in its management, collection and accounting. Although the First VAT Directive[2] required all Member

---

1 European Commission *Approximation of Taxes. Why ?* 1991 European File CC-73-91-368-N-C.
2 Directive 67/227/EEC, OJ 1967 L71/1301.

States to introduce VAT by 1 January 1970, the directive did not set out either the rate of VAT to be charged or specify the goods upon which it might be levied. The detailed application of VAT was a matter originally left to the discretion of the Member States.

VAT was introduced into the United Kingdom by the Finance Act 1972 in consequence of her intended accession to the European Communities. As a tax which was conceived in and created by Community law, the interpretation and application of VAT in the United Kingdom is governed, ultimately, by Community directives, the general principles of Community law and decisions of the Court of Justice.

For example, the Community doctrines of proportionality and of a fundamental right to respect for private property may apply to the question of due penalties established by national law for misdeclaration of VAT.[3]

Community law may allow Member States a degree of discretion to introduce their own specific national measures giving greater precision to Community directives or derogating from the requirements of the directive. Even in these areas, however, the lawfulness of the national measures is a matter to be determined ultimately by Community law.[4]

Thus, national measures which require the payment of national VAT on goods imported from another Member State on which VAT had already been paid, but which do not allow the VAT already paid to be set off against that national charge have been held to be contrary to Community law, in particular to Article 95 of the Treaty.[5] This article is also directly effective and may therefore be relied upon by individuals against any such claim to VAT.[6]

It is clear that no full and proper advice regarding VAT in the United Kingdom can be given unless regard is had to, and account taken of, the relevant Community legislation and case law.[7]

The Sixth VAT Directive

The most important directive from the point of view of the interpretation and application of VAT has been the Sixth VAT Directive [8] which first

3   See *W Emmett & Son Ltd v Customs & Excise Comrs* London VAT Tribunal LON 90/1316Z, unreported judgment of 7 October 1991.
4   See Case 324/82 *Commission v Belgium ('VAT on New Cars')* [1985] 1 CMLR 364.
5   Joined Cases 120/88, 119/89, 159/89 *Commission v Italy* [1991] ECR I-621, [1993] 1 CMLR 41.
6   Case 15/81 *Gaston Schul, Douane Expediteur BV v Inspecteur der Invoerrechten en Accijnzen (Gaston Schul 1)* [1992] ECR 1409, [1982] 3 CMLR 229.
7   See, eg Case MAN/91/650 *Next plc v Customs and Excise Comrs* [1993] 2 CMLR 993, Manchester VAT Tribunal.
8   Directive 77/388/EEC, OJ 1977 L145/1.

introduced common definitions and a uniform basis for the assessment of the tax. The Sixth VAT Directive has been amended and expanded on numerous occasions since its adoption and specific and limited derogation by Member States from its provisions have been authorised by the Commission under Article 27 of the Directive. It remains, however, the basic Community VAT document. Its provisions were originally implemented in the United Kingdom by amendments made to the Finance Act 1972 by the Finance Act 1977. The law was subsequently consolidated in the Value Added Tax Act 1983.

It has been suggested that, due to political pressures, the UK legislation failed to give full and proper effect to the provisions of the Sixth VAT Directive and has left inadequacies and inconsistencies between the UK law on VAT and the requirements of Community law.[9] One apparent inconsistency is that in UK VAT law a taxable person is a person who makes taxable supplies, but in Community law a taxable person is a person who carries out any economic activity, whether or not activities are taxable or exempt.

The Court of Justice has confirmed that unconditional and precise provisions of the Sixth VAT Directive may be relied upon by individuals directly before the national courts of the Member States against state authorities in the face of inadequacies in the implementing national legislation. [10]

One English judge has claimed that the Sixth VAT Directive should not be interpreted in the broad purposive manner which characterises other Community instruments, but in a strict and literal manner in the way of English taxing statutes. [11] Whatever the truth of this assertion, it is clear that the inadequacy or otherwise of the national legislation can only be determined if account is taken of the interpretation of the provisions of the underlying Community directive in the case law of the Court of Justice.[12]

Approximation of VAT rates

By 1992 there were thirty different VAT rates across the Community varying from zero-rating on a significant proportion of goods in the

9   Hoskin *Community Law and UK VAT* at p 34.
10   See Case 8/81 *Becker v Finanzamt Munster Innenstadt* [1982] ECR 53, [1982] 1 CMLR 499; Case 255/81 *Grendel GmbH v Finanzamt Hamburg* [1982] ECR 2301, [1983] 1 CMLR 379.
11   Brooke J in *Committee of Directors of Polytechnics v Customs & Excise Comrs* [1993] 2 CMLR 490 at 504 para 44, QBD.
12   See, eg the decisions of the VAT Tribunals in *Merseyside Cablevision Ltd* (1987) VAT Tribunal Reports 134, [1987] 3 CMLR 290 and *Bell Concord Educational Trust* (1986) VAT Tribunal Reports 165.

United Kingdom,[13] Ireland and Portugal to a higher rate of 38 per cent in Italy. The standard rate for VAT was 12 per cent in Spain, while in Denmark the standard rate was 22 per cent.

In June 1991 the Community's finance ministers agreed that each Member State should apply a standard rate of VAT not lower than 15 per cent. This unanimous agreement was reflected in the VAT Rates Directive[14] which provided from that the 15 per cent minimum standard rate should apply to all Member States from 1 January 1993 until 31 December 1996. The minimum standard rate to be applied thereafter is subject to the unanimous agreement of the Council of Ministers before the end of 1995. Up to two reduced rates of at least 5 per cent were also provided for in the directive, although zero-rating in force at the beginning of 1991 might continue up to 1997. Reduced rates can only be applied to a list of 'essential' goods and services set out in the directive. These include foodstuffs, water supplies, pharmaceutical products, medical aids, the provision of medical and dental care, admission to entertainment and sports facilities, hotel and holiday accommodation, funeral services, charity work, books and transport.

The long-term goal of the directive is that a common system of VAT as the sole turnover tax on goods and services should be adopted throughout the Member States of the Community. Thus the Member States' area of free action in the matter of VAT is decreasing all the time as the attention of the Community turns to tax harmonization with a view to abolishing all direct and indirect barriers to trade across the frontier-free Community.

A Community administrative organisation for VAT

As well as seeking to harmonise VAT rates, Community legislation has been introduced to create a new administrative structure for the levying of VAT across the Community following the abolition of tax checks at internal frontiers within the Community after 1992. Statistics on intra-Community trade will be established on the basis of information supplied in national VAT returns.[15]

---

13 See Case 416/85 *Commission v UK: Re Zero Rating* [1988] ECR 3127, [1988] 3 CMLR 169.
14 Directive 92/77/EEC, OJ 1992 L316/1.
15 Council Regulation (EEC) 3330/91, OJ 1991 316/1 as implemented by Statistics of Trade (Customs & Excise) Regulations 1992, SI 1992/2790.

Common principles for the collection of VAT

Directive 91/680,[16] which was implemented in the United Kingdom by the Finance Act 1992, establishes that until the end of 1996 VAT on cross-border sales between taxable persons internal to the Community should be paid in the country of consumption (the destination principle). In general, trade with non-taxable persons attracts VAT in the country of origin. From January 1997 the stated intention is that VAT on trade as between taxable persons should also be paid in the country of origin of the goods, but the introduction of this system is dependent on the unanimous agreement of the Council of Ministers.

Common rules on the deductibility of VAT: a proposal

Since 1983 there has been a proposal for a directive to establish a set of common rules for the deduction of VAT from business expenses.[17] The draft proposal sets out a range of goods and service (for example cars, accommodation, food, drink and business entertainment) on which VAT will not be deductible. No final proposal has yet been published and the process seems to have stalled for the present because of the inability of Member States to reach an agreement.

VAT on small and medium sized enterprises (SMEs)

Because of the apparent inability of Member States to reach an agreement, a Commission proposal for a directive to simplify the operation of VAT for small and medium sized businesses[18] has not been acted upon. It may be that these proposal will be revived in the future.

EXCISE DUTY

Excise duty is levied by Member States on alcohol, tobacco products and petrol and other mineral oil products. Excise duty on these products varies widely among the Member States. For example, in January 1990

---

16 Directive 91/680/EEC, OJ 1991 L376/1.
17 Proposed Twelfth VAT Directive COM (82) 870, OJ 1983 C37/8 as amended by COM (84) 84, OJ 1984 C56/6.
18 COM (84) 444 as amended by COM (87)524. See *OJ* 1986 C272/8.

the excise duty on spirits was over ECU 26 per litre of pure alcohol in Ireland compared to under ECU 1.5 per litre of pure alcohol in Greece. Less dramatically, but perhaps of more overall economic significance, in April 1992 the excise duty on leaded petrol in Italy was almost ECU 6 on 10 litres compared to ECU 2.7 in Luxembourg and ECU 3.6 in the United Kingdom.

It is clear that excise duty is seen by Member States not only as a valuable budgetary tool, but also as an instrument and reflection of social policy within the Member States. Thus, agreement on the equalisation of the rates charged by the Member States on these products has not been forthcoming. Agreement has however been reached on the way that excise duty is to be structured and applied so that all Member States calculate the excise duty charged on alcohol,[19] tobacco products[20] and mineral oils[1] on the same basis.

Directives have also been agreed setting the minimum rates of excise duty which may be charged by the Member States on alcohol,[2] cigarettes,[3] tobacco[4] and mineral oils.[5] In addition to setting minimum rates, these Directives also specify recommended target or 'reference rates' which should be taken into account by the Member State when setting their rates.

BUSINESS TAXATION

In order to encourage cross-border investment and activity the Commission has been concerned to reduce fiscal disparities among Member States in the area of business taxation. The Court of Justice has held that the corporation tax regimes of Member States may not distinguish between companies resident within that Member State and companies which are incorporated and resident within another Member State.[6] Thus, a German corporation subject to national taxation of its operations within the United Kingdom is entitled to the same treatment and tax breaks as any UK incorporated company.

---

19   Directive 92/83/EEC, OJ 1992 L316/21.
20   Directive 92/78/EEC, OJ 1992 L316/5.
1   Directive 92/81/EEC, OJ 1992 L316/12.
2   Directive 92/84/EEC, OJ 1992 L316/29.
3   Directive 92/79/EEC, OJ 1992 L316/8.
4   Directive 92/80/EEC, OJ 1992 L316/10.
5   Directive 92/82/EEC, OJ 1992 L316/19.
6   Case C-330/91 *R v Inland Revenue Comrs, ex p Commerzbank AG* [1993] ECR I-4017, [1993] 4 All ER 37.

In terms of specific regulation of direct taxation within the Member States, Community legislation exists as yet only in the area of transnational corporations. There has been a proposal for the harmonisation of tax relief regarding the carrying over of business losses into subsequent financial years which would apply to purely domestic companies.[7] This proposal has not yet been adopted and it is unclear whether it ever will be. Apart from this, current Community legislation in the area of company taxation requires a cross-border element.

The rationale for Community involvement is that differences in the taxation of company profits and capital gains within the internal market of the European Community may have an influence on companies' investment decisions. In order to maintain the 'level playing field' and prevent distortion in competition, an increasing number of directives dealing with issues of company taxation have been issued by the Community. Their aim is, ultimately, to set up a common and co-ordinated systems of corporation tax in the Member States which will have the effect, *inter alia*, of making cross-border trading and other income transactions less complex.

There has also been discussion regarding the possibility of harmonising the tax base for corporation tax by having a common method throughout the Member States for calculating the taxable profits on which corporation tax may be levied. This will ensure that firms that do business in several Member States will not be at a disadvantage compared to those who restrict their activities to only one state.

A directive has been adopted on a common system of taxation applicable to reorganisation across the Member State within the one corporate group[8] and to the taxation of dividend payments from a subsidiary in one Member State to its parent company in another.[9] An arbitration procedure between Member States' tax authorities designed to prevent double taxation of profit transfers between associated companies in different Member States has been set up by multilateral convention among the Member States.[10] All of these matters are implemented into UK law by the Finance (No 2) Act 1992.

At the time of writing there were published proposals from the Commission for a directive to ensure that Member States grant tax relief against the profits of parent companies for losses occurred by branches and subsidiaries of that company in another Member State[11] and for a

---

7 COM (85) 319, OJ 1985 C170/3.
8 Directive 90/434/EEC, OJ 1990 L225/1. See COM (93) 293 final, OJ 1993 C225/3 for current Commission proposals to amend this and the following directive.
9 Directive 90/435/EEC, OJ 1990 L225/6.
10 Instrument No 90/436/EEC, OJ 1990 L225/19.
11 COM (90) 595, OJ 1991 C53/30.

directive abolishing the taxation at source of interest and royalty payments made between parent companies and subsidiaries.[12]

The Commission has claimed that the centralist concept of the maximum harmonisation of national laws at Community level has been abandoned in the name of subsidiarity. Subsidiarity is the principle, embodied in Article 3b of the post-Maastricht Treaty of Rome, that the Community should take action only and insofar as the objectives of the proposed action cannot be sufficiently achieved by the Member States. Thus, in the field of company taxation further measures for harmonisation of national laws or other Community initiatives will be proposed only insofar as it can be shown that continuing differences in Member States' tax systems significantly affect the competitive situation and investment behaviour of business undertakings.

BIBLIOGRAPHY

Buckett *VAT in the European Community* (2nd edn, 1992) Butterworths.
Coopers & Lybrand *The 1993 EC VAT System: are you ready ?* (1992) CCH Editions.
A J Easson *Taxation in the European Community* (1993) Athlone Press.
Ernst & Young *VAT in Europe* (1989) Sweet & Maxwell.
Ernst & Young *The Future of Corporate Tax in the European Community* (1991) Kogan Page.
Hoskin *Community Law and UK VAT* (1991) Butterworths.
Hoskin *VAT Case Digest: UK and Community Law* (1991, looseleaf) Sweet & Maxwell.

12   COM (90) 571, OJ 1991 C53/26.

Chapter 20

TRADE LAW

INTRODUCTION

A common approach to restrictions on trade, between Member States, and with third countries, is one of the cornerstones of European Community law. The Community came into being as a customs union, and the rules relating to the free movement of goods and services within the Community and the common commercial policy as regards trade with non-Community states are among the most highly developed of the corpus of Community law.

This chapter focuses primarily on the former of these priorities, the removal of trade barriers within the Community, which, as the legal saga concerning the English Sunday trading regulations amply illustrated, has an increasingly important impact on the law of the United Kingdom.

WHEN IS COMMUNITY LAW RELEVANT?

Certain basic parameters should be noted at the outset. This aspect of Community law relates to 'goods', 'products which can be valued in money and which are capable, as such, of forming the subject of commercial transactions'.[1] This definition does not cover television signals or money which fall under the Community law relating to services and capital respectively. The law applies both to goods originating within the Community and to goods originating in third countries which are in 'free circulation' in the Community, that is, goods which have satisfied the

---

1   Case 7/68 *Commission v Italy* [1968] ECR 423.

277

import requirements, including the payment of customs duties or equivalent charges, in one of the Member States. Therefore, once a product from outside the Community gets into the Community system, it is treated as if it were a Community product. The nationality of the owner of the goods is irrelevant.

In general, the impact of Community law on a particular matter must be considered where the facts indicate a potential hindrance to the flow of trade between Member States. Three points arise immediately. Only a potential and not an actual adverse impact on trade need be shown; there is no *de minimis* requirement as in competition law, where the effect on trade must be appreciable; and goods must actually move between Member States in order to provide a 'Community element' justifying the intervention of Community law. As a result, Community law generally deals with the conduct of Member States in relation to goods originating elsewhere in the Community. The British Government then remains free to impose taxes on, or require standards to be met by, British goods notwithstanding that the result may be to hinder their sale in other Member States. The situation whereby goods produced in a particular Member State can be subjected to more stringent requirements than incoming goods from other states is known as reverse discrimination. The exception to this rule is that governments cannot impose restrictions on exports which have the object or effect of protecting the domestic market at the expense of the trade of other Member States.[2]

Community law is clearly relevant where one Member State prohibits or restricts the import of goods from another Member State. Its application extends, however, to a multitude of less obvious situations. Many of these instances will not concern rules which directly discriminate against imports, known in the Community jargon as 'distinctly applicable measures', but rather rules which are applied equally to all products, both domestic and foreign, known as 'indistinctly applicable measures'. Such rules, for example, technical and safety standards, although frequently introduced for the most commendable of reasons, may operate in practice as a barrier to trade.

All the major Treaty articles in this area have been held to be directly effective and can, therefore, be invoked in national courts. They are normally invoked against national governments: the provisions of the Treaty are, in many cases, explicitly addressed to the Member States, and in matters such as taxation, it is only the state which can act in the first place. The rules may be cited against all public bodies, as well as semi-

---

2   Art 34 of the Treaty, as interpreted in Case 15/79 *Groenveld v Produktschap voor Vee en Vlees* [1979] ECR 3409.

public bodies, such as quangos and professional associations, which exercise powers derived from public law. Examples from past cases include the Royal Pharmaceutical Society and the Irish Goods Council, a body set up by the Irish Government to organise a 'Buy Irish' campaign.[3] Accordingly, the Community regime applies not only to binding laws issued by governments but also to administrative acts,[4] and to non-binding, informal measures, such as promotional campaigns, which are capable of hindering its operation.

Community institutions (and thereby Community legislation) can also be challenged for obstructing the free movement of goods or for authorising Member States to do so, although frequently other objectives, such as the common organisation of the agricultural market, will take precedence. It is not entirely clear whether private parties can be sued under free movement of goods rules. In general, however, it may be said that the law discussed in this chapter is directed at official barriers to trade, whereas the Treaty rules on competition, Articles 85 and 86, exist to break down the trade barriers erected by private undertakings. However, obligations upon individuals not to obstruct the free movement of goods have been clearly upheld in the field of intellectual property rights.[5]

CUSTOMS DUTIES

Community law prohibits the imposition of customs duties and equivalent charges on imports and exports between Member States (Arts 12-17 EC). A charge equivalent to a customs duty covers any pecuniary charge, however small and whatever its designation and mode of application, which is imposed unilaterally on domestic or foreign goods by reason of the fact that they cross a frontier.[6] The fact that the charge is not discriminatory or is not imposed for protectionist reasons, or for the benefit of the state is irrelevant.[7] Certain charges levied as a recompense for a service actually rendered to the importer may be permitted, but within narrow limits. The service must tangibly benefit the importer,[8] and must be performed specifically for that reason, rather than for reasons of the

---

3   Cases 266-67/87 *R v Royal Pharmaceutical Society of Great Britain, ex p API* [1989] ECR 1295; Case 249/81 *Commission v Ireland* [1982] ECR 4005.

4   See, eg, Case 21/84 *Commission v France: Re Postal Franking Machines* [1985] ECR 1355.

5   See, eg, Case 15/74 *Centrafarm v Sterling Drug* [1974] ECR 1147, and generally Ch 14.

6   Case 24/68 *Commission v Italy: Re Statistical Levy* [1969] ECR 193.

7   Cases 2-3/69 *Sociaal Fonds voor Diamantarbeiders v Brachfeld* [1969] ECR 211.

8   Case 24/68 *Commission v Italy: Re Statistical Levy* [1969] ECR 193.

general interest,[9] as is often the case with health and safety and quality control inspections. It is easier to justify charges imposed to pay for services, such as inspections, which are required by Community law.[10]

In addition, certain charges may fall within the definition of internal taxation, which is not prohibited *per se*, but only where it is discriminatory or protective (see below). The difference between a tax and a charge is essentially that a tax is incorporated into an overall regime which operates systematically and according to objective criteria, irrespective of the origin of the product, rather than being imposed specifically on a particular product for a particular reason.[11] However, certain levies which appear to be in the nature of a tax because they are levied on domestic products and imports alike may be held to be illegal, as charges, where the proceeds of the levy are used exclusively to subsidise or otherwise benefit the domestic product and its producers.[12]

The Treaty articles relating to customs duties and equivalent charges are directly effective, so illegally levied charges can be challenged and recovered in national courts. Charges will not be recoverable where their burden has been passed on to the purchasers of the goods through price increases, but the (often onerous) burden of proving this rests with the national authorities.

It should also be noted in this context that, complementary to the abolition of customs charges, customs controls and other formalities have been considerably simplified under Community law. Border controls have been cut to a minimum, although Member States may still carry out routine checks on a non-discriminatory basis within their territory and standardised documents are used across the Community.

DISCRIMINATORY TAXATION

Under Article 95 of the Treaty Member States may not impose taxation which discriminates between similar domestic and imported products, or which affords indirect protection to domestic products. The rules apply not merely to differential tax ratings, but also to other aspects of tax law such as the basis of assessment for tax, permitted deductions, and the taxation of services ancillary to the supply of goods.[13] The Court of Justice has extended the rules to cover taxes imposed on exports, which are not

---

9   Case 39/73 *Rewe-Zentralfinanz v Landwirtschaftskammer Westfalen-Lippe* [1975] ECR 1039.
10 Case 46/76 *Bauhuis v The Netherlands* [1977] ECR 5.
11 Case 90/79 *Commission v France: Re Levy on Reprographic Machines* [1981] ECR 283.
12 Case 77/76 *Cucchi v Avez* [1977] ECR 987.
13 Case 20/76 *Schöttle v FZA Freudenstadt* [1977] ECR 247.

mentioned expressly in this context in the Treaty.[14] Both aspects of Article 95 confer directly effective rights on individuals which may be enforced in national courts.

The concept of the similarity of products, the central issue in this field, is to be interpreted broadly. Similar products are those which meet the same needs from the point of view of consumers and which compete in the same market,[15] although the question of market definition may involve a complex analysis of consumer habits, present and future.[16] The prohibition on protective taxation extends to the situation where imported products are taxed more than domestic products to which they are not 'similar' but with which they nevertheless compete in certain respects.[17] However, differential tax treatment of a type of product which is largely imported may be justifiable where it is based on objective criteria, and is effected in order to achieve acceptable economic aims.[18]

RESTRICTIONS ON IMPORTS

Article 30 of the Treaty prohibits quantitative restrictions on imports, both total and partial, and all measures having equivalent effect. Given that most quantitative restrictions had been lifted even before the Community came into being and that the Court of Justice has adopted a broad interpretation of the concept of measures having equivalent effect to quantitative restrictions, the vast majority of disputes have related to the latter category.

In *Dassonville*, the Court ruled against a Belgian law which required imports to be accompanied by a certificate of origin issued by the State in which they were manufactured. According to the '*Dassonville* formula': 'All trading rules enacted by Member States, which are capable of hindering directly or indirectly, actually or potentially, intra-Community trade are to be considered as measures having an effect equivalent to quantitative restrictions'.[19]

The definition laid down by the Court is extremely broad. As has been noted above, it covers any measure which could have an adverse effect on trade, regardless of the motives for its introduction. Importantly, it is capable of encompassing both measures which directly discriminate against imports and thus contravene the basic prohibition on discrimination

---

14 Case 142/77 *Statenskontrol v Larsen* [1978] ECR 1543.
15 Case 168/78 *Commission v France: Re Taxation of Spirits* [1980] ECR 347.
16 See, eg, Case 170/78 *Commission v United Kingdom: Re Excise Duties on Wine* [1980] ECR 417.
17 Case 168/78 *Commission v France: Re Taxation of Spirits* [1980] ECR 347.
18 Case 196/85 *Commission v France* [1987] ECR 1597; Case C132/88 *Commission v Greece* [1990] ECR I-1567.
19 Case 8/74 *Procureur du Roi v Dassonville* [1974] ECR 837.

on the grounds of nationality in Article 6 of the Treaty, and measures which apply to imports and domestic products alike, but which may have the net result of making imports more difficult or more expensive. The English Shops Act 1950, prohibiting the sale of certain goods on Sundays was a good example of a non-discriminatory or indistinctly applicable restriction—its terms applied equally to imports and domestic goods.

In fact, the *Dassonville* formula proved to be too broad to sustain and the Court adopted a more balanced approach in the landmark *Cassis de Dijon* case.[20] There were three aspects to the *Cassis de Dijon* regime. Firstly, Article 30 did indeed permit Member States to impose restrictions on trade on a non-discriminatory basis, but only where this was justified by certain 'mandatory requirements' of the public interest. These requirements included the effectiveness of fiscal supervision, the protection of public health, the fairness of commercial transactions and the defence of the consumer. The protection of the environment and of national socio-cultural characteristics were later added to the list. The end result was that Member States could not restrict the flow of trade within the Community in any way, unless they had a good reason of public policy for doing so.

Secondly, all measures imposed by Member States must have effects which are proportionate to their aims. Thirdly, there was a presumption that goods which have been lawfully produced and marketed in one Member State could be introduced, without further restriction, into the other Member States.[1]

The result of the Court's jurisprudence in this area is that the Article 30 regime can be contravened in a wide variety of situations.[2] Examples of national measures which have been held to contravene Article 30 include import formalities such as licences, even where they are to be granted automatically, food hygiene standards, price controls, public supply contracts, and marketing requirements.

By putting the onus on Member States to justify non-discriminatory rules before the Court of Justice, *Cassis de Dijon* seemed to encourage traders to challenge any attempts to limit their commercial freedom. The legal battles over Sunday trading restrictions in England and France were perhaps the most prominent but by no means the only manifestations of this legal climate. The Court now seems to regret the commercial uncertainty fostered by its previous caselaw and has taken the opportunity to retreat further from the broad brush approach adopted in *Dassonville*.

In *Keck*, the Court rejected a challenge to a French law prohibiting the resale of goods at a price lower than that for which they were purchased.

---

20   Case 120/78 *Rewe-Zentral v Bundesmonopolverwaltung für Branntwein* [1979] ECR 649.
1   Case 178/84 *Commission v Germany: Re Beer Purity Laws* [1987] ECR 1227.
2   See P Oliver *Free Movement of Goods in the EEC* (2nd edn, 1988) European Law Centre, Ch 7.

It held that provisions which apply to all affected traders operating within the national territory and which affect in the same manner, in law and in fact, the marketing of domestic products and of those from other Member States, do not fall within the *Dassonville* formula and so do not breach Article 30.[3] It seems clear now that rules which are truly non-discriminatory cannot be challenged on the basis of Community law. However, Member States will continue to have to justify non-discriminatory rules which in practical terms weigh more heavily on foreign traders.

This view appears to be confirmed by a subsequent judgment in which the Court ruled against a German law which forced Esteé Lauder to market its 'Clinique' range of products under a different name in Germany because the name allegedly misled consumers into thinking that the products had a therapeutic effect. The rule operated as a barrier to imports because the company had to adopt a different name in only one Member State and so incur additional advertising and packaging expenses. It therefore had to be justified on a public interest ground and the Court found that it was not necessary for consumer and health protection.[3a]

RESTRICTIONS ON EXPORTS

Article 34 prohibits quantitative restrictions and measures having equivalent effect on exports. It operates in a similar way to the Article 30 regime, particularly in view of the restrictions imposed on the latter by the *Keck* ruling. Whilst measures which directly discriminate against exports are not permitted, not all indistinctly applicable measures affecting exports are contrary to the Treaty. Only those measures which have as their object or effect the restriction of patterns of exports so as to provide an advantage for national production or for the domestic market, that is, protectionist measures, will be struck down.[4]

PERMITTED DEROGATIONS

Article 36 allows for prohibitions and restrictions on imports, exports and goods in transit for specified reasons. The permitted prohibitions and restrictions 'shall not, however, constitute a means of arbitrary

---

3 Cases C267-268/91 *Keck and Mithovard*, Judgment of 24 November 1993.
3a Case 315/92 *Verbond Sozialer Wetteberb v Esté Lauder Cosmetics*, Judgment of 2 February 1994; (1994) Financial Times, 8 February.
4 Case 15/79 *Groenveld v Produktschap voor Vee en Vlees* [1979] ECR 3409; Case 237/82 *Jongeneel Kaas v The Netherlands* [1984] ECR 83; Case C47/90 *Établissements Delhaize Frères v Promalvin* [1992] ECR I-3669.

discrimination or a disguised restriction on trade.' Measures must therefore be justified on objective grounds and, in practice, this has meant an investigation of the proportionality of the measure similar to that described above in relation to the *Cassis de Dijon* framework. Again, there is a presumption against restriction which must be rebutted.

The relationship between the permitted derogations of Article 36 and the mandatory requirements of the *Cassis de Dijon* case law, which only apply to indistinctly applicable measures,[5] has not been precisely enumerated. In practical terms, however, given that the list of mandatory requirements is wider in scope than the Article 36 classification and, moreover, is not exhaustive, indistinctly applicable measures should normally be considered under *Cassis de Dijon*, and distinctly applicable, or discriminatory measures, under Article 36. However, the Court has, on occasion, considered the validity of an indistinctly applicable measure under Article 36,[6] and frequently both sets of justifications are discussed.

Member States may derogate from Article 30 firstly on grounds of public morality. The Court of Justice has stressed that it is for each Member State to determine its own requirements of public morality in accordance with its own scale of values. However, certain common limits must be set according to Community law. In two British cases, import restrictions on certain pornographic goods have been first upheld, partly because there was no trade in such goods in the United Kingdom itself,[7] and then rejected, because the goods in question were not in fact prohibited within the United Kingdom.[8]

Public policy is potentially a very broad derogation but it has rarely succeeded in practice.[9] The same goes for public security, although the Court has upheld an Irish requirement that importers of petroleum products buy a certain proportion of their needs from the only Irish refinery, at fixed prices, in order to make sure that the refinery stayed in business and could thus be relied upon to provide essential supplies in times of crisis.[10]

The health derogation has been frequently invoked but again the Court has been reluctant to sanction restrictive measures. Measures must form part of a 'seriously considered health policy',[11] and meet a genuine health risk. The burden of proof is on the Member State and it must rebut the presumption that standards imposed on a product by other Member States are adequate to deal with the health risks which it poses.[12]

---

5   Case 113/80 *Commission v Ireland: Re Origin of Souvenirs* [1981] ECR 1625.
6   Case 124/81 *Commission v United Kingdom: Re UHT Milk* [1983] ECR 203.
7   Case 34/79 *R v Henn and Darby* [1979] ECR 3975.
8   Case 121/85 *Conegate v HM Customs and Excise* [1986] ECR 1007.
9   The one example is Case 7/78 *R v Thompson* [1978] ECR 2247, relating to the right of the state to mint coinage.
10   Case 72/83 *Campus Oil v Minister for Industry and Energy* [1984] ECR 2727.
11   Case 40/82 *Commission v United Kingdom: Re Newcastle Disease* [1982] ECR 2739.
12   Case 124/81 *Commission v United Kingdom: Re UHT Milk* [1983] ECR 203.

Of the other derogations, the protection of national treasures has not yet arisen directly,[13] and the protection of industrial and commercial property is dealt with in Chapter 14.

It should be noted that recourse to Article 36 is limited in two situations. Where the product in question is subject to a common organisation of the market, as in the sphere of agriculture, national measures may not interfere with the effective functioning of the market. Where Community legislation has been passed to harmonise the national standards relating to that product, Article 100A provides that the Commission must give its consent to any reliance upon Article 36, and two more grounds for derogation, the protection of the environment and of the working environment, are added.

Other Treaty provisions allow derogation from the free movement of goods rules: where a state is experiencing short-term economic difficulties (Art 103) or balance of payments difficulties (Arts 107-109) and in the interests of national security (Arts 223 and 224) where, for example, there exists the threat of war or serious internal disturbance.

STATE MONOPOLIES

Article 37 aims to ensure the observance of free movement principles by state trading monopolies. The term 'state monopoly' has been given a broad definition, extending beyond state undertakings in the strict sense, to any body through which a state 'supervises, determines or appreciably influences' imports or exports.[14] Total control of the market is not necessary; the body must merely play an effective part in trade between Member States. Many Member States import, export and market certain goods through such monopolies. An example in the British context is the (soon to be defunct) system of Milk Marketing Boards. Member States are not required to abolish such enterprises but to 'adjust' them so that they do not operate in a discriminatory manner. Accordingly, the Court has, in the past, ruled against an exclusive right to import or export a product,[15] and against a 'special equalisation' charge designed to make imported products cost the same as those marketed by the state monopoly.[16] The Court will, however, rule under Article 37 only where the measures specifically concern the exercise by the monopoly of its particular function.[17]

Article 37 does not extend to the provision of services by state monopolies,

---

13 It was mentioned in Case 7/68 *Commission v Italy: Re Export Tax on Art Treasures* [1968] ECR 423, but Art 36 has no relevance to taxes.

14 Case 30/87 *Bodson v Pompes Funebrès* [1988] ECR 2479.

15 Case 59/75 *Pubblico Ministero v Manghera* [1976] ECR 91.

16 Case 91/75 *Göttingen v Miritz* [1976] ECR 217.

17 Case 120/78 *Rewe-Zentral v Bundesmonopolverwaltung für Branntwein* [1979] ECR 649.

which, if anything, is more common than that of goods. Nevertheless, services monopolies may fall under Articles 59-66 on service provision (see below), or under Article 86 dealing with the abuse of a dominant position on the market (see Chapter 10).

TRADE IN SERVICES

In economic terms, and in practice, the distinction between trade in goods and trade in services is often esoteric. Trade in services is, however, dealt with by Community law under a separate chapter of the Treaty and is discussed in greater detail in Chapter 15. It is sufficient to make three points at this stage. Firstly, the definition of a service is broad—any activity which is done in return for remuneration, and residual—any operation which cannot be brought under the heading of movement of goods, persons or capital, will be classified under trade in services. Secondly, both providers and recipients of services have rights under Community law. Thirdly, there are considerable parallels between the law on goods and the law on services; barriers to trade in services which are discriminatory,[18] and, along the lines of '*Cassis de Dijon*', those which are non-discriminatory but cannot be justified as protecting the public interest, may breach Community law.[19]

TRADE WITH NON-COMMUNITY COUNTRIES

In addition to promoting the flow of trade within its borders, the Community also presents a common front to third country trading partners. A common commercial policy is in place across the Community consisting essentially of a uniform duty on particular products, the common customs tariff, also known as the EC's integrated tariff (TARIC), combined with a variety of additional provisions laying down trading rules specific to certain countries and to certain products. Following the European Economic Area Agreement, Austria, Sweden, Norway, Finland and Iceland are now treated, for trade purposes, as if they were Member States of the Community.

The common customs tariff is regularly updated by the Commission and published in the 'L' series of the *Official Journal*. Much of the Community's practice in this area is, however, contingent upon agreements reached at a wider international level, within the framework of GATT, the General

---

18 Case 33/74 *Van Binsbergen v Bestuur van de Bedrijfsvereniging voor de Metaalnijverheid* [1974] ECR 1299; Case 39/75 *Coenen v Sociaal-Economische Raad* [1975] ECR 1547.

19 Case C353/89 *Commission v Netherlands* [1991] ECR I-4069; Case C288/89 *Stichting Collectieve Antennevoorziening Gouda v Commissariaat voor de Media* [1991] ECR I-4007.

Agreement on Tariffs and Trade. There is no central Community customs administration, so the TARIC is actually applied at national level, and its uniformity must be ensured by national courts, with the aid of the Article 177 reference procedure.

As noted above, once a product has lawfully been imported into one of the Member States it is considered to be in free circulation in the Community, and subject to the same free movement rights as Community products. However, under Article 115, the Commission can authorise Member States to impose restrictions on goods from a third country which are in free circulation so as to prevent 'deflections of trade', that is, undue harm to its own market.

The common commercial policy is also concerned with unfair trading practices in international trade.[20] These matters tend to concern only a small number of specialist practitioners but it is useful to note that action can be taken on a Community level to deal with, for example, the dumping of products on the Community market at artificially low prices,[1] and the putting into circulation of counterfeit goods.[2] Anti-dumping is probably the area of most activity. 'Dumping' indicates that products are being sold in the Community at less than their normal value and the key comparison to be made is between the price of the product on the exporter's home market and the price at which it is being sold to the Community. If the Commission finds a significant differential and that the cheap foreign products are causing or threaten to cause material injury to a Community industry, it will issue an anti-dumping regulation, imposing a duty, payable by importers, on the products in question.

REMEDIES

Finally, it is worth outlining the various options open to a client with a grievance under Community trade law.

Firstly, complaint can be made to the Commission, which may negotiate with the Member State involved to have the restrictions lifted, and ultimately bring an Article 169 action before the Court of Justice. This is a cheap but neither a quick nor a reliable way to have a rule set aside.

Secondly, in some areas, such as Common Community Tariff assessments and anti-dumping proceedings, the grievance will be with measures, usually regulations, issued by the Commission. A direct challenge under the Article 173 action for annulment may be considered but is very difficult in respect of tariff regulations because importers are not generally regarded

---

20 The generic measure is Regulation (EEC) 2641/84, OJ 1984 L252/1.
1   Regulation (EEC) 2423/88, OJ 1988 L209/1.
2   Regulation (EEC) 3842/86, OJ 1986 L357/1; implemented by Regulaiton (EEC) 3077/87, OJ 1987 L291/19.

as having a sufficient interest in these measures to have standing to challenge them.[3] Direct challenges may, however, be brought to corrective anti-dumping regulations by producers and exporters who are charged with dumping,[4] by a complainant who initiates and participates in the investigatory process,[5] and, in certain circumstances, by importers who have to pay the extra duties.[6]

Thirdly, a complaint about potentially illegal restrictions on trade may be made to the national authorities. The British authorities are increasingly aware of the demands of Community law, and the *Francovich* case, which may allow damages actions to be brought on the basis of restrictions which are illegal under Community law, will doubtless enhance their sensitivity.

The most appropriate course of action, however, will frequently be a challenge to national measures in the national courts, which may then make a reference to the Court of Justice. The challenge may consist of an action for judicial review of national measures as being inconsistent with Community law. Alternatively, the national court action may be an indirect challenge to a Community measure: for example, an importer seeking to challenge a tariff assessment by the Commission should seek judicial review of the action of British customs officers in applying the Community tariff. Alternatively, many businesses take the simpler course of contravening the law and then basing their defence on Community principles. This was the primary tactic of the shops prosecuted under the Sunday trading legislation. The Sunday trading saga demonstrates the potency of the 'Euro-defence' if not to win actions, then at least, as cases travel to Luxembourg and back, to delay them for a number of years and frustrate the application of the law in the meantime.

In all the instances of national court actions, interim injunctions, to suspend the operation of British provisions, and even a *Francovich* type damages claim may be available.

BIBLIOGRAPHY

P Oliver *Free Movement of Goods in the EEC* (2nd edn, 1988) European Law Centre.
J-F Bellis and I Van Bael *Anti-Dumping and other Trade Protection Laws of the EEC* (2nd edn, 1990) CCH.

---

3   Case 40/84 *Casteels v Commission* [1985] ECR 667.
4   Eg Case 239/82 *Allied Corporation v Commission* [1984] ECR 1005.
5   Case 264/82 *Timex v Commission* [1985] ECR 849.
6   Case C358/89 *Extramet v Commission* [1991] ECR I-2501.

Chapter 21

TRANSPORT LAW

INTRODUCTION

Many aspects of British transport law now have their origin in European Community measures. The importance of transport, both internal and cross-border, for an economic conglomeration such as the Community can scarcely be exaggerated. For many years, however, political disagreement dictated that little progress was made towards establishing a coherent common Community transport policy. The completion of the Single Market in 1992 provided a considerable impetus towards the implementation of common rules with the objective of reducing the cost of cross-border transportation and increasing competition between different means of transport. Nevertheless, a large part of Community transport law consists simply of the application of more general Community legislative policies, such as freedom of establishment and free competition, in the sphere of transport.

As a result, Community law in this field is a mixture of regulations, which have direct application within the United Kingdom, although British legislation may be enacted to facilitate their operation, and directives, which take effect subject to British implementing measures.

ROAD TRANSPORT

Previously, Member States controlled access to the road transport market on the basis of quantitative criteria, rationing the number of journeys which could be made by non-national carriers and restricting or prohibiting altogether cabotage, the offering of services entirely within another Member State. From 1 January, 1993 a complete system of qualitative criteria is in operation. Carriers who can satisfy certain objective standards of professional competence and financial viability can obtain Community-wide permits entitling them to unlimited cross-border journeys.[1] Cabotage, however, will remain subject to a permit system for the time being.[2]

The progress in respect of passenger transport has been less dramatic. The principal Community measures lay down common definitions and authorisation requirements for different types of cross-border passenger service.[3] The Community has also acceded to ASOR, the international agreement regulating occasional passenger services.

The road transport sector has been traditionally subject to state-imposed price controls in certain Member States but again, 1992 has brought liberalisation, and the full exposure of road transport prices to competitive pressures.[4] The general Community regime to promote free and open competition is applied in this sector by a special regulation, albeit one which corresponds closely to the basic competition law regulation, 17/62.[5]

The Community has been very active in harmonising technical and safety requirements in this field. Such matters as maximum weights and dimensions for lorries, vehicle number plates, tyre treads, exhaust emissions, brakes and rear-view mirrors are subject to common rules.[6] As regards safety, Community legislation demands, for example, that speed-limiting devices be fitted to lorries and coaches,[7] and that vehicles be periodically checked for roadworthiness.[8] More generally, common Community driving licence criteria have been introduced, to improve general driving competence and assist the movement of drivers to work in other Member States.

The establishment of uniform competitive conditions for road transport requires also the harmonisation of social measures relating to the protection of drivers. Consequently, Community regulations lay down requirements as to the minimum age and competence of drivers and very specific rules on drivers' hours, backed up by compulsory installation of tachographs, the so-called 'spy in the cab', and a prohibition on the payment of wages according to distance travelled or amount of goods carried.

---

1   Regulation (EEC) 881/92, OJ 1992 L95/1 establishes the Community licence.
2   Regulation (EEC) 3118/93, OJ 1993 L279/1.
3   The basic measure is Regulation (EEC) 117/66, *JO* 1966 p 2688.
4   Regulation (EEC) 4058/89, OJ 1989 L309/1.
5   Regulation (EEC) 1017/68, OJ 1968 L175/1. This regulation applies also to rail and inland waterway transport.
6   For a full list, see *Directory of Community Legislation in Force* sector 13.30.10.
7   Directive 92/6/EEC, OJ 1992 L57/27.
8   The most recent measure is Directive 91/328/EEC, OJ 1991 L178/29; implemented by SI 1991/2229.

AIR TRANSPORT

Many of the Community rules applicable to air transport arise out of the Community's regime of competition law, reflecting the airline industry's long history of government protection and collusive and restrictive practices. Originally, the competition rules did not apply to air transport services but certain decisions of the Court of Justice have prompted the extension of the operation of Articles 85 and 86 to inter-state flights within the Community, and then to domestic flights and flights between the Community and third countries.[9]

The basic powers of the Commission in this sphere are laid down in a regulation equivalent to the general competition law Regulation 17/62.[10] Subsequent amendments have empowered the Commission to take emergency action against a carrier which is behaving in a predatory manner so as to threaten the existence of an air service, and laid down a special complaints procedure for the air transport sector.

Under the basic regulation certain types of agreement fall outside the operation of Article 85(1) in so far as they seek to promote technical improvement or co-operation. The Commission is also empowered to issue block exemption regulations under Article 85(3). Regulations have been promulgated dealing with airline computer reservation systems, joint planning and co-ordination of capacity, sharing of revenue and consultations on tariffs of scheduled air services and slot allocation at airports, and airport ground handling services. The approach of the Commission has been progressively to narrow the scope of the block exemptions as airlines have had more time to adapt to the demands of the competition law regime. This can be expected to continue. Further regulations deal in greater detail with the implications for fair competition of computer reservation systems, and establish a more equitable system for allocating take-off and landing slots at busy airports.

In recent years, considerable progress has been made in developing common Community rules to govern the air transport industry. The third phase of this multi-faceted program came into operation in July 1992. Access to the air transport market is promoted in a number of ways. The right of Member States to refuse authorisation to Community-based scheduled airlines wishing to serve its airports has been severely curtailed and capacity controls on airlines virtually abolished. Further, full rights to carry passengers between two Member States other than the state of registration, the so-called 'fifth freedom', have been introduced, as well as

---

9 Cases 209-213/84 *Ministère Public v Asjes* [1986] ECR 1425; Case 66/86 *Ahmed Saeed v Zentrale sur Bekampfung Unlauteren Wettbewerbs* [1989] ECR 803.
10 Regulation (EEC) 3975/87, OJ 1987 L374/1.

a limited right of cabotage, the carriage of passengers within another Member State. Many restrictions on air freight services have also been lifted.

Much effort has been made to liberalise airline fares. Recently, the previous strategy of price restrictions has been revised: fares are to be fixed by free agreement subject to a right of intervention of the Member States concerned, and of the Commission, where the fare is felt to be too high, or too low, relative to the cost of providing the service.[11]

As in the sphere of road transport, the Community aims to provide common qualitative criteria for airline operators and personnel. To this end, air carriers are now to be licensed on a Community-wide basis, and civil aviation personnel licences will be mutually accepted throughout the Member States. In addition, the Community has been active in ensuring compensation to passengers who have been denied passage because of overbooking by the airline, and limiting aircraft noise emissions.

MARITIME TRANSPORT

The competition Articles 85 and 86 are applied to sea transport by means of Regulation 4056/86.[12] As well as laying down basic procedural rules, the regulation sets out certain types of agreement which will not infringe Article 85(1), including ship pooling or exchange agreements and agreements to co-ordinate timetables, and grants a block exemption to liner conferences, that is, agreements between freight carriers on a particular route to operate under uniform or common freight rates and conditions. Parties to such agreements are subject to certain obligations of reasonable conduct and the exemption is lost if different prices or conditions are applied to the same cargo according to the port of loading or destination. Consortia and joint ventures are excluded but the Commission is in the process of producing an exemption for the former.

In a further move to ensure fair competition, the Community has taken action to monitor and act against unfair pricing practices by third country shipowners. The measures taken are the maritime services equivalent of anti-dumping regulations, and aim to combat practices which disrupt freight patterns and otherwise threaten or cause injury to Community interests.

In the field of safety at sea, Community rules exist in respect of ensuring adequate piloting of ships in the North Sea and the English Channel, and of safeguards regarding tankers entering and leaving Community ports in

---

11   Regulation (EEC) 2409/92, OJ 1992 L240.
12   OJ 1986 L378/4.

an effort to reduce pollution. Shipowners will also have to ensure minimum standards of health and safety on board ship.

As in other sectors, the single market has brought a significant liberalisation of the restrictions on cabotage. Cabotage will be permitted on non-regulated, freely negotiated freight services ('tramping' operations) and regular non-island freight services, although many exceptions have been made.[13] Of particular importance are the derogations relating to ships of less than 650 tonnes until January 1998 and regular passenger and ferry services, and island services until 1999.

Efforts have been made to develop a Community fleet. This would involve, principally, the establishment of a Community register of ships which would fly the Community flag, and the common definition of a Community shipowner.

RAILWAYS

National railway networks do not operate outside the territory of their home state and so do not, as such, compete with each other. They do, however, compete with other means of transport, and Community policy has focussed on ensuring fair conditions for this competitive process by removing the advantages for railway networks of their close connection with the state apparatus. Therefore, for example, the relationship between the railway and the state must be transparent, and the railway must produce separate accounts. Railways must also have financial and management autonomy and commercial independence to set international passenger and luggage tariffs.

INLAND WATERWAYS

Community law regulates access to the profession of carrier of goods by inland waterway on the basis of common criteria of professional competence. Certificates of professional competence are mutually recognised by the Member States. The reciprocal recognition of national boatmasters' certificates has also been provided for. Vessels using inland waterways within the Community are subject to common technical standards and must carry the requisite Community authorisation certificate.[14] Cabotage is to be permitted from January 1993.

---

13 Regulation (EEC) 3577/92, OJ 1992 L364/7.
14 Directive 82/714/EEC, OJ 1982 L301/1 is the basic measure.

INFRASTRUCTURE

The co-ordination of investment in infrastructure is an important part of the common transport policy, albeit one which is likely to concern governments rather than private parties. Member States must inform the Commission of their plans for infrastructure, and the Community, as well as making grants to specified infrastructure projects, is engaged in long-term planning with the aim of, for example, reducing road traffic congestion and developing an integrated rail network throughout the Community.

STATE AIDS

The general regime of regulation of state aids to undertakings of Articles 92-94 applies in the transport sector. Article 77, however, provides for an additional exception to the general rules, where subsidies meet the needs of the co-ordination of transport or represent reimbursement by the state to transport undertakings for public services provided by them. Secondary legislation has limited the circumstances under which Member States may take co-ordinating measures or impose public service obligations.[15] Public service obligations include, for example, the duty to accept passengers and goods at uncommercial rates and the duty to operate according to published schedules regardless of the actual demand for the service.

BIBLIOGRAPHY

Rosa Greaves *Transport Law of the European Community* (1991) Athlone Press.

---

15   Regulation (EEC) 1107/70, OJ 1970 L130/1.

Chapter 22

WORKPLACE HEALTH AND SAFETY LAW

INTRODUCTION

The general law relating to health and safety in the workplace in the United Kingdom has, since 1 January 1993, been based on Community law. Such matters as the duties incumbent upon an employer to provide his employees with a safe place of work, a safe system of work, suitable and appropriate personal equipment where reasonably necessary for the performance of their job, are now covered by UK regulations which seek to implement Community directives. The existing common law relating to health and safety, as well the provisions of such statutes as the Factories Act 1961 and the Health and Safety at Work etc Act 1974 which have not been expressly repealed by these new regulations, can only be properly understood, interpreted and applied in the United Kingdom in the light of the relevant provisions of Community law.

The Treaty basis for Community involvement in health and safety is Article 118a of the Treaty of Rome which provides that Member States should pay particular attention to encouraging improvements, especially in the working environment, as regards the health and safety of workers, and should endeavour to harmonise their legislation among themselves, while maintaining those improvements. In order to promote the dual objectives of an improvement of workers' health and safety combined with harmonisation of Member States' legislation, the Council of Ministers is required to adopt directives under the qualified majority voting procedure in consultation with the European Parliament as laid down in Article 189c. This concern with the health and safety of workers is part of the general social programme of the Community. Measures brought under Article 118a apply to all Member States of the Community including the United Kingdom. Further, Member States may now only undertake international commitments in this area within the framework of Community institutions.[1]

Prior to the 1986 Single European Act, Community legislation in the area of health and safety was essentially limited to piecemeal reforms, whether by way of detailed regulations or by directives in specific fields which included: the provision of safety signs at places of work;[2] exposure to radiation at work;[3] the prevention of major accident hazards of particular industrial activities, such as the production and processing or organic and inorganic chemicals and energy gases, oil refining and coal distillation, toxic waste disposal and electrolytic production;[4] the essential health and safety requirements to be taken into account in the design, maintenance and use of industrial machinery;[5] and the provision of a minimum standard of medical care on board merchant ships.[6]

The style of Community legislation in the light of the '1992 project' has, by contrast, been characterised by the use of directives to set out broad aims and approaches within which specific reforms are then carried out by more detailed 'daughter directives'. By the end of 1993 there were two such 'framework directives' in the field of health and safety. The first framework directive dealt with the harmonisation of measures relating to workplace exposure to various chemical, physical and biological agents. The second framework directive was concerned with the introduction of measures to encourage improvements in the safety and health of workers at work.

THE FIRST HEALTH AND SAFETY FRAMEWORK DIRECTIVE

The first Health and Safety Framework Directive[7] applies to all areas of commercial activity except air and sea transport. This directive imposes

1   See Opinion 2/91 *Re ILO Convention on Chemicals at Work* 19 March [1993] ECR I-1064, [1993] 3 CMLR 800.
2   Directive 77/576/EEC, OJ 1977 L229/12 as amended by Commission Directive 79/640/EEC, OJ 1979 L183/79 implemented into UK law by The Safety Signs Regulations 1980, SI 1980/1471.
3   Directive 90/641/EURATOM, OJ 1990 L349/21. Cf the Ionising Radiations Regulations 1985, SI 1985/1333.
4   Directive 82/501/EEC, OJ 1982 L230/1 implemented in the United Kingdom by Control of IndustrialMajor Accident Hazards Regulations 1984, SI 1984/1902.
5   Directive 89/392/EEC, OJ L183/9 implemented by the Supply of Machinery (Safety) Regulations 1992, SI 1992/3073.
6   Directive 92/29/EEC, OJ 1992 L113/19.
7   Directive 80/1107/EEC, OJ L27/80 as amended by Directive 88/642/EEC, OJ 1988 L356/74 and supplemented by Directive 91/322/EEC, OJ 1991 L177/22.

a duty on the Member States to make provisions limiting or prohibiting the use of any chemical, physical or biological agents present in the workplace and likely to be harmful to health with a view to protecting employees who might be exposed to such agents. Measures listed in the directive as appropriate to such an objective include: the establishment of maximum limit values and sampling procedures for the agents in question; the establishment of safe and suitable working practices; hygiene measures; medical surveillance of the health of workers; information and instruction to the workforce regarding the risks associated with exposure and how to avoid and minimise these; the provision of emergency procedures in the event of abnormal exposure. Specific procedures relating to the sampling and measurement of exposure to the agents, along with the assessment of the results of such sampling and measurement, were set out in the Annex to the 1988 directive. Additional measures as regards health surveillance, workers' rights of information where the appropriate limit values were exceeded, and access to the results of exposure measurements and of any biological tests indicating exposure are also set out in the directive for cases involving the following chemicals: acrylonitrile; asbestos; arsenic and its compounds; benzene; cadmium and its compounds; mercury and compounds; nickel and compounds; lead and compounds; chlorinated hydrocarbons.

The First Framework Directive was largely implemented within in the United Kingdom by the Control of Substances Hazardous to Health Regulations 1988, SI 1988/1657 as amended.[8]

Daughter directives dealing with other specified workplace hazards have since been adopted by the Community under the general scheme set up by the First Framework Directive. These include directives dealing with exposure to lead and its compounds,[9] exposure to asbestos,[10] exposure to noise in the workplace,[11] and banning the use of certain specified chemical agents and work activities.[12] The first three directives required employers to carry out assessments of the workplace to determine whether, how and where the provisions of the various directives might apply to their premises. They required records to be made and kept by the employers of their physical sampling and measurements, together with the biological monitoring of the workforce and assessments of the workplace impact of the agent in question. They provided, too, for special provisions and procedures to be triggered into action if the

---

8   See the Control of Substances Hazardous to Health (Amendment) Regulations 1992, SI 1992/2382.
9   Directive 82/605/EEC, OJ 1982 L247/12.
10 Directive 83/477/EEC, OJ 1983 L263/25 as amended by Directive 91/382/EEC, OJ L206/16.
11 Directive 86/188/EEC, OJ 1986 L137/28.
12 Directive 88/364/EEC, OJ 1988 L179/44.

samples indicate a particular level of exposure, designated as significant, below the maximum levels which are also set out in the relevant directives.

The First Framework Directive (and the daughter directives made under it) stress the importance of measurement and full information regarding an employer's existing activities in the protection of health and safety.

THE SECOND HEALTH AND SAFETY FRAMEWORK DIRECTIVE

The Second Framework Directive[13] is conceived as the bed-rock of a new Community-wide programme which is intended, in time, completely to replace the existing national legislation of Member States on health and safety at work with common basic standards framework as regards the safety and health of workers throughout the territory of the Community. The rationale for this project is that the legislative provisions of the present Member States which cover safety and health in the workplace differ widely and all, in any event, need to be improved.

The Second Health and Safety Framework Directive requires the introduction of measures actively to encourage improvements in the safety and health of workers at work.[14] The 1989 Framework Directive in fact imposes a number of basic duties on employers throughout the Community and applies to all sectors of activity, both public and private, with the possible exception of the police, army and civil protection services. The directive imposes a general responsibility on employers for the health and safety of workers as regards their presence in the workplace and in all aspects of work done by them. Part-time and temporary workers and those working on fixed term contracts are also included within Community health and safety protection.[15]

The Second Framework Directive lays down minimum standards and requirements as regards health and safety. It requires employers to inform, consult and involve their workers and their workplace representatives in the whole field of accident prevention and health protection. Employers are required to keep themselves informed of advances in workplace design and to evaluate the risks to the health and safety of employees in their choice of work equipment and the fitting out

13   Directive 89/391/EEC, OJ 1989 L 183/1.
14   Directive 89/391/EEC, OJ 1989 L183/1.
15   See Directive 91/383/EEC, OJ 1991 L206/19.

of workplaces. They have an obligation to train their workforce appropriately (to include refresher and updating courses) and adequately to direct them as regards the tasks required of them. Employers also have a general duty under the framework directive to develop coherent overall programmes and strategies for accurate risk assessment and for the elimination of avoidable risks and the reduction of the dangers posed by unavoidable risks. They have a duty to record and to notify the appropriate national authorities of occupational accidents and illnesses. The employers' duties extend to ensuring that workers from outside undertakings and establishments who are engaged in work in their undertaking have received appropriate instruction regarding health and safety risks. Appointment of safety supervisors is also required by the directive.

Interestingly, the directive expressly provides for workers and/or their representatives to be given the power to call in the appropriate health and safety authorities and to attend any workplace inspection by these authorities. In this way 'whistle blowers' in the work-place might be accorded a degree of protection against retaliation from their employer for bringing to light a hazard in the work-place. No such specific protection was given to the worker in the pre-existing UK legislative framework.[16]

The Second Framework Directive also imposes duties on workers to take individual care for their own health and safety and that of others who might be affected by their acts or omissions, in accordance with the training and instructions given to him by their employer. To this end, employees are required to co-operate with the employer on health and safety matters, to notify him of potential hazards and to use tools and equipment provided to them in a correct and safe manner.

Under the auspices of the Second Framework Directive a number of specific directives had been adopted by the end of 1993. These set out minimum health and safety requirements in the following areas: the constitution of a safe working environment/safe place of work,[17] for example in the provision of fire exits, proper ventilation; the provision and use of safe work equipment;[18] the provision and use of personal protective equipment[19] such as helmets, earplugs, goggles, face masks, gloves, shoes, barrier creams, safety harnesses etc; the manual handling

---

16 Workers acting as safety representatives and carrying out functions covered by s 2(4) of the Health and Safety at Work etc Act 1974 were given some degree of protection against employer retaliation.
17 Directive 89/654/EEC, OJ 1989 L393/1.
18 Directive 89/655/EEC, OJ 1989 L393/13.
19 Directive 89/656/EEC, OJ 1989 L393/18.

of loads where there is a risk of back injury,[20] requiring the employer to provide technical assistance and training; the use of video display screen equipment;[1] the exposure of workers to carcinogens at work;[2] exposure to biological agents at work;[3] the implementation of minimum safety and health requirements at temporary or mobile construction sites;[4] minimum requirements for the provision of health and safety signs at work;[5] minimum requirements for improving the safety and health of workers in the onshore and off-shore drilling industries;[6] minimum health and safety requirements for workers engaged in surface and underground mineral extraction from mines and quarries;[7] and minimum safety and health requirements for work on board fishing vessels.[8] The Working Time Directive,[9] which sets limits on the maximum average working week and provides for compulsory rest periods and minimum annual leave for all employees, was also adopted by majority voting under the justification that it was primarily a health and safety matter. A directive, ostensibly founded on health and safety considerations, which provided for the protection of employment rights of pregnant workers was also adopted,[10] but this is dealt with in Chapter 17 on sex discrimination.

At the time of writing there were proposals for and drafts of directives for further health and safety directives in the following areas: the harmonisation of minimum requirements for improving health and safety in the transport field[11]; exposure to workers to the risks arising from certain physical agents—noise, mechanical vibration, optical radiation and electromagnetic fields and waves;[12] the protection of workers from exposure to chemical agents;[13] the protection of young

20 Directive 90/269/EEC, OJ 1990 L156/9.
1   Directive 90/270/EEC, OJ 1990 L156/14.
2   Directive 90/394/EEC, OJ 1990 L196/1.
3   Directive 90/679/EEC, OJ 1990 L374/1 and Directive 93/88/EEC, OJ 1993 L268/71 which provides for the classification of biological agents into four infection risk groups. See also Directives 90/220/EEC, OJ 1990 L117/15 and 90/219/EEC, OJ 1990 L117/1 on the use and disposal of genetically modified organisms.
4   Directive 92/57/EEC, OJ 1992 L245/6.
5   Directive 92/58/EEC, OJ 1992 L245/23.
6   Directive 92/91/EEC, OJ 1992 L348/9.
7   Directive 92/104/EEC, OJ 1992 L404/10.
8   Directive 93/103/EEC, OJ 1993 L307/1.
9   Directive 93/104/EEC, OJ 1993 L307/18.
10 Directive 92/85/EEC, OJ 1992 L348/1.
11 COM (92) 234 final - SYN 420, OJ 1992 C25/17.
12 COM (92) 560 final - SYN 449, OJ 1993 C77/12.
13 COM (93) 155 final - SYN 459, OJ 1993 C165/4.

people at work;[14] and the protection of the health of workers and the general public against dangers arising from ionising radiation. [15]

IMPLEMENTATION IN THE UNITED KINGDOM

According to the UK Government the Management of Health and Safety at Work Regulations 1992 with its associated 'Approved Code of Practice',[16] when read together with pre-existing national legislation, implements the Second Framework Directive in full. In the 'Health and Safety Case Study' in the *Review of the Implementation and Enforcement of EC Law in the UK* [17] the Department of Trade and Industry provided a detailed breakdown of each article of the second framework directive showing which provision of national law was considered to implement it. These provisions range from the aforesaid 1992 regulations to provisions of the Health and Safety at Work etc Act 1974, the Fire Precautions Act 1971, the Employment Protection (Consolidation) Act 1978, the Trade Union Reform and Employment Rights Act 1993 and a variety of other statutory instruments.

A number of the daughter directives noted above have already been implemented in national law, by a series of statutory instruments: the Workplace (Health, Safety and Welfare) Regulations 1992, SI 1992/3004;[18] the Provision and Use of Work Equipment Regulations 1992, SI 1992/2932;[19] the Personal Protective Equipment at Work Regulations 1992,SI 1992/2966; the Manual Handling Operations Regulations 1992,SI 1992/2793; and the Health and Safety (Display Screen Equipment) Regulations 1992, SI 1992/2792.

THE RELATIONSHIP BETWEEN EXISTING UK LAW AND COMMUNITY LAW ON HEALTH AND SAFETY

The new UK health and safety regulations cannot be understood as standing on their own terms as ordinary domestic legislation; neither can

---

14 COM (93) 35 final - SYN 383 final, OJ 1993 C77/1.
15 COM (93) 349 final, OJ 1993 C245/5.
16 (HMSO 1992: ISBN-0 11 886630 4) SI 1992/2051.
17 See Annex B1 'Health and Safety Case Study' of the Department of Trade and Industry *Review of the Implementation and Enforcement of EC Law in the UK* (1993) pp 107-110.
18 These regulations apply to new workplaces with effect from 1 January 1993, and to existing workplaces from 1 January 1996.
19 These regulations apply to work equipment supplied after 1 January 1993, and to existing work equipment with effect from 1 January 1997.

they properly be explained under reference to the pre-existing cases and common law rules on health and safety, even where the new regulations apparently use the same terms and phrases (such as 'dangerous', 'safe', 'likely', 'adequate', 'suitable and effective') which have already been the subject of authoritative interpretation by the national courts. The introduction of Community law into this area marks a break with the past. Rather than seeking to determine how these words were interpreted by the domestic courts heretofore, better guidance will be obtained by looking at how the equivalent words, phrases and concepts which implement the same directives are currently understood and applied by other national jurisdictions within the Community. The final word on the correct interpretation of the law in this area will, of course, rest with the European Court of Justice.

Where the action before the national court is brought against an 'emanation of the state', such as a local authority or health board, then the doctrine of direct effect will allow the precise and unconditional provisions of the directives to be relied upon directly against that party, regardless of the provisions of the national regulations. In case involving only private parties, it is the duty of every national court (under Article 5 of the Treaty of Rome) to do all in its power to ensure that the national regulations are interpreted in accordance with the directive.

Further, all the Community directives considered above are aimed at the *improvement* of workers' health and safety. The Health and Safety Directives, therefore, effectively provide the floor level by which concepts such as a 'safe system of work' are to be understood. In so far as the national law allows for a standard below that permitted by the directive, then it must be disregarded. In so far as the duty at common law provides for a higher standard than that required by the directive, then the former should still be applied.

In addition, national regulations made in implementation of the directive cannot be used to lower the standards of protection which previously existed within national law. Thus, where civil liability existed against employers under previous national legislation, for example under ss 28 and 29 of the Factories Act 1961, any Community derived measures which replace the national regulations should also be construed so as to continue to impose civil liability on employers[20] and give full compensation for all loss suffered by the employee.

---

20 Section 47(2) of the Health and Safety at Work etc Act 1974 provides that breach of a duty imposed by 'health and safety regulations' made under the Act shall be actionable unless the regulations provide otherwise, but s 17(1) states that the failure of a person to observe any of the provisions of an 'approved code of practice' shall not, of itself, render him liable to any civil proceedings.

Given that the Second Framework Directive is part of the social programme intended to protect employees, any provision of the regulations which seems to limit the liability of employers must be read narrowly. For example, Article 5(4) of the Second Framework Directive allows for the possibility of a limited exclusion or limitation of employers' responsibility for their workers' health and safety to cases of exceptional and unforeseeable circumstances, the consequences of which could not have been avoided despite the exercise of all due care. By contrast s 2(1) of the Health and Safety at Work etc Act 1974 provides that it shall be the duty of every employer to ensure, only so far as is reasonably practicable, the health, safety and welfare at work of all his employees. Any reference to reasonable practicability as a limitation on the general duty of employers would not appear accurately to reflect the limited exclusion in cases of unforeseeable events as is set out in the directive. A duty limited by what is 'reasonably practicable' is a less burdensome than one limited simply by what is practicable or physically possible.[1]

It would appear that the retention of the reasonable practicability test indicates that the United Kingdom has sought to limit the duty of employers to a lower standard than that required in the Community provision. On this view, full and proper implementation in the United Kingdom of the Community Health and Safety Directives would have imposed a general duty on employers to ensure, *so far as is practicable*, the health, safety and welfare at work of all their employees.[2] The UK Government has argued, however, that the retention of the reasonable practicability test is in fact an accurate implementation within the United Kingdom of the relevant Community law. It is claimed that, while other Member States can couch their implementing laws in more absolute terms because their courts would apply the law with more flexibility and in accordance with the principle of proportionality, the UK tradition would be for the judges to apply an absolute text literally. Thus, it is necessary to make explicit to the United Kingdom courts that the test of proportionality should be considered by them in applying and interpreting the Community based legislation by making the appropriate test one of reasonable practicability. In any event, it is clear that the test of reasonable practicability in the context of the new legislation will have to be interpreted in a manner which is consonant with Community law. Previous case law on 'reasonable practicability' has to be applied with caution, since the context of its use will have changed to a European one.

1   Asquith LJ in *Edwards v National Coal Board* [1949] 1 KB 704 at 712.
2   Following the decision of the House of Lords in *R v Secretary of State for Employment, ex p the Equal Opportunities Commission* (3 March 1994 unreported) it would appear that any provisions of national legislation which are alleged to be contrary to the requirements of Community law may be challenged by way of judicial review procedure before the domestic courts.

Finally, all remedies available under the existing national law of Member State, for example interdict or injunctive relief should similarly be available to ensure the full protection of Community derived rights in this area.

The field of health and safety is one in which the Community will have an ever-growing involvement. Given the self-exclusion of the United Kingdom from the Social Chapter provisions of the Maastricht Treaty, the Commission has begun to construe the notion of provisions relating to 'health and safety' very liberally so as to allow Community workplace legislation of a broad social nature to be adopted under the qualified majority voting procedure.[3] The United Kingdom government has expressed its unease over Community legislation which, for example seeks to regulate the length of the working day and week and to provide for paid annual leave under the guise of health and safety considerations of workers. The possibility remains open that any such broad social legislation adopted under reference to health and safety considerations may be challenged before the Court of Justice on the basis that it has been passed using the wrong procedure and incorrect legal basis.

BIBLIOGRAPHY

R Baldwin and T Daintith *Harmonisation and Hazard: regulating workplace health and safety in the European Community* (1992) Graham & Trotman.

Health and Safety Executive *Workplace Health and Safety in Europe* (1991) HMSO.

Health and Safety Executive *Handbook of Labour Inspection in the European Community* (1991) HMSO.

A C. Neal and F B Wright *The European Communities' Health and Safety Legislation* (1992) Chapman & Hall.

A C Neal 'The European Framework Directive on the Health and Safety of Workers: challenges for the United Kingdom' (1990) 6 *International Journal of Comparative Labour Law and Industrial Relations* 80.

J Hendy and M Ford *Redgrave Fife & Machin: Health and Safety* (2nd edn, 1993) Butterworths.

Smith, Goddard and Randall *Health and Safety: the New Legal Framework* (1993) Butterworths.

---

3   Eg, the Working Time Directive 93/104/EEC, OJ 1993 L307/18.

INDEX